THE WRITER'S DAILY COMPANION

365
Inspirations
and Writing Tips

AMY PETERS

FALL RIVER PRESS

New York

FALL RIVER PRESS

New York

An Imprint of Sterling Publishing
1166 Avenue of the Americas
New York, NY 10036

Jacket design by Igor Satanovsky

ISBN 978-1-4351-5563-3

For information about custom editions, special sales, and premium and
corporate purchases, please contact Sterling Special Sales at 800-805-5489
or specialsales@sterlingpublishing.com.

Manufactured in China

2   4   6   8   10   9   7   5   3   1

www.sterlingpublishing.com

ACKNOWLEDGMENTS

HIS BOOK WOULD NOT HAVE BEEN POSSIBLE without the help of many people. I'd like to thank Pamela Liflander for her invaluable assistance in helping to make this book a reality. I would also like to thank the good folks at Sterling: Carlo DeVito for fostering such a great project and Iris Blasi and Joe Rhatigan for picking up the ball and really running with it. We make a great team!

Lastly, I would like to acknowledge my husband Peter, and two sons Max and Chet, for their boundless patience and support.

INTRODUCTION

WELCOME TO THE *WRITER'S DAILY COMPANION*. Inside this chunky volume you'll find everything you need to get your creative juices flowing. Whether you're honing your skills for writing fiction or nonfiction, screenplays, or poetry, or simply trying to keep a more compelling journal or blog, you'll find 365 inspiring quotations and informative tutorials that will aid in developing your unique voice. Each entry is meant to be read either at the start of your work, as you unwind when you're done, or as a little treat during the day when things are getting too stressful.

Writing is a solitary activity, but you don't have to feel that you are completely on your own. Hopefully, this book can provide fresh information and wise counsel from legendary authors ranging from the distant past to today's bestseller lists. Much of their advice will add a bit of cheer; all will encourage and inspire you on your path. There are also plenty of surprises that will make reading this daily devotional an enlightening practice that you will look forward to returning to as you follow your dream.

Each day of the week highlights a different aspect of a writer's life:

MONDAYS—Writers on Writing: Learn what the best in the business have to say about the writing process and what their work, and the works of others, meant to them.

TUESDAYS—Motivation: Use these tips and tricks to help you keep writing even when you've hit a wall, and to help you gain the courage to share your work.

WEDNESDAYS—Writing Class: Try your hand at dozens of different formats, broadening your writing experience. You may find that you excel at a whole new category of written works that you've never before considered.

THURSDAYS—Editing: Understand the nuts and bolts every writer needs to master. This section runs the gamut from punctuation to mastering the active voice, as well as the secrets of creating a truly compelling work.

FRIDAYS—Biography: While the works of great writers remain, their own stories are often unknown. Here's your chance to meet fifty-two of the most interesting writers in history, including some of your current favorites. Learn what motivated them to write and how their past shaped their prose.

SATURDAYS—Books Writers Should Read: Explore this stimulating survey of fifty-two books you must have under your belt. These are the "best of the best" in many different genres and styles, so you can measure your work against the masters, and see exactly how they got the job done.

SUNDAYS—Writing Prompt: Wrap up each week with an exercise allowing you to take on one of fifty-two topics. I know that it's sometimes tough to stay on track, or even get started. Here are some great ideas and the writings they may have inspired, so you can see how a simple idea can lead to a great work.

I hope these pages fill you with the optimism and promise of fulfillment that only writing can bring.

MONDAY | WRITERS ON WRITING

> The role of the writer is not to say what we can all say but what we are unable to say.
>
> *—Anaïs Nin*

THERE ARE COUNTLESS REASONS WHY SO MANY people are unable to make their voices heard. Perhaps social restrictions bind a person. Consider the character Celie in *The Color Purple.* During the early years of her life, she was unable to have her voice heard because she was a poor, black woman. Author Alice Walker gave a voice to all women like Celie, women who had been historically—and even in current times—suppressed.

Likewise, Marjane Satrapi gave voice to oppressed Iranians in her graphic novel, *Persepolis.* Or, take the dramatic case of Harriet Beecher Stowe, who in writing *Uncle Tom's Cabin,* an exposé on slavery in pre–Civil War America, inspired a country to change. Abraham Lincoln famously said of Stowe and her work, "So this is the little lady who started this great big war." These authors speak for those who were "unable to say."

There are many reasons to write, ranging from recording personal memories, offering advice, creating poetry, or documenting a historical era. All of these reasons are important. As Nin says, though, one of the unique and powerful tools a writer holds is the ability to speak for the oppressed, the disenfranchised, or those similarly unable to have a voice in society.

TUESDAY | MOTIVATION

> The indispensable first step to getting the things you want out of life is this: decide what you want.
>
> —*Ben Stein*

SOMETIMES THE MOST SAGE AND SOUND OF ADVICE is also the most straightforward. Such is the case with humorist, author, and commentator Ben Stein's kernel of wisdom. There are times when the seemingly simple stuff can trip a person up. You think you know the endgame but have you really defined your goals?

Begin by deciding what you want to achieve as a writer. Have you always dreamed of writing a successful novel? Or, do you have the desire to keep your writing to yourself, cataloging family recipes or tracing your genealogy? Maybe you want to master haiku or write for a local newspaper.

Take the time to reflect and to delineate your writing desires. Then put the goal in writing, determining a time frame for achieving your goal. By defining what you want, you're creating a type of road map to follow, helping you to steer clear of distracting detours. As baseball player Yogi Berra put it, "If you don't know where you are going, you might wind up someplace else."

WEDNESDAY | WRITING CLASS

Write a short biography about your best friend.

B EGIN WITH A REAL HOOK OR GRABBER SENTENCE. You want to draw in your reader immediately, so write a first sentence that will get your reader's attention as well as begin to illuminate what is interesting about this person. After crafting this first sentence, continue writing, including basic facts—full name, birth date, place of birth, and current home address. Next, describe why this person is your best friend. What draws you to this person? What will draw your reader's focus to this person? Show by using examples.

THURSDAY | EDITING

The key to revision is learning to look at your
work with an editor's eye.
—The Writer's Digest Writing Clinic

A N EDITOR'S JOB IS TO MAKE THE WRITER LOOK better. Editors are trained to look at a piece of written work and help the writer tie up the loose ends. S/he makes sure that there are no superfluous characters, red herrings, or plotlines that go nowhere. S/he tries to ask questions of the text that the writer can answer by changing the story. And, an editor makes sure that the point the writer is trying to make is clearly definable.

A good editor makes sure the language is tight: not too flowery and not too staid. S/he makes sure that each piece of writing has a "voice," a unique cadence or rhythm, or sense of humor or deep understanding.

Good writers are not always good editors, and certainly, good editors are not always good writers. However, you need to take on the editor's role when you are ready for the revision stage. First, walk away from your text for at least twenty-four hours. Then, as you read through your material, take an editor's approach and see how you can tweak your work to make it better.

FRIDAY | BIOGRAPHY

> In a time of universal deceit—telling the truth
> is a revolutionary act.
>
> *— George Orwell*

GEORGE ORWELL (1903–1950) WAS THE PEN NAME of Eric Arthur Blair. Born in Bengal, India, and raised in England, his early schooling began at St. Cyprian's School, in Sussex, where he met Cyril Connolly, who later published many of Orwell's essays. He was sent on scholarship to the exclusive boarding school, Eton, where Aldous Huxley was one of his teachers. Blair joined the Indian Imperial Police and served in Burma from 1922 to 1927. Returning west, he lived an impoverished life in Paris and London, making little money as a tutor and a bookshop assistant while he began writing. He fought and was wounded during the Spanish Civil War, and during World War II he found work as a war correspondent and editor, writing for the BBC, the *Observer*, and the *Tribune*. At the same time he continued to write books, all of which met with little success. As one biographer put it, "his first amateurish efforts arose smiles."

Yet he kept writing, worked his professional connections, and concentrated on the political message. He abhorred both communism and imperialism. After the war, these two themes repeated in his best-received works, *Animal Farm* (1945) and *Nineteen Eighty-Four* (1949). During most of his career, Orwell was best known for his journalism and essays. Unfortunately, he was able to enjoy fame from his novels only briefly: he died of tuberculosis in 1950.

SATURDAY | BOOKS TO READ

Silent Spring by Rachel Carson

> It would be unrealistic to believe that one
> book could bring a complete change.
> —*Rachel Carson*

WRITERS OFTEN IMAGINE THAT THEIR WORK WILL bring about social change, but few really succeed. Even author and scientist Rachel Carson underestimated the power of her own 1962 book, *Silent Spring*. This important book changed our collective world view about the dangerous effects of chemicals on the environment, and it continues to affect our consciousness today. It's a wonderful example of how clear and forceful writing can effect change.

Silent Spring took on dichlorodiphenyltrichloroethane (DDT), condemning its effects. During the 1940s and 1950s, DDT had come into widespread use as an agricultural insecticide. It helped farmers grow bigger crops and gain larger yields. Carson, a scientist, recognized and researched the detrimental effects of the chemical. Critics—many intimately involved in the chemical business—accused Carson of being a "hysterical woman." Yet readers flocked to the book. It leaped to the top of the *New York Times* bestseller list, staying in the number-one position for thirty-one weeks.

Among Carson's fans was President John Kennedy. After reading the book, he asked his Science Advisory Committee to study the impact of insecticides on the environment. The committee's report vindicated Carson and her work and led to the ban of DDT and other chemicals. Her work also paved the way for books such as Al Gore's *An Inconvenient Truth*.

SUNDAY | WRITING PROMPT

If I could live anywhere in the world . . .

MANY OF US WISH WE LIVED EITHER SOMEWHERE more exciting or more peaceful, and this topic allows us to dream big. There are, however, a few of us who realize that we are sitting on a literary gold mine. For example, Peter Mayle tackles the joys of living abroad in a tiny French village in his bestselling books about his life in Provence. Interestingly, he is able to capture the flavor of this region and introduce it as a character in and of itself in both his fiction and nonfiction works—a tradition he has continued for more than a decade.

Mayle is known for bringing the sights, sounds, smells, and gustatory world of France to the page. He does this by recreating a rich and unique setting that was quite foreign to the majority of his readers when his first book, *A Year in Provence,* was published in 1989. His books revolve around his experiences with a community of characters where the mundane becomes interesting, and where the readers feel that they intimately understand his life and his neighbors.

Even if you think nothing ever happens in your own hometown, think again. Practice this technique, and write about your neighborhood, or write about a place where you've always fantasized living. See if you can bring these locales to life, where the community itself plays a central role, not just as a setting, but as a character.

MONDAY | WRITERS ON WRITING

> We are a species that needs and wants to understand who we are. Sheep lice do not seem to share this longing, which is one reason why they write so little.
>
> *—Anne Lamott*

ART IN ALL OF ITS FORMS HELPS US TO CONSIDER THE immense question of how does art speak to and reflect the human experience. Whether imagining the motivation and passion behind the great Spanish artist Pablo Picasso's wartime painting *Guernica* or considering the meaning of French composer Claude Debussy's *La Mer,* art helps us to consider what it means to be human.

An essential aspect of the writer's journey is this same examination of what it means to be human. Since the time of Aristotle, scholars have encouraged humans to engage with words and to search for meaning. Keith Oatley, PhD, Professor Emeritus, Department of Human Development & Applied Psychology at the University of Toronto, decided to test this theory of Aristotle's: Do humans find that they are better able to understand and experience life through their reading, particularly by reading fiction?

The results were clear: participants who read fiction were better able to relate to their peers and to engage in social interaction. Also significant was the participants' abilities to show increased empathy, which was attributed to their increased understanding of human nature as found through their reading. Through their work, writers can reap the same rewards. By writing about the world around us, we are better able to empathize and to understand the intricacies of life.

TUESDAY | MOTIVATION

> As I've learned . . . no one knows "enough"
> about grammar. This causes a lot of people
> to feel insecure and alone, as if they're the
> only ones whose grasp of the language is
> less than adequate.
>
> —June Casagrande

DON'T LET THE FACT THAT YOU HAVE NOT ENTIRELY mastered the rules of the English language stop you from writing. The rules are not really so cut and dried to begin with, and the ones that are can be easy to master. Once you understand the fifty-two tips found every Tuesday in this book, you'll automatically increase your knowledge. There is a whole cottage industry of books on grammar just waiting to be read, each of which offers sound advice. I know; I had to read all of them to write this book.

And while good grammar is important, there are plenty of writers who spit directly in its face. Some writers choose to write ungrammatically for effect; others don't know better and get away with it. Still others make mistakes, even when they think they know it all. If your goal is to be published in books or magazines (and possibly on the web), there is always at least one backup grammarian on staff: they're called copyeditors, and they're happy to help make you sound even better.

My advice is to think creatively first, and then worry if you've written it correctly. Chances are that you'll capture your audience with your wit and prose, and the style will follow.

WEDNESDAY | WRITING CLASS

Write a book review for a book you didn't like.

IT'S EASY TO DESCRIBE WHY YOU LIKE A BOOK. Sometimes, though, it can be hard to pinpoint why you don't. For this exercise, choose a book you didn't care for. Give the full name of the book, and include the subtitle if there is one. Include the author's full name, the illustrator's full name (if applicable), and the year in which it was published. Give examples from the text to support your reasons for disliking the book. For instance, it's not enough to say that the author didn't develop her characters well. You need to draw examples from the work to support your claims and make a convincing case.

THURSDAY | EDITING

*For all my longer works I write chapter outlines
so I can have the pleasure of departing from
them later on.*

— Garth Nix

REGARDLESS OF WHETHER YOU'RE WRITING A LONGER work or a short piece, you have to start with an outline. The second step is to write a brief synopsis of your story detailing its beginning, middle, and end. Even if you end up deviating from this, as Nix does, you'll know that you've at least thought through your original idea and that it has a logical progression or arc.

Then, write a master plot list for each of your characters, beginning with the main one and working your way down the pecking order. This list substantiates why those characters are in the story.

Now the fun begins. Before you write one word of the actual work, you need to create a backstory for every character, even if you don't use it. Flesh out who these people are and how they interconnect in the story, and identify their motivations and how they will affect the plot.

Once you've finished your piece (or if it's large, at the end of each chapter), go back and compare what you've done to these lists. If you've strayed off course, figure out why and whether or not your new idea is better than your original.

FRIDAY | BIOGRAPHY

> I believe that world literature has it in
> its power to help mankind, in these its
> troubled hours, to see itself as it really
> is, notwithstanding the indoctrinations
> of prejudiced people and parties.
>
> —*Aleksandr Solzhenitsyn*

ALEKSANDR SOLZHENITSYN (1918–2008) WROTE books that shed a true light on what was happening behind the Iron Curtain: how many talented people were wasting away in prison camps. As a child, he wanted to be a writer, but without the right schooling available to him, he chose to study mathematics. It was to play a beneficial role: on at least two occasions he credits mathematics for saving his life.

During World War II, because of his mathematical knowledge, he was placed as the commander of an artillery-position-finding company. In February 1945 he was arrested for his unflattering portrayal of Stalin in private correspondence and writings. He was sentenced to eight years in a detention camp in July 1945. A month later, the full term of his status was changed to "exiled for life."

In exile, Solzhenitsyn taught mathematics and physics in a primary school and wrote prose in secret. His first work was published in 1962: *One Day in the Life of Ivan Denisovich.* Printing of this work, which reflected his years in the camps, was discontinued almost immediately. He spent the next thirty years writing and evading the Soviet government. At his return to Moscow in 1994 he was treated as a hero.

SATURDAY | BOOKS TO READ

Scoop by Evelyn Waugh

> I think that Hemingway made real discoveries
> about the use of language in his first novel,
> *The Sun Also Rises*. I admired the way he made
> drunk people talk.
>
> —*Evelyn Waugh*

ENGLISH AUTHOR EVELYN WAUGH PUBLISHED *Scoop* in 1938, and it's one of the best examples of social satire in the modern era. Waugh was known for his sharp wit as well as his precise use of language. He was also known for his strong opinions, calling Faulkner's writing "intolerably bad," accusing James Joyce of being a "lunatic," and claiming that Raymond Chandler's writing was essentially about drinking shots of whiskey.

Waugh brought his biting wit to the social satire, *Scoop*. In it, a young London journalist, William Boot, is sent to cover a civil war in the fictional African country of Ishmaelia, when his editors at *The Daily Beast* (from which Tina Brown got the name for her online news site) mistake him for another novelist with the same name. While his inept editor dines on canapés and drinks sherry back in London, Boot, a nature writer, gamely tries to cover the events unfolding on the ground in Ishmaelia. Through a series of fortunate strokes, Boot is able to get the big scoop. But, upon returning to London, the credit for the news goes to the other novelist, and Boot returns to obscurity.

Scoop demonstrates why Waugh is considered one of the greatest satirical writers of his generation.

SUNDAY | WRITING PROMPT

I like animals . . .

ANIMALS HAVE A UNIVERSAL APPEAL FOR READERS. And it doesn't seem to be limited to the domesticated few or the exotic wild beasts that roam the African plains. The late James Alfred "Alf" Wight, who wrote under the name James Herriot, made a career as a mild-mannered British veterinarian who had a penchant for sharing stories about all sorts of creatures, great and small. His art was the ability to share his unique relationship with a wide variety of animals, letting the reader experience what his life was like and often imagine the life of the animals themselves.

Try your hand at this same task. Whether you love dogs, cats, iguanas, birds, or snow leopards (not in your house, of course), see if you can share what is truly unique about your relationship with your pet or the pet you always wished you had.

MONDAY | WRITERS ON WRITING

> Confronted by an absolutely infuriating
> review, it is sometimes helpful for the victim
> to do a little personal research on the critic.
> Is there any truth to the rumor that he had no
> formal education beyond the age of eleven?
> Was he ever arrested for burglary?
>
> —*Jean Kerr*

JEAN KERR IS AN AMERICAN AUTHOR, BEST KNOWN for her humorous novel *Please Don't Eat the Daisies,* published in 1957. Some critics wrote off Kerr's musings on family life as trite, but the public didn't agree. Her book became a bestseller, a movie, and a popular television series.

Although Kerr is jesting about doing a background check on the infuriating critic, her point is valuable. Have a sense of balance about the role of the critic, whether it's your local librarian, a review in a newspaper, or a friend.

One of the values of all artistic endeavors is that its evaluation is subjective. When French artist Claude Monet first unveiled his Impressionist works, they were widely panned. Now, history has proved his artwork to be of the master class: it's beloved and regarded as exceptionally well executed. Andy Warhol's pop art masterpieces, including his soup can paintings, were met with scoffs by many who felt the paintings were nothing more than commercial bunk. Wrong again. The paintings now grace the walls of many major art museums and sell for tens of millions of dollars. If you receive a less-than-glowing review, keep calm, carry on, and consider the source.

TUESDAY | MOTIVATION

> [My friend] asked me, "Do you ever write
> poetry?" and I said, "No"—I'd never thought
> of doing so. He said: "Why don't you?"—and
> at that point I decided that's what I would do.
> Looking back, I conceived how the ground
> had been prepared.
>
> —W. H. Auden

I T LOOKS AS IF BRITISH POET AUDEN KNEW RHONDA Byrne's *The Secret* at least half a century before that book was even written, and certainly before it rocketed to the top of all of the bestseller lists. Published in 2006, *The Secret* has sold tens of millions of copies and been translated into dozens of languages. Its premise? The power of positive thinking.

Positive thinking brings energy and optimism and helps focus our goals and dreams. But why does it work? Recent scientific research shows that there is a strong mind-body connection.

Neurologists describe it as "neurons that fire together, wire together." In other words, you have the capacity, by affirming your goals, to effectively rewire your brain. Every time Auden thought or spoke of being "a very good poet" he was, in fact, gathering neurons together and reinforcing his belief that he would become a successful poet. Wire your neurons together by affirming your belief in your abilities as a writer.

WEDNESDAY | WRITING CLASS

Write a blog entry about a recently released movie.

KEEP IT SHORT, 250 WORDS OR LESS. ACCORDING to BlogPulse, the search engine for blogs, there are 126 million blogs on the Internet. That means web surfers have lots of choices when it comes to choosing a blog, so don't waste their time with a wordy blog post. If your entry is too long, readers are likely to skip over it altogether. Make sure you create a zippy headline that uses the film's name. Encapsulate the essence of your piece in the headline. Use bullet points so your reader can discern information with a quick scan. Write like you talk. It's okay in this format to be more casual with language. That's not to say, however, that it's okay to have typos. Be scrupulous in checking for grammatical errors. Sloppy blog entries will turn off potential readers.

THURSDAY | EDITING

James Blish told me I had the worst case of
"*said* bookism" (that is, using every word
except *said* to indicate dialogue). He told
me to limit the verbs to *said, replied, asked,*
and *answered* and only when absolutely
necessary.

—*Anne McCaffrey*

THIS IS A FINE LESSON ON WRITING DIALOGUE THAT was first learned by the beloved science fiction writer and creator of the *Dragonriders of Pern* novels. McCaffrey is teaching us to let our characters speak for themselves. In order to write believable and compelling dialogue, don't worry about describing how they're saying it. "Susan sneered" is often too much information, and it makes the rest of the dialogue less effective. A better way is to focus on the naughty comeback, such as "Don't be a dolt, Alice. Just whack his head off." The readers then have the opportunity to infer for themselves what Susan is doing with her face, without being instructed. Keeping dialogue cues to a minimum lets the true essence of your story shine.

"Susan sneered" does work when it's a complete sentence, as a retort to the conversations of other characters in the scene. In this way, you're making your verbs do the heavy lifting, creating ambiance when there's no need for more dialogue.

FRIDAY | BIOGRAPHY

> He . . . invariably began with patter and
> palaver, like a conjurer at a fair. . . . Then
> he established his people with bold, bril-
> liant strokes, like a great cartoonist. But the
> barb was always a surprise, adroitly prepared,
> craftily planted, and to catch him at it is an
> exercise for a detective.
>
> —*Francis Hackett*

O. HENRY (1862–1910) WAS THE PEN NAME FOR
William Sydney Porter. As a child in North Carolina,
Porter was always reading. He started working in his uncle's
drugstore at the age of fifteen, and four years later he was
licensed as a pharmacist.

Porter then moved to Texas and in 1887 found a job
drawing maps at the Texas General Land Office. The salary
was enough to support his family, and he began to write
articles for local magazines and newspapers. Eventually,
he became the editor and publisher of *The Rolling Stone*, a
satirical magazine that folded in 1895. At the time, Porter
was working at a bank and was charged with embezzlement;
he fled the country for Honduras. He later returned to the
United States and spent three years in a federal penitentiary.
While in prison, he assumed a pen name and published his
first story, "Whistling Dick's Christmas Stocking" (1899).
A friend of his in New Orleans would forward his stories to
publishers, so they had no idea the writer was imprisoned.
Porter was released on July 24, 1901, for good behavior. He
moved to New York City and went on to write 381 stories,
including the beloved holiday story "The Gift of the Magi."

SATURDAY | BOOKS TO READ

A Room of One's Own by Virginia Woolf

> Women, then, have not had a dog's chance of writing poetry. That is why I have laid so much stress on money and a room of one's own.
>
> —*Virginia Woolf*

WHEN THE BOOK-LENGTH ESSAY *A ROOM OF One's Own* was published in 1929, it met head-on with controversy. It's an important essay for writers to read because it makes such a compelling argument for a complete change in worldview.

Woolf believed in a "materialist approach," suggesting that if women had the same advantages as men, including access to education, they would be on equal footing. In *A Room of One's Own*, Woolf said, "A woman must have money and a room of her own," in order to write fiction. Woolf recommended that the room have a lock and that 500 pounds be provided ($40,000 in today's American dollars). Woolf came from a literary family and took degree-level courses at King's College in London. While at King's College, she met some of the reformers of women's education—encounters that helped to shape this famous essay.

When viewed through today's cultural lens, the book still conveys a profound message that bears revisiting: women are just as capable as men at creating meaningful art.

SUNDAY | WRITING PROMPT

The meaning of freedom . . .

THE NOTION OF PERSONAL FREEDOM IS AUTHENTICALLY American in many respects. It's a topic that has been tackled by many a writer, and often the end product is something unique. In a sense, that's the nature of freedom: to express it any way you choose.

Jonathan Franzen's 2010 bestseller *Freedom* places this ideal at the core of his novel where he explores individual characters and the choices they make. Yet this topic lends itself equally well to essays, poems, or any type of writing. It can be viewed as political or personal, historical or current. No matter how you choose to take it on, make sure you look at every angle: what some consider freedom, others may interpret as reckless or selfish. You might also want to explore how one person's freedom impacts others.

MONDAY | WRITERS ON WRITING

> Writing is a way of talking without being
> interrupted.
>
> —*Jules Renard*

F RENCH AUTHOR JULES RENARD, WHO LIVED FROM
1864 to 1910, was known for his pithy summations
of everyday life. For instance, he penned, "The horse is
the only animal into which one can bang nails," or, "As I
grow to understand life less and less, I learn to love it more
and more."

Along with these quirky insights, Renard expressed one
of the key tenets of writing: authors have the unique ability
to express a thought, idea, or philosophy without the threat
of interruption. How many times in the course of daily life do
you have the opportunity to get your thoughts across without
any interruption? Or, without the *threat* of interruption?

As a writer, you must also create a work space that pro-
vides a sanctuary from the interruptions of your daily life
and get away from the responsibility of answering phone
calls, replying to e-mails, walking the dog, or talking to the
neighbor.

TUESDAY | MOTIVATION

> Half of being smart is knowing what you're
> dumb at.
>
> —*David Gerrold*

WITHIN DAYS OF SEEING THE 1966 *STAR TREK* television series premiere, David Gerrold made a decision to submit a proposal for a two-part episode. The sixty-page outline was summarily rejected by *Star Trek* producer Gene L. Coon. Gerrold was undeterred. He sought out advice from experts, knowing he was "dumb at" certain aspects of writing for television.

His perseverance was rewarded when Coon finally produced his episode, "The Trouble with Tribbles." It became one of the most-watched episodes of the popular series. Later, Gerrold's novelette *The Martian Child* won Hugo and Nebula awards.

Never be afraid to ask for help. All writers, no matter how accomplished, continue to read for knowledge, to ask colleagues for advice, and to seek out thoughtful critics. Just as you wouldn't expect to master a complicated computer software program without any assistance, you shouldn't expect to conquer the art of writing without some support along the way.

WEDNESDAY | WRITING CLASS

Write a caption for a family photo.

PICK A PHOTO YOU ESPECIALLY LIKE. IT CAN BE from a recent vacation, a friend's birthday party, or a family reunion. Write a caption that includes the five W's—what, where, when, who, and why—and do this in fifty words or less. Use a series of short sentences rather than writing one ungainly sentence. Use strong verbs to convey any action in the photo.

THURSDAY | EDITING

When you do common things of life in an uncommon way, you will command the attention of the world.

—George Washington Carver

THIS QUOTE REMINDS ME OF AN OLD BASF TELEVISION commercial, when the ubiquitous tagline for the world's leading chemical company was "We didn't invent the _____ we just made it better." In the same way, Carver, the noted scientist, botanist, and inventor, didn't "invent" the peanut, he just taught farmers how—and why—they should grow it.

In literature, there are very few new ideas. Mostly, stories and novels are just mixes of existing plotlines. Even this practice is not new; writers have been embellishing on the ideas of others at least since Shakespeare's day, and probably well before. And this exercise cuts across all types of writing, including "remixing" song lyrics.

When you're editing your final work and realize that your great idea wasn't entirely your own, the best thing to do is come clean. You can subtly acknowledge that your work pays homage to another's, which is better than waiting for a reviewer to point this out well after publication.

FRIDAY | BIOGRAPHY

> Poetry is the opening and closing of a door,
> leaving those who look through to guess
> about what is seen during a moment.
>
> — *Carl Sandburg*

CARL SANDBURG (1878–1967) WORKED AS A reporter for the *Chicago Daily News,* covering labor issues and writing his own feature in relative obscurity. In 1914, a group of his poems appeared in the nationally circulated *Poetry* magazine. Two years later his book, *Chicago Poems,* was published, and the thirty-eight-year-old author found himself on the brink of an international career.

More poetry followed, along with *Rootabaga Stories* (1922), a book of children's tales. Sandburg's publisher, Alfred Harcourt, suggested he write a biography of Abraham Lincoln for children. Sandburg researched and wrote for three years, instead producing a two-volume biography for adults in 1926: *Abraham Lincoln: The Prairie Years.* This was his first financial success. He moved to Michigan and devoted his time to completing *Abraham Lincoln: The War Years,* for which he won the Pulitzer Prize in 1940.

Sandburg continued his prolific writing in Michigan throughout the war, and afterward moved his family with their herd of prize-winning goats and thousands of books to Flat Rock, North Carolina. Sandburg's *Complete Poems* won him a rare second Pulitzer Prize in 1951. His broad range of writing—from poetry to prose, fiction and nonfiction, for adults and children—made him the quintessential American writer of the early twentieth century.

SATURDAY | BOOKS TO READ

The Lord of the Rings by J. R. R. Tolkien

> By the time the reader has finished [*The Lord of the Rings*]. . . he knows as much about Tolkien's Middle Earth . . . [as] he knows about the actual world.
>
> —*W. H. Auden*

T*HE LORD OF THE RINGS* WAS PUBLISHED IN 1955. Although intended to be a children's story to follow on the heels of his popular book, *The Hobbit,* it became something entirely different. English author J. R. R. Tolkien wrote the work as a single book, taking more than twelve years to complete it. Along the way, he decided to focus on an adult audience. The wide-ranging story was published in three volumes: *The Fellowship of the Ring, The Two Towers,* and *The Return of the King.*

The Lord of the Rings is the sweeping and epic fantasy set in Middle Earth. This parallel world is filled with magical people and places, along with a myriad of mythical creatures including dwarfs, elves, halflings, and dangerously powerful orcs.

The trilogy's ongoing popularity (it has sold more than 150 million copies) is due to Tolkien's creation of a setting so rich and complex that readers feel as if they have actually experienced this world. *The Lord of the Rings* brought fantasy writing to the mainstream and created the foundation for other fantasy writers who have used Tolkien's template.

SUNDAY | WRITING PROMPT

My strongest memory . . .

THIS CLASSIC PROMPT CAN BE INTERPRETED IN A VARIETY of different ways. It could be a profoundly positive experience (such as giving birth or seeing your first grandchild), or it could be a way to revisit something that changed the direction of your life. It could be the smell of your first home, an experience from your early working years, or, as in the case of Stephen King's imagination, a childhood trauma.

In his novella, *The Body*, which was later made into the major motion picture *Stand By Me* (directed by Rob Reiner), King creates a first-person account of a childhood memory as told by a thirty-year-old man. The technique of foreshadowing is employed in a unique way. Most of the story is a straight retrospective of what happened, but comments, or entire chapters that relate to the "present" are interspersed. This gives a clear perspective that this narrative is a memory, yet lets the reader see not only what happened but also how it has affected the narrator in a way that's far more engaging than just a recounting of events.

MONDAY | WRITERS ON WRITING

I can't write five words but that I change seven.
—*Dorothy Parker*

A MERICAN WRITER DOROTHY PARKER IS CONSIDERED one of the grand doyennes of America's literary scene during the first half of the twentieth century. She recognized that writing is a process of constant revision. Like most accomplished writers, Parker spent more time editing, deleting, reorganizing, and cutting and pasting (remember, these were the days before computers) than she did on the actual writing.

Unfortunately, some writers get a bad taste in their mouths when it comes to rewriting. Perhaps, they flash back to childhood days when having to rewrite a paper at school was taken as bad news. Rewriting is not punishment and not torturous. As Parker describes it, rewriting and editing is an opportunity to improve and better express your ideas.

As Henry David Thoreau said, "Not that the story need be long, but it will take a long while to make it short." Ironically, it may take longer for you to make a story short than it took you to make it long. Don't despair. It's all part of the writing process, and you'll come to enjoy editing and revising as much as the writing.

TUESDAY | MOTIVATION

> I'm a slow writer: five, six hundred words is
> a good day. That's the reason it took me 20
> years to write those million and a half words
> on the Civil War.
>
> —*Shelby Foote*

REMEMBER THAT ALL WRITING COUNTS AND THAT all writing is cumulative. If you're struggling to get started, daunted by the stack of blank paper in front of you or the glare of your computer screen, then set a word-count goal for each day's writing. It's both liberating and inspiring to have this clearly defined goal in mind.

Alex Haley, author of *Roots*, disciplined himself, even when ill, to write six hundred words a day. Hemingway famously penned five hundred words a day. J. G. Ballard, author of the bestselling *Empire of the Sun,* aimed for one thousand a day, "even if I've got a hangover." Mega-bestselling author Nicholas Sparks commits himself to writing two thousand words each day.

Like the fable of the tortoise and the hare, slow and steady can most assuredly win the race. Consider the math. If an average novel weighs in at 80,000 words, then it would take only 160 days, writing at a pace of 500 words per day, to complete a first draft: less than half a year.

WEDNESDAY | WRITING CLASS

Make a one-panel comic strip about getting your hair cut.

THINK OF THIS AS WRITING A SHORT STORY, A *REALLY* short story of no more than fifty words. Come up with a plot. Maybe, the stylist misunderstands and gives you the wrong haircut or dyes it the wrong color. Or, your stylist gets called away for an emergency, leaving you with lopsided hair. Try to make the story funny and compelling. Remember that your pictures do some of the talking for you. For instance, if you depict yourself with lopsided hair, you don't need to describe your hair in prose. Your reader will get this information visually. Don't fret about the quality of your drawing. If necessary, use stick figures or computer clip art that you can paste into the panels.

THURSDAY | EDITING

Place yourself in the background.
—*Strunk and White,*
The Elements of Style

THIS ADVICE IS ALWAYS GOOD, UNLESS YOU'RE writing a memoir, where you are center stage. If not, even if your work is "all about you," make sure the reader doesn't know it.

This editing tip is a slam against the omniscient narrator, also known as the "third person omniscient" point of view. This method of storytelling employs a narrator (you) who knows the thoughts and feelings of all of the characters in the story, as opposed to "third person limited," which adheres closely to one character's perspective.

Basically, the kings and queens of editorial style are saying that no one likes a know-it-all. Readers don't want to be blatantly told how you would like them to feel about your characters. Instead, they would rather figure it out themselves through their individual interactions.

One way around this is the "multiple points of view" technique, which seems to have taken hold in current literature. These books read like short stories because each character is allowed to present his or her point of view in his or her own chapter. This is great fun to read once in a while, but after reading five or six of these novels in a row, I find that it gets tedious. However, it is still more engaging than the omniscient view because you, the author, remain in the background.

FRIDAY | BIOGRAPHY

> I've learned that people will forget what you said, people will forget what you did, but people will never forget how you made them feel.
>
> —*Maya Angelou*

M AYA ANGELOU (1928–2014) WAS BORN AS Marguerite Johnson. She is one of America's best-known poets and autobiographical writers. But before her literary career took off, she worked as a singer, actress, dancer, civil rights activist, book editor, lecturer, and professor.

Life was not always easy for her. Angelou's parents divorced when she was only three, and she was sent to live in rural Arkansas. When she was seven, she was sexually molested by her mother's boyfriend. This traumatic event psychologically scarred her, and she remained mute for the next five years. As a teen, she studied dance and drama, but she dropped out to become San Francisco's first African American female cable car conductor. She later finished school.

Angelou knew how to surround herself with powerful and influential leaders in every field. She studied modern dance with Martha Graham, danced with Alvin Ailey, and in 1958 joined the Harlem Writers Guild, where she met Dr. Martin Luther King, Jr. In the mid-1960s, she moved to Africa, where she met Malcolm X. Later, guided by the novelist James Baldwin, she finally put pen to paper and wrote what she knew. The first volume of her five-volume auto-biography, *I Know Why the Caged Bird Sings,* was published in 1970 to international acclaim. In all, she wrote more than thirty bestselling works.

SATURDAY | BOOKS TO READ

In Cold Blood by Truman Capote

> I got this idea of doing a really serious big work—it would be precisely like a novel, with a single difference: Every word of it would be true from beginning to end.
>
> —*Truman Capote*

PUBLISHED IN 1966, TRUMAN CAPOTE'S *IN COLD BLOOD* became an immediate bestseller. And to think that the book never would have been written if Capote had not read a slim, three-hundred-word piece buried in the back of the *New York Times* about the random and brutal murder of the Clutter family in rural Kansas.

In Cold Blood tells the story of Dick Hickock and Perry Smith and their murder of the four members of the Clutter family. Capote describes everything from the details of the Clutter family's last day to the particulars of the crime scene and the intricate facts about the prosecution and defense cases. It's a chilling and compelling page-turner.

With *In Cold Blood*, Capote created a new genre: narrative nonfiction. Although the idea of a nonfiction novel doesn't seem radical today, in 1966 the concept was unheard of. Capote's writing in this book paved the way for future New Journalism writers such as Tom Wolfe, Norman Mailer, and Joan Didion. Capote's book also provided the blueprint for perennially popular television shows about crime, like *CSI* and *Law and Order* (which focuses both on the crime and on the legal processes that follow).

SUNDAY | WRITING PROMPT

The nature of friendship . . .

FRIENDSHIPS HAVE BEEN AT THE CORE OF MANY GREAT pieces of writing for years, but one of my favorite novels about the nature of friendship is *The Divine Secrets of the Ya-Ya Sisterhood* by Rebecca Wells. Reviews compared it to the work of Fannie Flagg, who wrote another wonderful book about friendship, *Fried Green Tomatoes at the Whistle Stop Cafe.*

Wells's second novel continues the story of her character Siddalee Walker, who revisits her mother's lifelong friendships with three women, collectively known as "the Ya-Ya's," via a scrapbook. The anecdotes about the Ya-Ya's are very amusing, and through them, Siddalee is able to understand her mother on a different level.

You can write about the friendships of others, as Wells did, or explore your own unique relationships with the people with whom you've surrounded yourself. That's the most interesting angle of the nature of friendship: you can't choose your family, but you *can* choose your friends.

MONDAY | WRITERS ON WRITING

> Writing is like meditation or going into an ESP trance, or prayer. Like dreaming. You are tapping into your unconscious. To be fully conscious and alert, with life banging and popping and cuckooing all around, you are not going to find your way to your subconscious, which is a place of complete submission.
>
> —*Carolyn Chute*

CAROLYN CHUTE, AUTHOR OF THE BESTSELLING *The Beans of Egypt, Maine,* published in 1985, describes isolation as essential to the writer's art. Finding complete submission has not always been easy for her. Chute spent decades getting by as a waitress, chicken factory worker, hospital floor scrubber, shoe factory worker, potato farm worker, tutor, canvasser, teacher, social worker, and school bus driver before finding success as a writer. Now she lives an isolated life at a rural Maine outpost. A sign by her driveway reads, "Woa. Visitors Turn Back." If you choose not to heed the warning, you'll find a compound with stacks of tires, rusty furniture, and a pen of Scottish terriers. And an AK-47 rifle.

Chute has taken an extreme route to finding complete submission. You do not have to move to a rural enclave. However, writers need to create a peaceful environment conducive to tapping into the subconscious, getting to the heart of an idea. If you're waiting to hear the timer on your clothes drier, you're probably unable to access some of your deepest thoughts. For Chute and most writers, their craft is not possible with life "banging and popping . . . all around."

TUESDAY | MOTIVATION

> John Cheever wrote some of his early
> stories in his underwear. . . . Thomas Wolfe
> reportedly wrote parts of his voluminous
> novels while leaning over the top of a
> refrigerator. Flannery O'Connor sat for two
> hours every day at a typewriter facing the
> back of a clothes dresser.
>
> *—Kent Haruf*

DON'T WORRY. SPORTING ONLY YOUR SKIVVIES is not a requirement for becoming a successful writer, nor is proximity to the refrigerator. What is necessary is to develop a routine for your writing, just as you have other daily routines, like making your bed or fixing breakfast.

Start by choosing a place to write. Perhaps it's at your kitchen table, with a mug of coffee at the ready, or at your desk in a quiet corner of your home. Some writers opt for a spot away from home, like J. K. Rowling, who writes in restaurants where she nurses one cup of coffee, or Maya Angelou, who favors the sterile environment of hotel rooms. Wherever you choose, pick a place with few distractions.

Kent Haruf, author of the bestselling *Plainsong*, goes to extreme measures to ensure he is not distracted. When he writes, it's in the basement of his family home in a small room that once served as a coal cellar. There, Haruf takes off his glasses and pulls a stocking cap snugly over his eyes. "It's the old notion of blinding yourself so you can see," says Haruf. He types on a manual typewriter, finding that this writing blind helps to free up his mind to become more spontaneous. Only once, he notes, did his fingers stray off home row.

WEDNESDAY | WRITING CLASS

Create instructions for making a sock puppet.

YOU'RE GOING TO INSTRUCT THE READER HOW TO transform a plain white sock into a puppet with personality. Start with a materials list. Along with the sock, will the crafter need scissors, paper, scraps of fabric, glue, pipe cleaners, and/or buttons? Make sure to include everything needed in this bulleted list. Then, describe, step-by-step, how to make and personalize the puppet. Number these instructional steps. Tell your reader how to create a puppet by adding eyes, nose, hair, clothing, and any other details. Assume that your reader has never created a sock puppet. Don't take even the smallest step for granted.

THURSDAY | EDITING

> Aim for vividness in describing.
> —*Frederick C. Crews,*
> The Random House Handbook

A RE YOU LETTING YOUR ADJECTIVES AND ADVERBS do their job? Can the reader get a good idea of setting based solely on your language? These are questions to ask yourself when you're in the final rounds of editing.

Vivid language is particularly important for nonfiction writing, when you're trying to bring to life a particular place or time. It can make the difference between a boring article and captivating reading. But be careful not to overdo it and step into the muck of "purple prose." This happens when each scene is dripping in description or is overly dramatic—so much so that the reader says, "Enough, I'm so not interested."

Dialogue is another place where vivid language makes for better reading. Choose colorful words and expressions for your characters that are believable. Let them have a sense of humor, or pathos, or whatever emotion they're trying to convey. Let them see, hear, touch, and so on, and be able to describe what they're experiencing, so the reader can enjoy the ride.

FRIDAY | BIOGRAPHY

> I feel no need for any other faith than my
> faith in human beings. Like Confucius of old,
> I am so absorbed in the wonder of earth and
> the life upon it that I cannot think of heaven
> and the angels.
>
> *— Pearl S. Buck*

PEARL S. BUCK (1892–1973) WAS BORN IN Hillsboro, West Virginia, but grew up in China where her parents were missionaries. Buck was sent back to America to attend Randolph-Macon Woman's College in Virginia. After graduation, she returned to China and lived there until 1934, returning to the United States only to complete a master's degree at Cornell University.

Buck did not begin to write until the 1920s. But when she did, she was able to introduce the hidden world of China to a curious American audience. Her first novel, *East Wind, West Wind*, appeared in 1930. It was followed by *The Good Earth* (1931), *Sons* (1932), and *A House Divided* (1935), together forming a trilogy about the Wang family. *The Good Earth* remained on American bestseller lists for almost two years and earned her several awards, including the Pulitzer Prize. Her personal interest in East/West relations led to some activity in political journalism. In 1938, she became the first American woman to be awarded the Nobel Prize in Literature, "for her rich and truly epic descriptions of peasant life in China and for her biographical masterpieces."

SATURDAY | BOOKS TO READ

Rebecca by Daphne du Maurier

> Last night I dreamt I went to Manderley again.
> It seemed to me I stood by the iron gate
> leading to the drive, and for a while I could
> not enter, for the way was barred to me.
>
> —*Daphne du Maurier*

WITH THE PUBLICATION OF *REBECCA* IN 1938, Daphne du Maurier became one of the most popular writers of the day. The book remains a staple on most lists of the 100 best mystery novels of all time.

In this spellbinding psychological thriller, du Maurier uses an extended flashback to lay out the events. The unnamed narrator, who is safely ensconced in a hotel room with her husband, relates the harrowing events that led to their harried retreat from Manderley, the family estate.

Rebecca had a profound impact on the future of the Gothic novel. Often compared to the classic of the genre, *Jane Eyre* (although the *New York Times* says du Maurier, "served up more sinister fare than the Brontës"), *Rebecca* set a new and different standard. While containing the traditional elements—a ghostly, nightmarish atmosphere and an impressionable young woman—*Rebecca* deviates on one key point: the brooding heroine of this book is not innocent.

Following the successful publication of *Rebecca*, Gothic novels enjoyed a renaissance, with authors such as Mary Stewart, Virginia Coffman, and Barbara Michaels writing many bestselling works.

SUNDAY | WRITING PROMPT

The scariest thing that ever happened to me . . .

I LOVE THIS PROMPT BECAUSE YOU CAN LET YOUR imagination run to your deepest fears or logically revisit your darkest memories. By exploring your scariest moment, you might find that your memory of a real event doesn't hold up to the facts. Or, you might find that you've blocked some of the most upsetting details and can now face them with the perspective of time.

Horror and thriller writers have been exploring this topic for hundreds of years. To my mind, the ones who are most successful choose a fear people don't even know they have. Take the novel *Jaws* by Peter Benchley as the perfect example. Before the novel, and later the movie, most beachgoers never gave a thought to what lurked beneath the depths of the sea. After the movie was released, the beaches, especially in the Northeast where the story took place, were emptied, and everyone was afraid to go into the ocean.

See if you can transfer your fears to others—or face them yourself—by tackling this prompt.

MONDAY | WRITERS ON WRITING

> It is necessary to write, if the days are not to
> slip emptily by. How else, indeed, to clap the
> net over the butterfly of the moment? For
> the moment passes, it is forgotten; the mood
> is gone; life itself is gone. That is where the
> writer scores over his fellows: he catches the
> changes of his mind on the hop.
>
> —*Vita Sackville-West*

B RITISH AUTHOR VITA SACKVILLE-WEST, AUTHOR of the prize-winning narrative poem *The Land*, cites the absolutely necessity of writers to ply their trade. Once bitten by the bug, writers find it "necessary to write" lest the days "slip emptily by." Just as so many of us won't miss a day at the gym, writers develop the need to write every day to keep their heart and soul intact.

Beyond the visceral need to put pen to paper, writers also feel the need to record the moment. As Sackville-West so aptly describes, once the moment passes it is quickly forgotten. Sackville-West says that writers have the privilege and the duty to record what unfolds in front of them, from the mundane, odd bits of everyday life to the profound moments.

We are constantly bombarded by news, trivialities, and other information, even more so in this age of technology. The job of every writer is to record ideas, information, and even the context of the day before they are lost.

TUESDAY | MOTIVATION

> It's so easy to fool yourself into thinking that
> you're working hard. It's so easy not to write.
> So you use any trick you can to make yourself
> know there's work to be done. That's why I
> wear a jacket and tie when I sit down to write.
>
> —*Robert Caro*

THE KEY WORD HERE IS *WORK*. WRITING IS ONE OF your jobs. You may only have fifteen or thirty minutes available for writing each day, but while you're at your computer or your journal, writing is your work.

Make it official by getting ready for work. Take a shower, brush your teeth and hair, and get dressed. If it's morning, get out of your pajamas. If you've just finished exercising, change out of your workout gear and put on other clothes. You don't need to wear a suit, but you need to distinguish the time you're writing from other times of the day.

While it's true that John Cheever often wrote while wearing nothing but his underwear (see page 39), he first went to his windowless office (in the basement of the apartment building in which he and his family lived) fully clothed in his business suit, disrobed, carefully hung up his suit, and went to work in his boxers. When finished, he donned his clothes and rode the elevator back to his apartment. In that way, Cheever must have felt that he "went to work."

WEDNESDAY | WRITING CLASS

Create an anagram using an author's name or
the title of a book.

A N ANAGRAM IS THE REARRANGEMENT OF LETTERS
in one word or phrase into another word or phrase.
For instance, the letters in *dormitory* can be re-formed to
spell "dirty room." Likewise, the letters in *debit card* can be
rearranged to spell "bad credit." *Alice B. Toklas* becomes
"sociable talk"; *E. M. Forster* becomes "terse form"; and the
book title *Ulysses* becomes "sly uses."

THURSDAY | EDITING

> Do not overdo the literary device of
> hyphenating words that are not usually
> linked: the stringing-together-of-lots-and-
> lots-of-words-and-ideas tendency can
> be tiresome.
>
> —The Economist Style Guide

THERE'S NO SINGLE RULE TO HELP YOU DECIDE when two words should be run together as one word or should be hyphenated. However, there are some general guidelines that can help you determine when words can or should be hyphenated, and when they should not.

Words with common or short prefixes, like *biplane, prepay, subcommittee, underdog,* or *asexual,* do not require hyphenation. However, some prefixes require hyphenation when closing them up would confuse the intended meaning, for example *recreate* versus *re-create.* Longer words, especially ones that run consonants together, can be hyphenated, such as *cross-reference, major-general,* or *submachine-gun.* Using numbers as an age is also a good use of hyphenation, as in "eighty-year-old woman."

Use of hyphens can help avoid ambiguities when three words are used together. For example, high-school results can mean something entirely different than high school results.

FRIDAY | BIOGRAPHY

> Kipling strikes me personally as the most
> complete man of genius (as distinct from
> fine intelligence) that I have ever known.
> —*Henry James*

RUDYARD KIPLING (1865–1936) WAS A BRITISH author and poet. In 1907, he was awarded the Nobel Prize in Literature, making him the first English-language writer to receive the prize, and he remains its youngest recipient.

Born in India, Kipling's parents considered themselves Anglo-Indians: a term used in the nineteenth century for people of British origin living in India. Yet Kipling would spend the bulk of his life elsewhere. Most of his life was spent away from India, until he returned at the age of seventeen to work as a civil servant for Anglo-Indian newspapers. His literary career began with a collection of verse, *Departmental Ditties* (1886), but subsequently he became chiefly known as a writer of short stories. A prolific writer, he achieved fame quickly. By 1889, he returned to England via Japan and America. He met and married an American and lived in Vermont for five years in the 1890s. *The Jungle Book* was published in 1894, becoming an instant children's classic all over the world.

SATURDAY | BOOKS TO READ

The Odyssey by Homer

> Of all fictions, the marvelous journey
> [as in Homer's *Odyssey*] is the one
> formula that is never exhausted.
>
> —*Northrop Frye*

IT IS VIRTUALLY IMPOSSIBLE TO OVERSTATE THE IMPACT of Homer's epic poem, *The Odyssey*. Everyone from William Shakespeare and James Joyce to Matt Groening, the creator of *The Simpsons*, has credited Homer with influencing their work.

Although details are sketchy about Homer's life, it's believed that Homer was blind and that he probably composed his two greatest works—first *The Iliad* and then *The Odyssey*—between 700 and 800 BCE. Both of these works are referred to as epic poems: they are stylized, yet easy-to-understand, narrative poems.

The Odyssey tells the story of Odysseus as he returns to Greece after the fall of Troy. There are pirates, six-headed monsters, interactions between humans and the gods, cannibals, shipwrecks, cases of mistaken identity, fraught love interests, treachery, greed, and more.

If you've ever read a book about a journey—say, John Steinbeck's *Travels with Charley* or Jack Kerouac's *On the Road*—you can thank Homer for the inspiration. In writing *The Odyssey*, he set the bar high for road trip narratives.

SUNDAY | WRITING PROMPT

My first flight . . .

YOU DON'T HAVE TO TAKE THE POINT OF VIEW of a bird or be a professional pilot-turned-writer like Richard Bach to explore your feelings about flight. A former U.S. Air Force pilot, gypsy barnstormer, and airplane mechanic, Bach is the author of fifteen books about flight, ranging from the classic allegory *Jonathan Livingston Seagull* to his memoirs and his novels.

Bach adds a spiritual bent to flight, but you don't have to do so. You might be moved by the sheer technology of it or the travel abilities that it affords. See if you can connect with the excitement and mystery, and how it has changed your worldview. Use descriptive language to capture the essence of your experience instead of relying on a purely narrative form.

MONDAY | WRITERS ON WRITING

> The pages are still blank, but there is
> a miraculous feeling of the words
> being there, written in invisible ink
> and clamoring to become visible.
>
> —*Vladimir Nabokov*

B EFORE PUTTING WORDS ON PAPER, WRITERS FEEL
the ideas and themes in their minds. Nabokov, famed
for his love of words and wordplay, certainly had a constant
stream of words swirling through his mind.

All writers, like this famed Russian novelist, author
of the bestselling *Lolita*; *Speak, Memory*; *Ada, or Ardor: A
Family Chronicle*; and *Pale Fire,* have words "clamoring to
become visible." Consider the optimism of Nabokov's statement. He regards it as miraculous that the words are there,
ready to be committed to print. Remember that you, too,
have the words and ideas at the ready. If you keep this in
mind, the blank pages will be less intimidating when you
sit down to write.

Like Nabokov, you can use your words to create descriptive details and puns to get your creative juices flowing. You
can also use your knowledge of language to create new words,
which Nabokov was masterful at doing.

TUESDAY | MOTIVATION

Make everybody fall out of the plane first,
and then explain who they were and why
they were in the plane to begin with.
—*Nancy Ann Dibble*

NANCY ANN DIBBLE WROTE *ELEMENTS OF FICTION Writing: Plot* under the pseudonym Ansen Dibell. In it, she outlines the ways in which a writer can create a strong and compelling plotline.

One way to do this is to remember as you write that you don't have a large window of time to grab your reader's attention. Many book buyers choose a book based on the strength of the first page, so it's important to create a strong and compelling opening to your work.

Consider some of the famous first lines in literary history:

» "124 was spiteful."—Toni Morrison, *Beloved*

» "Mrs. Dalloway said she would buy the flowers herself."—Virginia Woolf, *Mrs. Dalloway*

» "For a long time, I went to bed early."—Marcel Proust, *Swann's Way*

» "In the town, there were two mutes and they were always together."—Carson McCullers, *The Heart Is a Lonely Hunter*

Imagine you are that customer in the bookstore who makes a decision based solely on the power of the first line. To paraphrase the poet T. S. Eliot, "If you start with a bang, you won't end with a whimper."

WEDNESDAY | WRITING CLASS

Write an entry about a happy dream.

KEEP YOUR WRITING NOTEBOOK AT THE SIDE OF your bed so you can begin writing as soon as you wake up. Don't get dressed or take a shower before writing in your dream journal. It's important to write about dreams as soon as you awaken so your thoughts come directly from your subconscious. Write in the present tense, as it will help you to remember your dream as you write. Describe any sensations and emotions you felt. Describe the characters and action of your dream. Don't worry about creating pitch-perfect prose here; just let your writing flow. Write the date of the dream in your journal, and give your dream a title. The more you track your dreams, the better your dream recall will become.

THURSDAY | EDITING

> If you want a happy ending, that depends, of
> course, on where you stop your story.
> — *Orson Welles*

ONE OF THE TRICKIEST PARTS OF WRITING IS determining when you're done. Even if you've outlined your ideas and followed your original course, you may be tempted to keep the story going. This is particularly true if you've "fallen in love" with your characters.

One tip to determine if you're finished, or at least close to being done, is to make sure that you have both a climax to your story and a denouement. Many writers confuse these as the same thing. The difference is that the climax is the story's ultimate high point, while the denouement is when everyone in the story, and the reader, understands the final outcome of the action.

For example, in Shakespeare's *Romeo and Juliet*, the climax occurs when Friar Laurence's plan is put into action: Juliet pretends to be dead, but Romeo doesn't realize she's still alive and commits suicide. The denouement is when Prince Escalus tells everyone that the deaths are the result of the families' feuds and everyone feels guilty. The story ends with everlasting sadness.

FRIDAY | BIOGRAPHY

When I write, I forget that it's not real.
I'm living the story.

—Stephenie Meyer

S TEPHENIE MEYER (1973–) WAS BORN IN HARTFORD, Connecticut. She grew up in Phoenix, Arizona, and attended Chaparral High School in Scottsdale. She then attended Brigham Young University, where she received a BA in English in 1997.

Meyer is a member of The Church of Jesus Christ of Latter-day Saints, and her religious convictions strongly influenced the themes of marriage and family in her writing. Meyer had never even thought about writing fiction before waking up from a dream in 2003. At the time, she was a stay-at-home mother of three young sons. Her dream was so compelling that it began to affect the daylight hours of her life. Household chores, chauffeuring her children around town, and every mundane errand she ran became infused with plot ideas that she was unable to shake. Late at night when her children were asleep, Meyer began to write. Her older sister, Emily, encouraged her to keep at it, and after three months of late-night writing, Stephanie Meyer had written her first novel, *Twilight*.

With the encouragement from her older sister, Meyer submitted her manuscript to various literary agencies. Of the fifteen letters she wrote, five went unanswered, nine brought rejections, and the last was a positive response by the New York literary agency Writers House, that sold the project at auction to the publishing company Little, Brown and Company. *Twilight* was published in 2005 and debuted at number five on the *New York Times* bestseller list.

SATURDAY | BOOKS TO READ

Grimm's Fairy Tales
by The Brothers Grimm

*But iron slippers had already been put upon the
fire, and they were brought in with tongs, and
set before her. Then she was forced to put on
the red-hot shoes, and dance until she dropped
down dead.*

—*Jacob and Wilhelm Grimm,
from "Little Snow-White"*

WHEN JACOB AND WILHELM GRIMM PUBLISHED their first collection of fairy tales in 1812, it was with an eye toward educating their readers about the history of language and folklore. They certainly were not writing with children in mind. The brothers, both librarians and professors, were more interested in studying the history of language and considered themselves patriotic folklorists.

Of course, we don't read these stories to study language. We enjoy them for their captivating stories of dragons, evil witches, magical forces, enchantments, and fairy godmothers. Grimm's fairy tales include "Cinderella," "Rapunzel," "Hansel and Gretel," "Snow White," "Sleeping Beauty," "Tom Thumb," "Rumpelstiltskin," and "The Fisherman and His Wife."

Grimm's Fairy Tales teach us how to create a story with a truly compelling plot regardless of the simplicity of the theme. Most of their fairy tales were simple battles between good and evil. The reader always knows who will win in the end: the adventure is how they got there.

SUNDAY | WRITING PROMPT

People are easily corrupted . . .

POWER CORRUPTS, BUT SO DO MONEY, BEAUTY, sex, freedom, and even health. These themes have been explored as long as stories have been recorded, going back as far as the Bible and William Shakespeare.

Have you had any experiences with a person who has become morally or politically corrupt? Or, can you imagine a situation where someone becomes corrupt because of a twist on his or her extenuating circumstance? Do people need to be persuaded to become corrupt, like Shakespeare's Macbeth, or does it happen on its own? All of these ideas pose a challenge to the writer of both fiction and fact. The question is, can you get to the bottom of it?

MONDAY | WRITERS ON WRITING

If my doctor told me I had only six minutes to
live, I wouldn't brood. I'd type a little faster.
—*Isaac Asimov*

AMERICAN SCIENCE FICTION AND POPULAR SCIENCE writer Isaac Asimov needn't have worried about typing faster. In his seven-decade life, he wrote and edited more than five hundred books. He wrote almost ten thousand letters and postcards. Clearly, Asimov liked to type, and although his advice here is given with a bit of a wink and a nod, there's tremendous value in his view.

To be a writer means to write. It is as simple as that. Writing is sort of an odd hybrid. It requires the mental energy to create ideas and craft language. It also demands a physical regimen of sitting and working. Professional writers, like Asimov, have trained themselves to write by creating a routine and structure.

Science shows that you can rewire your brain to create a writing routine and form a writing habit. When Albert Einstein decided he needed to develop the ability to think more creatively, he remodeled his brain by playing the violin. Winston Churchill painted landscapes. Both said that these exercises helped them develop their abilities to think in new ways. Einstein's second wife, Elsa, credited the violin and music with helping Albert develop his scientific theories: "Music helps him when he is thinking about his theories." Perhaps without Einstein's violin there would have been no $E = MC^2$.

TUESDAY | MOTIVATION

I do not try to dance better than anyone else.
I only try to dance better than myself.

—*Mikhail Baryshnikov*

THERE'S ONLY ONE BAR THAT YOU NEED MEASURE up to as a writer and that is the one you set for yourself. Ballet dancer Mikhail Baryshnikov was born in communist Russia. Although his talent as a dancer was apparent from a young age, the Soviet system of training dancers did not recognize his early genius. Further, because his short stature made it impossible for him to tower over his ballerina partners, he was relegated to secondary roles.

Undeterred, he continued to dance with the famed Bolshoi Ballet, and although not a star, he continued to work to "dance better than myself." These efforts paid off when in 1974, during a grueling tour with the Bolshoi, he defected from the Soviet Union and became the principal dancer for the American Ballet Theater. Today, he is recognized as one of the greatest ballet dancers of the twentieth century.

Just as Baryshnikov set out to dance for himself, you must write for yourself. Even if your vision is to have a work published, you must first write a work that's pleasing to you and that meets the standards you have set for your own writing. Comedian Bill Cosby says, "I don't know the key to success, but the key to failure is trying to please everybody." Please yourself first and then others will be pleased, too.

WEDNESDAY | WRITING CLASS

Write an essay on why it is (or is not) important
to eat organic food.

B REAK YOUR ESSAY INTO THREE PARTS: INTRODUCTION,
body, and conclusion. In your introduction, use your
thesis statement to define your views on organic food. Is
organic food essential for better health, or is the hype
much ballyhooed? Start your essay with a grabber to get
your reader's attention, such as using an interesting fact. In
the body of your essay, support your thesis statement. If
you think organic food is overpriced and under-regulated,
give evidence. In your conclusion, sum up your argument.
Remember, the goal of an essay is to persuade. When you're
done, ask yourself if you believe that you could change someone's mind about organics.

THURSDAY | EDITING

My play was a complete success. The
audience was a failure.

—Ashleigh Brilliant

WHEN YOU ARE WRITING FOR AN AUDIENCE, you need to identify if they are coming to your work with a certain set of expectations. That means you have to understand their needs and make sure that you give 'em what they want.

All forms of successful writing are created with a specific audience in mind. Each word, each sentence, should be aimed at your target audience. A romance novel has an entirely different cadence than a thriller. A military biography will use a different vocabulary than one written about a famous painter. The advice from a doctor is usually given in an authoritative tone; the advice found in a relationship book is much more relaxed.

The differences are even greater in the magazine world. Take automobile magazines, for example. These are entirely audience-specific and use descriptive language found in no other media. The writers know that their readers get pleasure from thinking about cars in just this way. Without knowing your audience, you can write the greatest piece that will never get published.

FRIDAY | BIOGRAPHY

> What I write when I force myself is generally just as good as what I write when I'm feeling inspired. It's mainly a matter of forcing yourself to write.
>
> —*Tom Wolfe*

T OM WOLFE (1930–   ) WAS BORN IN RICHMOND, Virginia, to an affluent family that afforded him the privilege of pursuing a career in the arts. In December 1956, he began working for the *Springfield (Massachusetts) Union* and has been writing ever since. Although he is best known as a novelist, Wolfe spent more than twenty-five years writing investigative nonfiction and is credited for helping to create New Journalism.

In 1962, Wolfe was a reporter for the *New York Herald Tribune* and its Sunday supplement, *New York* magazine. His first book, *The Kandy-Kolored Tangerine-Flake Streamline Baby*, was a bestseller, and in 1968 he published two nonfiction bestsellers on the same day: *The Pump House Gang* and *The Electric Kool-Aid Acid Test*. In 1979, Wolfe published *The Right Stuff*, a book about the United States' manned space program, which was awarded the American Book Award for nonfiction.

Wolfe invented many now-popular American phrases, including "the right stuff," "radical chic," "the Me Decade," and "good ol' boy." His first novel, *The Bonfire of the Vanities*, initially appeared in serial form in *Rolling Stone* magazine and was subsequently published in book form in 1987.

SATURDAY | BOOKS TO READ

When Pride Still Mattered
by David Maraniss

[Maraniss] forges a near-perfect synthesis of fine writing and fascinating material. [*When Pride Still Mattered*] may be the best sports biography ever published.

—*Ron Fimrite*

WINNING ISN'T EVERYTHING, IT'S THE ONLY thing," Green Bay Packers' coach Vince Lombardi famously uttered. Or did he? In *When Pride Still Mattered*, the bestselling 1999 biography of this legendary coach, David Maraniss examines the truths and the myths behind this larger-than-life character.

In this award-winning book, Maraniss considers whether the famed coach was a motivator, a manipulator, a bully, or a great leader. Maraniss deftly describes how Lombardi was able to muster the inner and outer strength to coach the Green Bay Packers to back-to-back-to-back National Football League titles and back-to-back Super Bowl titles.

The strength of the book lies in its honest portrayal of a legendary figure. Rather than presenting a hagiographic view of Lombardi, Maraniss develops a picture of the entire man—conflicted, eager to win, filled with a single-minded devotion, and at times difficult but always human.

SUNDAY | WRITING PROMPT

Sports are important . . .

COMPARING SPORTS TO ANY ASPECT OF LIFE IS overused, but only because it is often so true. Sports are a microcosm of what happens in the real world: the failures and triumphs of everyday life.

And, many believe that sports are important in terms of growth and development, on both the personal as well as the community level. This aspect was clearly portrayed in the book *Friday Night Lights* by H. G. Bissinger, which was later used as the basis for the hit television series. Bissinger recorded how one Texas high-school football team had a transformative effect over everyone involved, from the players to the spectators.

Take on this topic if you have a strong opinion about sports. Delve into the deeper issues of your favorite pastime, and see if what you write holds up to the standard set by this excellent nonfiction book.

MONDAY | WRITERS ON WRITING

> Everywhere I go I'm asked if I think the
> university stifles writers. My opinion is that
> they don't stifle enough of them. There's
> many a bestseller that could have been
> prevented by a good teacher.
>
> —*Flannery O'Connor*

AMERICAN AUTHOR FLANNERY O'CONNOR WAS made of stern stuff. After a diagnosis of lupus at a young age, O'Connor knew she had to make every minute count, and she focused her time on honing her writing.

Flannery O'Connor knew firsthand about university writing programs. She was accepted to the acclaimed University of Iowa's Writers Workshop in 1945 and received her master of fine arts degree in 1947. While completing her degree, she also developed the beginning for her critically acclaimed novel *Wise Blood.*

O'Connor's quote above can be read as tongue-in-cheek. After all, her time at the University of Iowa writing program helped her pen her own acclaimed book *Wise Blood.* Although not a bestseller upon publication, it has sold tens of thousands of copies for six decades. In *The Habit of Being,* a compendium of more than eight hundred letters written by O'Connor during her lifetime, she offers words of wisdom to aspiring writers, including the crucial virtue of creating a writing habit. "I'm a full-time believer in writing habits. You may be able to do without them if you have genius but most of us only have talent and this is simply something that has to be assisted all the time by physical and mental habits or it dries up and blows away."

TUESDAY | MOTIVATION

> [This one-inch picture frame on my desk]
> reminds me that all I have to do is to write
> down as much as I can see through a one-
> inch picture frame. This is all I have to bite
> off for the time being.
>
> —*Anne Lamott*

JUST AS PUTTING ONE FOOT IN FRONT OF THE OTHER results in walking, writing, even in small bits, adds up, often to complete stories or even novels. Just remember steady as she goes: sentence by sentence, paragraph by paragraph, page by page.

If you're struggling to put words on the page, try Lamott's advice for a week or so. Write one carefully crafted sentence. A week's worth of sentences will provide you with a page of written work.

When he was writing his masterwork *Ulysses*, James Joyce sometimes spent a whole day creating one sentence. After 265,000 words, that's a lot of days' sentences. In fact, it took Joyce seven years to write *Ulysses*. That works out to only 104 words per day.

WEDNESDAY | WRITING CLASS

Describe the most memorable first day of school.

I T COULD BE YOUR CHILD'S FIRST DAY OF KINDER-garten, your brother's first day of high school, or your own first day of college. Choose a first day, and describe all of the events surrounding it. Describe the setting: What year was it? What was the weather like?

Show the emotion of the day through examples of people's behavior and actions.

If it is your child's first day of kindergarten, how did she feel as you walked her to the bus or to the school's doors? What were you feeling? If you are describing your first day, what emotions did you feel?

THURSDAY | EDITING

> Ellipsis points suggest faltering or fragmented
> speech accompanied by confusion, insecurity,
> distress, or uncertainty, and they should be
> reserved for that purpose.
>
> —The Chicago Manual of Style

M AKE SURE THAT YOUR PUNCTUATION IS NOT the most memorable part of your work. This can occur if you are overdoing it with some form that's not often used, like ellipses. Nothing says "purple prose" more than a piece of writing covered with ellipses. But if you use them as instructed here, and use them sparingly in your work, they can be quite effective.

When I see ellipses, they immediately bring to mind the music that's played before the big reveal in a murder mystery. From the directions above, it's clearly not the way they were intended to be used. Focus here on the directive that points out "confusion or distress." If your story has these elements, by all means incorporate this technique. But if not . . . stop worrying about it and take them out.

In general, I find that they are more effective in the middle of a sentence than when they are left dangling at the end. However, they work nicely in dialogue when one speaker interrupts another.

FRIDAY | BIOGRAPHY

A book must be the axe for the frozen sea inside us.

—*Franz Kafka*

GERMAN-LANGUAGE NOVELIST FRANZ KAFKA (1883–1924) is known for his uncanny ability to make the reader completely uncomfortable and feel almost hopeless but yet still wanting to turn the page. His life in Bohemia (now the Czech Republic) was filled with a similar hopelessness, beginning with his relationship with his father.

Hermann Kafka, a major influence on Kafk'a work, was a dominant, imposing businessman, who overshadowed Franz's childhood years. Their conflicted relationship was a theme that revealed itself in some of Kafka's best-known works, including his story "The Verdict," in which a rigid and dictatorial father, confined to a bed, passes judgment on his sensitive and assiduous son.

Kafka never earned an income as a writer: instead, he worked for insurance companies. His profession shaped the formal, cold language of his writings, which avoided sentimental interpretations. Because of his Jewish heritage, Kafka felt isolated and oppressed living among the Germans in Bohemia. He had difficulties getting his work published, and he suffered both physically (tuberculosis) and mentally (depression and chronic insomnia). He was comforted by his girlfriend Dora Diamant, who was forbidden to marry Kafka because of his lax religious upbringing. His university friend Max Brod became his editor, biographer, and literary agent, and Brod saw to it that Kafka's unpublished works were later published posthumously.

SATURDAY | BOOKS TO READ

1776 by David McCullough

1776 treats war as theater. The outcome is known, but the story is so gripping that it's easy to turn the pages as if the fates of nations were still at stake.

—*Bob Minzesheimer*

IN WRITING THE BESTSELLING *1776*, PULITZER Prize–winning author David McCullough took a new tack on history. Rather than create a sweeping view of the Revolutionary War—the type of panoramic vista he had employed in his previous books, such as *Truman* and *John Adams*—he chose to focus on a single year to showcase the events precipitating one of the nation's most pivotal moments. In fewer than three hundred pages, he captures the *zeitgeist* that surrounded America and its war for independence.

In *1776*, McCullough also presented the points of view of both the American and English leaders. He opens with King George III speaking to the British Parliament, passionately arguing that England should wage war against the Americans he viewed as traitors. McCullough shows that many members of Parliament were strongly opposed to war. George Washington is also portrayed as a flawed and sometimes fragile leader. As McCullough writes, Washington is often a demoralized man, lacking confidence in his abilities to rally the sad-sack, ragtag troops enlisted to him.

Although there have been thousands of writings about the Revolutionary War, McCullough brought this epic period to new life by presenting it in an innovative way.

SUNDAY | WRITING PROMPT

My favorite music group . . .

NOT ALL OF US WILL EVER BE LUCKY ENOUGH TO hang out with our favorite music group. Danny Sugarman was. Author Jerry Hopkins was trying to write a biography of Jim Morrison, the lead singer for The Doors, to no avail. Then, he met Sugarman, a teenage admirer of The Doors who parlayed his affection into an office job with Morrison. When Hopkins met Sugarman years later, together they created the classic *No One Here Gets Out Alive*.

First, see if you can narrow down which of your musical interests you're most influenced by, or who you think most influences the culture, past or present. Then, determine how you would do the research to really get the inside scoop about the band, and combine that with your personal thoughts and feelings about the musicians involved and their music.

MONDAY | WRITERS ON WRITING

> When a man is in doubt about this or that in
> his writing, it will often guide him if he asks
> himself how it will tell a hundred years hence.
> —*Samuel Butler*

VICTORIAN NOVELIST SAMUEL BUTLER WOULD BE interested to know that his books have stood the test of time. They are very much alive and well, both online and at brick-and-mortar bookstores more than one hundred years after his death. He wrote the popular Utopian satire *Erewhon* and *The Way of All Flesh*, both of which remain in print as do his translations of Homer's *The Iliad* and *The Odyssey*. It's not imperative that your writing be relevant in a hundred years. You may be keeping a journal of personal thoughts and may not be interested in publishing it or in its longevity. However, Butler makes a key point: if you write for publication, it's interesting to consider what the value of the writing will be in the future.

Since we don't have a crystal ball, it isn't easy to determine the value of writing and its future impact (although Butler had a pretty sure bet with his translations of classic works like the Greek poet Homer's). Instead of looking forward one hundred years, look beyond the next five or ten, and ask yourself the question, "Does my work touch on universal themes that will remain relevant?"

TUESDAY | MOTIVATION

> Do it every day. Make a habit of putting your observations into words and gradually this will become instinct. This is the most important rule of all and, naturally, I don't follow it.
>
> — *Geoff Dyer*

ONE OF THE FIRST BENEFITS YOU'LL DERIVE FROM creating a daily routine for your writing is a "loosening" of your writing style. After only a few weeks, you'll find that you're less inhibited and that you're better able to develop more natural rhythms with your language.

A daily writing schedule will also increase your confidence in your ability to write. Each time you sit down to write, it will, one hopes, become easier and more enjoyable. Writing daily will also help you be a better judge of your writing and help you be a more effective critic of your own work. Because of the continuity of your work, you'll be able to read through your writing and distinguish what makes your writing better from one day to the next. As the weeks glide by, you'll likely see a huge improvement in the quality of your writing.

Author Geoff Dyer may joke about not following through on his writing routine, but in reality he believes in it. "Personally, I am very prone to the 'I can't be bothered' attitude to life. But this brings no contentment. On the contrary: it ends up . . . goading me into action, into bothering."

WEDNESDAY | WRITING CLASS

Write a haiku about your favorite season.

H AIKU ARE SHORT POEMS OF SEVENTEEN SYLLABLES. The syllables are divided among three lines, 5/7/5. Here's a classic example of this form written by Matsuo Bashō, a Japanese haiku master who lived in the seventeenth century:

> *Winter solitude*
> *in a world of one color*
> *the sound of the wind*

Choose a season and write three lines describing it. Try to incorporate one word about color. Also, feel free to deviate from the 5/7/5 rule. That's just a guideline to which you need not strictly adhere.

THURSDAY | EDITING

> These days, the passive voice has a very bad
> reputation.
>
> — *C. Edward Good,*
> A Grammar Book for You and I . . . Oops, Me!

IN ORDER TO GROUND YOUR NARRATIVE VOICE
with consistent tone, you have to be able to differentiate
between the active and passive voice. The passive voice adds
any form of the verb *to be* to the past participle of a second,
transitive verb. Did I lose you already?

First, the past participle is the *-ed* version of any regular
verb (*walked, talked, spied,* etc.). The past tense of irregular
verbs ends in other ways. When either is combined in one
sentence with the *to be* verb, you get the passive voice, which
is not direct language and is thought to slow down the action
and confuse the reader. ("Betty and Tony had kissed while
Tommy was watching.")

Active voice constructions can occur in any tense (past,
present, or future), but each time, the subject of the sentence
is doing something directly to the object. ("Tommy watched
Betty and Tony kissing.") Better, right?

Not always. Some experts, like Wood, believe that the
passive voice is justified when the action becomes the subject
of the sentence. ("The salmon was cured with sugar, and then
was salted.")

FRIDAY | BIOGRAPHY

> A good writer is an expert on nothing except himself. And on that subject, if he is wise, he holds his tongue.
>
> —*John le Carré*

JOHN LE CARRÉ (1931—) IS THE PEN NAME OF David John Moore Cornwell. He was born in Poole, Dorset, England, and was educated at the public boarding school of Sherborne, at the University of Berne (where he studied German literature), and at Lincoln College, Oxford, where he graduated with a first-class honors degree in modern languages. He taught at the posh Eton school from 1956 to 1958 and was a member of the British Foreign Service from 1959 to 1964. Apart from spying, he also earned money selling bath towels and washing elephants. He started writing novels in 1961, and since then he has published twenty-two books. His third novel, *The Spy Who Came in from the Cold* (1963), became an international bestseller, at which time he was able to leave the Foreign Service and write full time.

Although he's famous for his espionage novels, he says that his time in the Foreign Service did not influence his writing. He insists that everything he writes is a work of his own imagination. He also notes that his current class stature is far beyond his meager upbringing. His mother left his family when he was very young, and le Carré did not meet her until he was twenty-one. He says, "I am wonderfully badly born. My father was a confidence trickster and a jail bird." He rarely gives interviews and is reluctant to receive literary prizes and awards, although he is most deserving. Instead he prefers to live as a recluse on the Cornish cliffs.

SATURDAY | BOOKS TO READ

A Farewell to Arms
by Ernest Hemingway

> I think Hemingway was one of the half-dozen
> greatest living writers, a Titan of the age we
> live in. I put him with Joyce, Eliot and Yeats
> among the real founders of what is called the
> modern movement in writing.
>
> — *Cyril Connolly*

A *FAREWELL TO ARMS*, PUBLISHED IN 1929, IS A semi-autobiographical novel. Like the soldier in this storied book, Ernest Hemingway was an ambulance driver on the Italian front during World War I. And, like his protagonist, Hemingway was injured in the line of duty and fell in love with his caregiver. A stirring love story, *A Farewell to Arms* is also a profound antiwar statement.

With this novel, Hemingway established himself as one of the leading voices of modernist writing. In reaction to what he felt were the overwritten and overly elaborate books of the nineteenth century, Hemingway created a distinctive spare prose using short declarative sentences. Collagelike, he layered these staccato sentences to create depth in his writing. Hemingway excluded all but the most necessary description. Adverbs and adjectives were used sparingly. This style of writing has since earned the sobriquet "Hemingwayesque."

SUNDAY | WRITING PROMPT

Two disparate experiences of the same place . . .

I N THIS PROMPT, YOU WILL EXPLORE TWO DIFFERENT points of view of the same location. Can two people see the same world in totally different ways, based on their personal frames of reference? Are some doors open to one, and not the other? Can they live in the same house and live two entirely different lives?

For example, in the bestselling novel *Little Bee*, author Chris Cleave switches his story between different narrative voices, all experiencing life in the same places. First there's Little Bee, a sixteen-year-old Nigerian orphan who stows away to Britain to escape certain death. Then there's the upper-middle-class English couple who's intrinsically connected to her. The setting of the novel switches from the beaches of Nigeria to present-day London, and all of the characters share their impressions of each of these locations.

You don't have to employ the tool of switching narrators to get this point across. It's more important to be able to see the world through two or more different lenses.

MONDAY | WRITERS ON WRITING

> When you are describing, / A shape, or sound, or tint; / Don't state the matter plainly, / But put it in a hint; / And learn to look at all things, / With a sort of mental squint.
>
> —*Lewis Carroll*

AUTHOR OF THE BELOVED CLASSIC, *ALICE'S Adventures in Wonderland*, Lewis Carroll hits the nail on the head when he describes what sets the great writers apart from the good ones. Authors who develop a "mental squint," or the ability to look at things and events with a different perspective, are the writers whose works often gain staying power.

Carroll did just this in writing Alice's grand adventures. Other authors had written children's stories, but Carroll, by taking a different view, created the ultimate children's fantasy. What child hasn't dreamed of adventuring in an alternate universe (in this case, the rabbit hole)? Carroll captured this fantasy on the pages of his bestselling novel.

James Joyce, in his books *Ulysses* and *Finnegans Wake*, developed his own "mental squint" by creating new words, including *quark*. Quark has since been taken on by the scientific community to describe one of the fundamental particles of physics. Physicist Murray Gell-Mann, who won the 1969 Nobel Prize, chose the word from *Finnegans Wake* because he was intrigued by Joyce. Joyce also famously created the word *tattarrattat*, to signify a knock at the door.

TUESDAY | MOTIVATION

> Simple means getting rid of extra words.
> Don't write, "He was very happy" when
> you can write "He was happy." You think
> the word "very" adds something. It doesn't.
> —*Scott Adams*

S COTT ADAMS IS THE CREATOR OF THE LONG-running comic strip *Dilbert*, a satiric view of office life. This comic appears in two thousand newspapers worldwide in sixty-five countries and twenty-five languages.

By necessity, Adams has to prune his sentences. In the strip he creates for daily publication, he must tell his readers a story with fewer than fifty words, all fitting into a space measuring a few square inches. In this compressed area, he can create a story that is both humorous and satirical, capturing the essence of Dilbert's cubicled work life.

Entire stories can be told with even fewer words. Although its authorship has not been definitively proven, a heart-wrenching short story is rumored to have been written by Ernest Hemingway with just six carefully chosen words: "For sale: baby shoes, never worn." Hemingway was said to have called it his best work.

Try writing a story as if it were a tweet, using only six words. Then, tell the same story with fifty words. After the experience of creating a story with a scant six, an allotment of fifty words will seem a virtual treasure trove. Then reverse the process, writing a story with fifty words and then reducing it to six.

WEDNESDAY | WRITING CLASS

Write about a little-known detail of the
American Civil War.

WRITE ABOUT THE CIVIL WAR BY FOCUSING A
unique light on the theme, or find an unusual or
little-known fact. For instance, the chance of surviving a
wound in Civil War days was 7 to 1; in the Korean War,
50 to 1. If you were writing about this fact, then you would
want to elucidate the types of medical care available to Civil
War soldiers. Were there medics? Hospitals? Anesthesia for
surgery? Painkillers? How were patients transported? Were
they able to return home after their recovery? A good place
to start your research is at Google Books (www.books.google
.com). On this site, you will find firsthand accounts of the
Civil War that are in the public domain.

THURSDAY | EDITING

> If dialogue doesn't take up any more space
> than exposition, use dialogue.
> —The Writer's Digest Writing Clinic

HERE'S THE MOST IMPORTANT RULE ABOUT DRAMATIC writing: show, don't tell. One way to keep the action going is to have the characters narrate what they are doing as they do it. This will also help you stay in the active voice.

Showing puts the reader directly in the main character's world through actions, thoughts, senses, and feelings. It's the art of speaking to the imagination. Telling is the act of passing along information. It gives the readers insight without engaging them because it doesn't put them right into the story.

Active dialogue is one of the best ways to help your reader into your scene. "Claudia was sad" is telling. "'I could cry all night,' said Claudia" is showing.

Other techniques to show rather than tell include moving your characters from one location to another: if your characters remain in the same space, or are too focused on their "inner world," you are telling. Lastly, creating ambiance and vivid settings help put the reader directly into the action, especially if you can have your characters add to the descriptions through dialogue.

FRIDAY | BIOGRAPHY

> Imagination is the beginning of creation. You imagine what you desire, you will what you imagine and at last you create what you will.
> — *George Bernard Shaw*

GEORGE BERNARD SHAW (1856–1950) WAS BORN in Dublin, the son of a civil servant. He did not complete a formal education due to his dislike of organized training. He moved to London in 1876, where he established himself as a leading music and theater critic. He began his literary career as a novelist, publishing five unsuccessful novels between 1879 and 1883. He then switched direction and changed to writing plays in order to illustrate his criticism of the English stage. In total, he wrote more than sixty plays, many of which continue to be performed. When he was awarded the Nobel Prize for Literature in 1925, the committee stated that "Shaw's radical rationalism, his utter disregard of conventions, his keen dialectic interest and verbal wit often turn the stage into a forum of ideas."

These ideas were influenced by his political leanings. Shaw was a dedicated socialist and a charter member of the Fabian Society, an organization established in 1884 to "promote the gradual spread of socialism by peaceful means." He met Charlotte Payne-Townshend, an Irish heiress and fellow Fabian; they married in 1898. Her inheritance enabled him to write without seeking further work. The long marriage was never consummated. However, she was a key aide to his writing, learning shorthand so she could record his words and later type them for him.

SATURDAY | BOOKS TO READ

The Art of Eating by M. F. K. Fisher

> In a properly run culture, Mary Frances
> Kennedy Fisher would be recognized as
> one of the great writers this country has
> produced in this century.
>
> *— Raymond Sokolov*

PUBLISHED IN 1954, *THE ART OF EATING* WEAVES information about food—in the form of practical tips for housewives during World War II, including how to best use rationing coupons, how to grow your own pearl, or how to warm an orange on a radiator for a divine effect—with culture, natural history, and philosophy.

The Art of Eating was published when the American diet consisted of boiled ham, broiled grapefruit, cheese balls, deviled eggs, three-bean salad, and tuna-potato chip casserole. Yet through her writing, M. F. K. Fisher was able to elevate the way Americans viewed food. Think of her as one of the original foodies, a person who recognized the importance of considering where food comes from and the cultural importance of dining and entertaining, long before these ideas became commonplace. With this book, M. F. K. Fisher created a new genre: food writing. Without her groundbreaking work, we might not have celebrities like Anthony Bourdain.

SUNDAY | WRITING PROMPT

I just can't seem to get along with anyone . . .

DON'T BE SURPRISED: MANY WRITERS FEEL THIS way. That's why they choose the solitude of writing over other more social pursuits. But just because you like to be alone doesn't mean that you can't get along with others.

Take Quasimodo, for example. In *The Hunchback of Notre Dame*, Victor Hugo created an enduring character who was forced into isolation because of the cruelty of others. He was taught to believe that the world would reject him because of his deformities. Yet once he overcame his emotional burdens, he was able to love and be loved back.

Can you think of a time when you weren't capable of forming relationships, only to find out that misguided thoughts were all that was holding you back? Have friendships sprouted from the most unlikely situations?

MONDAY | WRITERS ON WRITING

> The maker of a sentence launches out into the infinite and builds a road into Chaos and old Night, and is followed by those who hear him with something of wild, creative delight.
>
> *—Ralph Waldo Emerson*

E SSAYIST, POET, AND FATHER OF THE AMERICAN Transcendentalist Movement as famously displayed in his 1836 essay *Nature*, Ralph Waldo Emerson's writing style emphasizes the idea of compression. To form an essay, a great deal of information must be distilled into a relatively short piece. Emerson was a master of condensing and distilling information and constructing sentences that created organization out of the chaos of ideas.

Writers, who have infinite words and ideas buzzing around their brains, are constantly being called upon to select appropriate language, choosing just the right word. Different types of writing call for different language. The language choice and tone in a satirical novel, for example, should be different from the word choice of a memoir. If you are writing a romance novel, your language will differ from that used in an action thriller.

Having an infinite selection of words at their fingertips is one of the greatest gifts exceptional writers have. Because of this vast abundance, there will always be books to be written and stories to be crafted. It falls to the writer, Emerson says, to choose and craft language that best illuminates and describes your ideas.

TUESDAY | MOTIVATION

> It's doubtful that anyone with an Internet
> connection at his workplace is writing
> good fiction.
>
> —*Jonathan Franzen*

L ET'S FACE IT. IF YOU'RE WRITING AT A COMPUTER, the temptation to log on and surf the web is almost irresistible. Rather than getting down to business, you might feel like checking your e-mails, finding some new tunes to download, or even read the paper under the guise of research. Don't fall into this rabbit hole of temptation and procrastination. You know this rabbit hole, the hole you fall into when you start surfing at 8 a.m. and from which you don't emerge until it's time for lunch. And, you haven't written a word.

When you turn on your computer to begin writing, set a timer, perhaps for as few as thirty minutes. Press "Start" and begin writing. Don't let your mind wander; simply write. It can be anything—a continuation of where you left off the day before or even a silly poem. Do not check your e-mails, surf the web, or give into any other Internet distraction during the half hour. After a week of thirty distraction-free minutes every day, try setting your timer for sixty minutes. Then, reward yourself with a quick peek out the computer window that has become the rest of the world.

Jonathan Franzen, author of the bestsellers *The Corrections* and *Freedom*, leaves nothing to chance. He has permanently blocked the Ethernet port on his obsolete Dell laptop. "What you have to do," he says, "is you plug in an Ethernet cable with superglue, and then you saw off the little head of it."

WEDNESDAY | WRITING CLASS

Create a question/answer riddle about nature.

Use an element of nature to create a riddle. An example:

QUESTION: I am the red tongue of the Earth;
I've been known to bury entire
cities. Who am I?

ANSWER: I am lava.

RIDDLES HELP WRITERS THINK OF IMAGES IN NEW ways and to consider language in a different light. It is helpful when creating a question/answer riddle to imagine how the elements of nature would be viewed by an extraterrestrial being. As funny as this may seem, you are trying to strip away preconceived notions and replace them with a new idea. For instance, in the riddle above, the lava flow of a volcano has been re-imagined as a red tongue, which may be how aliens flying over Earth would perceive a volcano.

THURSDAY | EDITING

> I was working on the proof of one of my poems all the morning, and took out a comma. And in the afternoon? In the afternoon—well, I put it back again.
>
> —*Oscar Wilde*

COMMAS ARE MEANT TO CLARIFY, BUT OFTEN THEY are overused and end up making your writing more distracting or complicated. A copyeditor I used to work with would tell me over and over again, "Don't be a comma-kaze." She was warning me not to terrorize the reader with commas: keep them to myself.

The rules for commas are simple. You use them when you are making a list that consists of more than two elements. ("I need my shoes, socks, and slippers.") You use them before dialogue begins. ("She said, 'No Sam, not tonight.'") Or use them when it ends. ("'Susie is so boring,' her sister told me."). You use them before the words *and*, *but*, and *or* when you are joining two independent clauses or when you are starting a sentence with an introductory clause. ("While I like steak, hamburgers make my stomach turn.") They surround a clause. ("Rob, the most handsome man in the room, sauntered toward me.") You use them when two adjectives describe the same noun. ("Honey makes a sweet, sticky mess.") And that's about it.

FRIDAY | BIOGRAPHY

In my writing, as much as I could, I tried to
find the good, and praise it.

—*Alex Haley*

ALEXANDER MURRAY PALMER HALEY (1921–1992)
was born in Ithaca, New York, where his father was a
graduate student at Cornell University and his mother was
a music teacher. Through the stories of his Tennessee grandparents, Haley first heard about Kunta Kinte, his African
ancestor who had come to shore in Maryland aboard a slave
ship from Gambia. Inspired to further research, Haley was
able to document Kinte's life, a ten-year research process,
which he later turned into *Roots*, the novel that won him a
Special Award from the Pulitzer Board in 1977.

Haley was enrolled at Alcorn State University at age
fifteen. Two years later he dropped out of college. His father
felt that Haley needed discipline and convinced his son
to enlist in the military when he turned eighteen. Haley's
writing career began after he entered the U.S. Coast Guard
in 1939. During his enlistment, he was paid by other sailors
to write love letters to their girlfriends. He retired from the
military after twenty years of service and then began his
own writing career, becoming a senior editor for *Reader's
Digest*. His first successfully published article was an interview appearing in *Playboy* magazine in 1962, and he quickly
became known as a consummate interviewer. His first major
work was published in 1965, *The Autobiography of Malcolm X*,
which he cowrote.

SATURDAY | BOOKS TO READ

The Bell Jar by Sylvia Plath

> She is now a famous poet, but few read poetry.
> On April 14th, Harper & Row published [the
> novel] *The Bell Jar* for the first time in America.
> For the past seven weeks—to the astonishment
> of many—it has been on the bestseller list.
> What could have caused this wide popularity,
> this second posthumous career as a novelist?
> —*Richard Locke*

SYLVIA PLATH'S *THE BELL JAR* WAS ORIGINALLY published in England in 1963 under the pseudonym Victoria Lucas. It was not published in America until 1971, pursuant to her ex-husband and mother's wishes. Upon its U.S. publication, it was an immediate bestseller, climbing the *New York Times* bestseller list.

The Bell Jar is Plath's poignant fictional memoir. In this, her only novel, Plath tells the story of a young writer, Esther Greenwood, who descends into mental illness. This parallels Plath's own emotional spiral caused by bipolar disorder. A month after the book was published in England, Plath committed suicide at the age of thirty.

The Bell Jar deals with a myriad of feminist issues, including career aspirations and sexual encounters. In writing about this and other double standards, Plath was setting the foundation for future feminist writers as varied as Camille Paglia and Naomi Wolf.

SUNDAY | WRITING PROMPT

9/11 changed my worldview . . .

THE EVENTS OF SEPTEMBER 11, 2001, CHANGED THE way we will forever look at the world and our own lives. These events and their effects have influenced the work of many authors who continue to struggle with the subtle shifts, missed messages, and the cultural divides between the West and the Middle East. A quick glimpse on Amazon. com reveals that there are more than 180 nonfiction titles, not to mention the dozens of novels, collections of poetry, and children's books that explore this theme.

When you are thinking about the prompt, you can also think beyond the actual day, the "where were you" moment. It's interesting to explore how 9/11 continues to affect you right now. The novel, *Saturday*, by Ian McEwan, explores a post-9/11 world from the perspective of a London doctor, many years after the event. It was first published in 2005, but the opening scene of a plane flying with a wing on fire over London is just one of the novel's chilling connections to this historical event.

MONDAY | WRITERS ON WRITING

> Dancing in all its forms cannot be excluded
> from the curriculum of all noble education;
> dancing with the feet, with ideas, with words,
> and, need I add that one must also be able to
> dance with the pen?
>
> — *Friedrich Nietzsche*

FRIEDRICH NIETZSCHE, A NINETEENTH-CENTURY German philosopher, lauds the gifts of the writer. Just as so many sit in theaters and applaud the dancer, the musician, the singer, or the actor, Nietzsche encourages readers to appreciate those who dance with the pen. And, just as other artists help define the culture of a society and to educate audiences about these cultures, writers do the same.

Dancing with the pen offers writers the chance to provide readers with what Nietzsche describes as "a noble education," in particular when dealing with issues of social justice and understanding varied cultures and viewpoints on life. The prolific French writer Voltaire said, "The instruction we find in books is like fire. We fetch it from our neighbors, kindle it at home, communicate it to others, and it becomes the property of all." Perhaps, you've left a performance of musical theater, humming the catchy tunes from it for several days. After reading a book, you similarly "hum" when you share ideas and thoughts about the book with others who might be inclined to read it. In this way, books *are* like flame and enable writers to spread and to disseminate information.

TUESDAY | MOTIVATION

> Every minute that you spend planning . . . saves
> ten minutes in the execution of those plans. . . .
> This gives you a return of . . . 1,000 percent, on
> your investment of mental, emotional, and
> physical energy.
>
> —*Brian Tracy*

IMAGINE A 1,000 PERCENT RETURN ON A FINANCIAL
investment. You'd be a fool not to invest. The same is true
of author and motivational speaker Brian Tracy's equation for
using your time efficiently.

His formula boils down to a simple premise: by doing
some nominal planning and organizing first, you will be
more effective and efficient when you sit down to write.
Gather all the supplies you need to write. Leave them in the
spot designated for your writing. If you write at the computer, leave any notes or other materials you'll need nearby.
Make sure that when you finish writing you leave the area
tidy so it is ready for you to begin the next day.

As simple as this strategy sounds, it is very effective.
If you leave yesterday's coffee cup parked by the computer,
you'll be forced to bring the cup to the kitchen sink or dish-
washer. You've made an unnecessary distraction for yourself.
You have wasted time and kept your brain off the work at
hand: writing.

Likewise, keep your notes and journals at the ready near
where you write. If you have to stop midstream to fish your
notes out of a jacket pocket that is hanging in the hall closet,
you've delayed your writing again.

WEDNESDAY | WRITING CLASS

Write a limerick about your favorite animal.

I N THE 1800S, ENGLISH AUTHOR EDWARD LEAR popularized the limerick in his popular *Book of Nonsense*. One of his best known limericks, though not from this book, is:

> *There was a Young Lady whose eyes,*
> *Were unique as to colour and size;*
> *When she opened them wide,*
> *People all turned aside,*
> *And started away in surprise.*

There are some basic rules of thumb when it comes to writing limericks. Lines one, two, and five rhyme with one another and typically contain seven to ten syllables. Lines three and four are shorter, five to seven syllables, and also rhyme with each other. Limericks are meant to be funny, verging on bawdy.

THURSDAY | EDITING

> The story is not what happens; the story is who it happens to.
>
> —*Peter Rubie*, How to Tell a Story

W HILE PLOT IS IMPORTANT, CHARACTERS DRIVE your story. If you can develop characters who evoke a strong emotional reaction, then your work will be more successful. This is true with both fiction and nonfiction: readers need to become engaged in the lives of the people they read about in order for them to "buy into" the story.

Don't limit yourself to developing characters that people must fall in love with, or even like. Sometimes, a negative visceral reaction can be even more compelling. Take, for example, the novel *The Silence of the Lambs*. In this bestselling book, author Thomas Harris brought back one of his favorite characters who he first introduced in another novel, *Red Dragon*. Hannibal Lecter is certainly a monster, but he is a compellingly awful person, so much so that his character has become part of the lexicon, existing outside of the original work.

FRIDAY | BIOGRAPHY

> There was something unusually vivid about her writing. That's why even if one disagrees with it — as I did frequently— it was unusually stimulating. She showed you things you hadn't seen before; she had a way of reopening questions.
>
> *—Leon Wieseltier*

SUSAN SONTAG (1933–2004) WAS BORN IN NEW York City, grew up in Tucson, Arizona, and attended high school in Los Angeles. Exceptionally bright, Sontag graduated from high school before her sixteenth birthday. Her greatest dream, which she aggressively pursued, "was to grow up and come to New York and write for *Partisan Review* and be read by 5000 people." She received her BA from the University of Chicago and did graduate work in philosophy, literature, and theology at Harvard University and Saint Anne's College, Oxford.

Prolific and versatile, Sontag was the author of four novels, as well as dozens of short stories and essays. But she also made films, wrote and directed plays, and broke new ground in criticism, bringing vivid writing to cultural reporting that, she believed, had become dull and lacking in style and aesthetics. One of her most famous works was an essay, "Notes on Camp," published in 1964 and still widely read. For the next twenty-five years, she continued as a successful essayist, although she did not enjoy the work: a long essay could take up to a year to complete. But, it was through her essays that she was able to develop a singular voice.

SATURDAY | BOOKS TO READ

Aesop's Fables by **Aesop**

> I am sure the grapes are sour.
> —*Aesop*

"THE FOX AND THE GRAPES." "THE HARE AND the Tortoise." "The Boy Who Cried Wolf." "The Town Mouse and the Country Mouse." Virtually every child hears these tales during the early years of life. These fables have become part of the Western literary tradition and culture. Who hasn't ever uttered those famous words, "Oh, it's just sour grapes"?

Aesop was a slave and storyteller who lived in Greece around 600 BCE. He did not intend the fables for children. Rather, they were meant for adult listeners: cautionary tales about politics and the ills of society. Aesop collected the fables from varied sources. Some can be traced to papyrus found in Egypt and written hundreds of years before Aesop lived.

The first English edition of *Aesop's Fables* was published in 1484, primarily for adults. It was not until the 1700s that philosopher John Locke advocated using the fables to teach moral values to children.

To this day, Aesop's more than 650 tales continue to charm and educate. With their gentle, nonjudgmental tone, they impart the values of Western culture. From "appearances can be deceiving" to "don't count your chickens before they are hatched," we can thank Aesop for some of the most commonly used and beloved adages of our day.

SUNDAY | WRITING PROMPT

Why is it that . . . ?

I LOVE THE WORD THAT DAVID FELDMAN CREATED for his series of books that explore this same prompt: *imponderables*. For him, there is no science or pop culture question too obscure to investigate. His wide-eyed approach to the world has created a series of bestsellers as well as many an engaging read, and the answers to lots of the world's tough questions. (Although he hasn't tackled "when will there be peace in the Middle East?")

You might say that this prompt is too broad: that every piece of writing is an attempt to answer this question on some level. While that might be true, I'm thinking of the prompt in terms of the intersection between knowledge and creativity. What do you understand about this universe of ours that few others realize? Then, how can this information become the basis for a compelling work of fiction, or even a revealing exposé?

MONDAY | WRITERS ON WRITING

> Whatever an author puts between the
> two covers of his book is public property;
> whatever of himself he does not put there
> is his private property, as much as if he had
> never written a word.
>
> —*Gail Hamilton*

MARY ABIGAIL DODGE WAS BORN IN 1833 IN Massachusetts, the youngest of seven children. An accident at the age of two left her blind in one eye. Dodge felt herself deformed from this accident and decided that marriage most likely was not in her future. Instead, she devoted herself to writing.

Dodge was an early advocate of women's rights who placed a high value on privacy—so much so that she created a pen name for herself: Gail Hamilton. Gail came from her middle name and Hamilton was the name of the town in which she was born. Under this name she wrote political commentary, essays, children's stories, and a novel.

Dodge's penchant for privacy is especially relevant in today's world. Whatever is written and published is public. More concerning is the idea that every word written on a computer is public. Just assume that any words you write and send via e-mail, post on a blog, or place on a website are public words. Too many writers have been caught off guard, finding their words they felt should have been protected by copyright are not always safe on the web. To paraphrase Dodge, "Whatever an author puts on the Internet is public property." Writer beware.

TUESDAY | MOTIVATION

Close the door. Write with no one looking
over your shoulder.

—*Barbara Kingsolver*

E ASIER SAID THAN DONE, YOU MIGHT SAY, AS MANY
of us are faced with myriad daily distractions. The phone
is ringing, the washing machine is whirring, kids are clamoring, dogs are barking. If you can't literally shut the door, it is
still possible to shut out many distractions. Consider changing
your schedule to allow yourself a few minutes of peace and
quiet at one end of each day. Wake up thirty minutes early or,
if you are a night owl, stay up late. Turn off the television. Turn
off the ringer on your phone, and let the answering machine
pick up incoming calls; that's what it's there for. Be sure to eat
before you sit down to write. A hungry stomach is as much of
a distraction as a ringing telephone.

Evelyn Waugh said that "anyone could write a novel,
given six weeks, pen, paper, and no telephone or wife."
Actually, it is possible to write and to write well even with
a phone and a partner. Canadian writer Alice Munro took
twenty years to write her first book when she was raising her
three children. She found time to write while her children
napped or while dinner cooked in the oven. But her perseverance paid off: her first volume of short stories, *Dance of the
Happy Shades*, won the Governor General's Award, Canada's
highest prize for literary fiction.

Identify your distractions. Make a written list. By iden-
tifying distractions, you can often eliminate them. Are the
neighbors noisy? Wear earplugs. Are you distracted by the
clutter on your desk? Clear it off.

WEDNESDAY | WRITING CLASS

Write a love letter to your favorite celebrity.

G ET IN THE MOOD FOR WRITING A LOVE LETTER by setting the scene. Light a scented candle, dim the lights (not so much that you can't see), and begin. Make the salutation count. Instead of "Dear Mr. Clooney," use something more dramatic like "To my dearest George." From there, exalt your beloved. Remember this is a paean to a true love. Tell why you love this person, and recall the moment you first fell for him or her. Describe things you have in common. Write about the qualities that set your beloved apart. Close with as much passion as you opened your letter. For example: "I look forward to seeing you in my dreams, my beloved."

THURSDAY | EDITING

> Blessed is the man, who having nothing to
> say, abstains from giving wordy evidence of
> the fact.
>
> — *George Eliot*

YOUR WRITING COULD BE CONSIDERED WORDY if you choose expressions when a simple word would be sufficient. Wordiness makes your writing seem at worst cliché and at best difficult to follow.

When you are reviewing your work, look for instances where you can get to the same meaning in fewer words. Here are some of my favorite wordy examples and how they could be more succinct:

» any and all = choose one: any OR all

» due to the fact that = because

» for the purpose of = to

» for the simple reason that = because

» in connection with = about

» in order to = to

» in spite of the fact that = although

» in the near future = soon

» in view of the fact that = because

» is located in = is in

» on the part of = by

» owing to the fact that = because

» rarely ever = rarely

FRIDAY | BIOGRAPHY

> Take care of the luxuries and the necessities
> will take care of themselves.
>
> —*Dorothy Parker*

DOROTHY PARKER (1893–1967) WAS BORN in Long Branch, New Jersey, to Jacob (Henry) Rothschild, a garment manufacturer, and Eliza Annie (Marston) Rothschild. Parker was educated at a Catholic school and, upon graduation, moved to New York City.

In 1916, Parker's first poem was published in *Vogue*, and on the strength of her work, she was offered an editorial position at the magazine. She published her first collection of poems, *Enough Rope*, in 1926, and beginning in the next year, she wrote book reviews for the *New Yorker*—a magazine she contributed to until the mid-1950s. Her first collection of poems, *Enough Rope,* was published in 1926. Parker's poems were sardonic, dry, elegant commentaries on love or the shallowness of modern life. She relied on dialogue rather than on description. Among her best-known pieces are "Big Blonde," which won her the O. Henry Memorial Award, and "The Waltz."

Parker and her second husband, Alan Campbell, moved to Hollywood in the 1930s, where Parker found work as a screenwriter. With Lillian Hellman and Dashiell Hammett, she helped found the Screen Writers' Guild. But the time spent in Hollywood also earned her a place on the Hollywood blacklist, after she'd become an outspoken advocate of civil rights and associated herself with communist causes.

SATURDAY | BOOKS TO READ

Ulysses by James Joyce

> *Ulysses* is the most important contribution
> that has been made to fictional literature in
> the twentieth century. It will immortalize
> its author. . . . It is likely that there is no one
> writing English today that could parallel Joyce's
> feat, and it is also likely that few would care
> to do it were they capable.
>
> —*Dr. Joseph Collins*

ALTHOUGH JAMES JOYCE'S *ULYSSES* WAS FIRST published in Paris in 1922 with a printing of just one thousand copies by famed bookseller Sylvia Beach, it was not until 1933, when a United States Circuit Court judge ruled that the work was not obscene, that the path was cleared for publication in the United States.

In *Ulysses*, Irish author Joyce recounts a day in the life of Leopold Bloom. As a child, Joyce loved Greek poet Homer's *The Odyssey*, and he based the structure of *Ulysses* on the ancient tale. Ulysses is split into eighteen sections, which correspond to the episodes in *The Odyssey*.

The book is notable for its stream-of-consciousness style, innovative prose, extraordinarily rich and diverse vocabulary, and unusual structure. Joyce and *Ulysses* are credited by myriad authors with influencing their work, including Jorge Luis Borges, Arthur Miller, Anthony Burgess, Umberto Eco, Camille Paglia, Woody Allen, Philip Roth, Amanda Cross, and Salman Rushdie.

SUNDAY | WRITING PROMPT

This is my family . . .

WHEN I WAS GROWING UP AS A READER, SOME of my favorite books were the "family sagas." I loved to read the novels of Belva Plain, such as *Evergreen*, or Mario Puzo's *The Godfather*, that follow one family from their immigrant beginnings to realizing the American Dream, all the while dealing with the different sets of difficulties that come with achievement.

These novels are just one way to explore the concept of family. Another is the memoir, where you investigate your family's past to define who you are now. Whether you prefer to write fact or fiction, your family can be the beginning of a great story. Start with a little visit to one of the Internet's genealogy websites to see if you can dig up something about your past that you didn't know or fully understand. Or, you might have enough drama in your own nuclear family to fill many a page.

MONDAY | WRITERS ON WRITING

> Writing, I think, is not apart from living.
> Writing is a kind of double living. The writer
> experiences everything twice. Once in reality
> and once in that mirror which waits always
> before or behind.
>
> — *Catherine Drinker Bowen*

AMERICAN AUTHOR CATHERINE DRINKER BOWEN won the National Book Award in 1958 for *The Lion and the Throne*, her biography of Sir Edward Coke, an English jurist and Parliament member during the late 1500s and early 1600s. As his biographer, Bowen had to re-experience and reinterpret his life within a twentieth-century mirror looking back several hundred years. This is the challenge for all writers: to capture, through their own and unique lens, the "doubling living."

History is always being re-examined and rescrutinized. Take Pulitzer Prize–winning author Stacy Schiff's best-selling book *Cleopatra*. Schiff takes on the larger-than-life queen of Ancient Egypt, whom everyone from Michelangelo to Shakespeare has revered and worshiped as a beauty and goddess figure. Schiff, through her research, paints a different picture, a portrait of a brilliant strategist and cunning politician. The mirror now asks, "Who is right?"

Perhaps all of these artists' views are accurate on some level. Every time history is recorded, it is through the filter of the writer's sensibilities. It is virtually impossible for any writer—whether writing fiction or nonfiction—to write without some slight personal bent. That is what makes writing and reading interesting, after all.

TUESDAY | MOTIVATION

> I believe more in the scissors than I do in
> the pencil.
>
> —*Truman Capote*

TRUMAN CAPOTE HAD HIS OWN UNORTHODOX method for writing. He believed that he could only write if he was horizontal, so he'd lie on the couch and pen his books. At the start of the day, he'd work with a cup of coffee at his side. As the day wore on, the coffee cup would turn into a sherry glass and, finally, a classic martini.

As unorthodox as his horizontal method was, Capote had a very orthodox and prudent belief in the power of editing his work. When writing *In Cold Blood*, considered the first nonfiction novel, Capote covered the brutal murder of the Clutter family in rural Kansas. His finished work is a bit under four hundred pages. Capote culled these words from thousands of pages of transcripts and police reports and hundreds of hours of interviews and courtroom testimony. In this sense, he really did have to do more with his figurative scissors than with his pen, condensing thousands of pages of material into a relatively slim volume.

Try this exercise. Write a two-page short story, essay, or news article. Then, rewrite the piece to fit on one page. Or, choose a piece from the newspaper and rewrite it to half its original length. These exercises help you tighten your writing and cut unnecessary words.

WEDNESDAY | WRITING CLASS

Write a magazine feature article about the
newest food trends.

START THE ARTICLE WITH A LEAD (OPENING SENTENCE
or sentences) that grabs your readers' attention. It can
be a quote, an anecdote, or, often most effective, a surprising
statement. Instead of opening with a fairly standard and
straightforward "more and more, people are trying exotic
new foods," try something with more zing: "The navel
orange is being left behind as foodies everywhere are favoring
pummelos, blood oranges, kaffir limes, and other exotic
citrus." Follow this lead with the body of the feature, which
supports your lead statement. Conclude with a paragraph
summarizing your article.

THURSDAY | EDITING

Use orthodox spelling.
—*Strunk and White*, The Elements of Style

T HERE ARE TWO WAYS TO LOOK AT THE EVOLUTION of language: descriptive and prescriptive. Descriptive theory refers to the idea that language is constantly evolving: new words are added to the lexicon; old words take on new meanings. Prescriptive theory says no: it refers to a dictionary approach that features an arbiter that can say, "Let me tell you about words, and how they should be used."

Regardless of which camp you reside in, nothing drives professional editors and lay readers crazier than when writers make up words without defining them, or try to create dialect with funky spelling. These two techniques are neither descriptive nor prescriptive: they're just annoying and make the reader work too hard to get to what you are trying to convey.

The bible of words, the *Oxford English Dictionary*, contains 171,476 words in current use and 47,156 obsolete words. Until you've exhausted the possibilities these words present, stick with them and their correct spelling.

FRIDAY | BIOGRAPHY

> Talent is cheaper than table salt. What separates the talented individual from the successful one is a lot of hard work.
>
> —*Stephen King*

STEPHEN EDWIN KING (1947–) WAS BORN IN Portland, Maine. King was raised by his single mother and moved frequently throughout his childhood, always returning to Maine. Beginning in his sophomore year at the University of Maine, he wrote a weekly column for the school newspaper. He graduated in 1970, with a BA in English and planned to teach high school. While he waited for a teaching position, he worked as a laborer at an industrial laundry, and he continued writing, focusing on short stories that would appeal to men's magazines.

In the mid-1960s, King wrote "The Glass Floor," which became the first piece of writing to earn him a paycheck when *Startling Mystery Stories* published the story. King took a public school teaching job in Hampton, Maine, in 1971, where he spent evenings and weekends honing his craft, turning out short stories and developing novels. In the spring of 1973, his first book, *Carrie*, was accepted for publication. The advance was paltry: $2,500. However, the money advanced on the paperback sale was $400,000; enough to allow him to leave teaching and write full-time. He continues to write every day.

SATURDAY | BOOKS TO READ

A Short Guide to a Happy Life
by Anna Quindlen

> Don't ever forget the words on a postcard
> that my father sent me last year: "If you win
> the rat race, you're still a rat."
>
> —*Anna Quindlen*

PUBLISHED IN 2000, ANNA QUINDLEN'S *A SHORT Guide to a Happy Life* has a storied ancestry. Advice has long been a journalistic staple. As far back as the seventeenth century, newspapers printed columns addressing questions submitted anonymously. From *The Power of Positive Thinking* to *The Seven Habits of Highly Effective People* and, more recently, *The Secret,* self-help and advice books make up one of publishing's strongest categories.

One of the bestselling books in the category has been *A Short Guide to a Happy Life.* In it, Quindlen focuses on personal happiness and appreciating the small things in life—watching the sun rise, listening to your favorite music, eating (and really savoring and enjoying) good food. But unlike other self-help tomes, *A Short Guide to a Happy Life* is able to back up its advice with science—focusing on and appreciating the simple things in life, Quindlen says, *does* make people happier. The diminutive book, clocking in at just sixty-four pages, struck a universal chord. It instantly earned a place on the *New York Times* bestseller list and became one of *Publishers Weekly*'s bestselling books of 2000.

SUNDAY | WRITING PROMPT

So many people are selfish, greedy, and unfriendly . . .

I DON'T BELIEVE THAT THIS PROMPT REFERS TO ALL of human nature, but it does provide a wide platform for exploration and a reason to pull out your metaphorical soapbox. Instead of blaming mother, society, or religious intolerance, see if you can find the underlying reason why we just can't all get along.

A good place for inspiration for this prompt is the novel *Blindness* by Portuguese Nobel Prize–winner José Saramago. His international bestseller is set in an unnamed city where a large percentage of the population finds itself in a white, milky haze. As the epidemic spreads, the government panics and quarantines victims in an old mental asylum, where people quickly lose their civility even before real desperation sets in.

Another to consider is Dr. Seuss (Theodor Geisel) and his classic *How the Grinch Stole Christmas*, which goes to show that you don't have to be heavy handed in order to explore this important theme.

MONDAY | WRITERS ON WRITING

Fill your paper with the breathings of your heart.

—*William Wordsworth*

WORDSWORTH IS CONSIDERED TO BE A FATHER to the European Romantic era, which took place during the second half of the eighteenth century. In reaction to the Industrial Revolution as well as to the impositions of the aristocracy, Wordsworth wrote poetry that embraced deeply felt emotions—awe, wonder, terror—and focused on the role of unharnessed nature.

With this in mind, it is not surprising that he came up with a turn of phrase that refers to writing as the "breathings of your heart." Put another way, Wordsworth is encouraging you to resist putting any barriers between your mind and your words. He felt that just as the act of breathing comes without thought, so, too should your writing.

Don't be overly analytical. Try not to filter your thoughts as they pass from your mind to the paper, says Wordsworth, and write on emotionally evocative topics that are of importance to you.

TUESDAY | MOTIVATION

> You don't have to be great to start, but you
> have to start to be great.
>
> —*Joe Sabah*

PERHAPS THE GREATEST ENEMY OF ANY WRITER IS the bugaboo of procrastination. That's right, the devilish voice, whispering in your ear to put it off until tomorrow. Or next week. Or, even, next year. Banish that pesky voice from your thoughts.

Procrastination is not always about time management, as is sometimes suggested. A person can keep a detailed planner and still fall prey to procrastination. In fact, 20 percent of Americans define themselves as chronic procrastinators. You might think procrastinators put off tasks because the work is unpleasant, but often pleasurable tasks are also delayed, like redeeming a gift card or cashing a check. Another downside to procrastination: science shows that procrastinators are more susceptible to colds and the flu and more likely to suffer from insomnia. Procrastinators are also apt to have gastrointestinal issues.

Joe Sabah is correct. If you're a nonstarter, you'll never be great. Nonstarters are nonaccomplishers. Don't put off your writing. Instead, be willing to take the risk and to begin and to maintain a regular writing routine.

WEDNESDAY | WRITING CLASS

Create the setup for a mystery that takes
place on a cruise ship.

B Y PLACING YOUR MYSTERY ON A CRUISE SHIP YOU
have created a closed setting, one in which all of the
passengers could be considered possible suspects, similar to
the model used by mystery maven Agatha Christie in *Murder
on the Orient Express*. Know before you begin who committed
the crime, even if the setup doesn't feature that character.

Write until the crime has been committed, and then
stop. Make sure to introduce at least four characters: the
victim, the detective, and two or more suspects.

THURSDAY | EDITING

Avoid clichés like the plague.
—Samuel Goldwyn

A CLICHÉ IS AN EXPRESSION OR IDEA THAT HAS been so overused that it becomes either a stereotype of a person or place (e.g., *New York is dirty*; *New Yorkers are mean-spirited*) or signals a predictability (e.g., *happy as a clam*). A cliché does offer an instant, vivid depiction or comparison; so much so that it does the work for you. While it's tempting to draw on them, most consider writing that is full of clichés a sign of inexperience or unoriginality.

Along with clichés, I would also avoid using similes and metaphors. Even if you spent all of junior high school working these into your essays or short stories, there really is no place for them in adult writing. When you are not wasting time comparing and contrasting, you'll figure out how to write directly what you mean. Use vivid description and details to get your point across. The one exception is when you can create a metaphor that is so shockingly new and brilliant that others might use it in the future.

In fact, most phrases now considered clichéd were originally regarded as striking, but lost their force through overuse. For example, Salvador Dalí once said, "The first man to compare the cheeks of a young woman to a rose was obviously a poet; the first to repeat it was possibly an idiot."

FRIDAY | BIOGRAPHY

> A whale-ship was my Yale College and my
> Harvard.
>
> — *Herman Melville*

H ERMAN MELVILLE (1819–1891) CAME FROM A well-established New England family, but when his father died when Melville was just twelve, the family was left penniless. As a young man, Melville was a schoolteacher in England when he heard the call of the sea and found work as a cabin boy on international voyages. On one voyage aboard the *Acushnet* to the South Seas, Melville jumped ship in the Marquesas Islands in the Pacific, and in July 1842, he lived among a reputedly cannibalistic tribe of Typee natives. He used this experience as the basis of his first novel, *Typee,* as well as *Moby-Dick,* which was published many years later. All of Melville's work was published as fiction because he felt that no one would believe the stories to be true.

Melville had difficulty getting his work published in the United States. Although *Typee* was published in 1846 in London to critical acclaim and commercial success, Melville found it difficult to publish his work in the United States. It wasn't until he returned to Boston that he eventually found a publisher for his second novel, *Omoo*, as well as for *Typee*. The novels, however, did not generate enough royalties to support Melville. During his life, only his first three books gained much attention. When he died in 1891, he was almost completely forgotten. It was not until the "Melville Revival" in the twentieth century that his work won recognition, especially *Moby-Dick,* now considered a great American novel. Ironically, it did not receive much praise when it was published.

SATURDAY | BOOKS TO READ

The Catcher in the Rye by J. D. Salinger

> What really knocks me out is a book that, when you're all done reading it, you wish the author that wrote it was a terrific friend of yours and you could call him up on the phone whenever you felt like it. That doesn't happen much, though.
>
> —*J. D. Salinger*

THE 1951 NOVEL *THE CATCHER IN THE RYE* WAS originally intended for adults, but it quickly became an anthem for adolescent readers as they identified with the book's protagonist, Holden Caulfield. Sixty years after publication, the book still sells at a rate of 250,000 copies per year. Total sales are an estimated sixty-five million.

In *The Catcher in the Rye*, Salinger created a coming-of-age tale of an alienated adolescent. Salinger used a subjective, first-person voice to allow readers into Caulfield's mind and into his heart. Before this novel was published, authors usually portrayed teens in the mold of once-radio hero Jack Armstrong, a happy, popular teenager. Salinger broke this mold and opened the door for William Golding's *Lord of the Flies* and Evan Hunter's *The Blackboard Jungle*.

The Catcher in the Rye was published to lukewarm reviews and held the dubious rank of most censored high-school book for decades. As journalist and author Andrew Gopnik says, "In American writing, there are three perfect books, which seem to speak to every reader and condition: *Huckleberry Finn, The Great Gatsby,* and *The Catcher in the Rye*."

SUNDAY | WRITING PROMPT

I have a disability . . .

I USED TO TELL MY CHILDREN THAT EACH OF US HAS a disability: that no one is perfect. Yet what was once a family secret in today's society has become something of a badge of honor, mostly due to the proliferation of inspiring "overcoming the odds" legends. Some of the most compelling and enduring stories are often about those who rise above their limitations to achieve greatness.

Many biographers are constantly on the lookout for just such a person, and you can use this prompt to explore the life of the famous and their little-known shortcomings, such as the blindness of Louis Braille, or the stuttering of James Earl Jones. You might know someone intimately who has mastered their disability, alone or with the help of others.

While you don't have to be a victim of cerebral palsy who can paint with his feet like Christy Brown, as reported in his autobiography turned major motion picture, *My Left Foot*, you can explore how you work within the confines of your own disability every day and manage to thrive.

MONDAY | WRITERS ON WRITING

> I had been emotionally depleted by [writing
> *The Book of Daniel*]. So I sat around for a year.
> And I was staring at the wall . . . and I began
> to write about the wall, and I realized that this
> house was the first house on the hill built at
> that time. And then I imagined what things
> looked like from the bottom of the hill. From
> one image to another, I was off the wall and
> in a book.
>
> —*E. L. Doctorow*

AMERICAN AUTHOR E. L. DOCTOROW IS THE author of the bestsellers *Ragtime* and *Billy Bathgate*, among others. He has also been the victim, like the majority of authors at one time or another, of writer's block.

His suggestion for getting started? Doctorow illustrates that ideas can be harvested from virtually everywhere. You do not need to find a profound idea to begin writing. If you are stuck, look around you, choose something from your physical environment, as Doctorow did, and begin writing.

Are you staring at your kitchen table? At your front yard through your office window? Use this as a fertile seed for your writing. What makes your kitchen table or your front yard different from the others on your street or in your town? Doctorow realized that his house was the first one built. What was that like, he wondered, for the residents of the house, living there without neighbors? This is just how he started writing *Ragtime*, published in 1975, which became a nationwide bestseller. Good thing he looked at the wall.

TUESDAY | MOTIVATION

> Do be kind to yourself. Fill pages as quickly
> as possible; double space, or write on every
> second line. Regard every new page as a
> small triumph. Until you get to Page 50.
> Then calm down, and start worrying about
> the quality. Do feel anxiety— it's the job.
>
> —*Roddy Doyle*

REGARD EVERY NEW PAGE AS A *LARGE* TRIUMPH. There is a deeply felt satisfaction in seeing a page become filled with type. Filling pages daily will help you develop a writing rhythm, which can only be accomplished with a sense of inner confidence.

Novelist Don DeLillo, while working on his book *The Names*, overcame writer's block by creating an unorthodox method of quickly filling blank pages. "I devised a new method—new to me, anyway. When I finished a paragraph, even a three-line paragraph, I automatically went to a fresh page to start the new paragraph. . . . The white space on the page helped me concentrate more deeply on what I'd written."

Try double- or even triple-spacing your lines to fill the page. Or, write one sentence at the top of each page. Soon, a stack of blank paper will become filled with your writing. Use one of these techniques to get your writing going. Then, as the pages pile up, begin focusing on the characteristics and condition of your writing as well.

WEDNESDAY | WRITING CLASS

Write a news story about the opening of a
new business.

P ERHAPS A BIG-BOX RETAILER HAS COME TO TOWN
or a local resident has opened a coffee shop. Choose
a newly opened business and create a news story about it.
There are seven key questions to answer in your story:

» Who?

» What?

» When?

» Where?

» Why?

» How?

» Why does it matter?

The first five questions are fairly straightforward, but
the last two are a bit trickier and often of greater interest
to your reader. If a big-box store has opened in your area,
how did this happen? Were there zoning issues to be met?
Increasingly, these retailers are finding resistance from local
municipalities. Include the backstory that describes how a
store came to open its doors. Finally, why does this new business matter to your reader? In particular, you need to answer
this last question to make your story newsworthy.

THURSDAY | EDITING

> A novel's whole pattern is rarely apparent at
> the outset of writing, or even at the end; that is
> when the writer finds out what a novel is about,
> and the job becomes one of understanding
> and deepening or sharpening what is already
> written. That is finding the theme.
>
> —*Diane Johnson*

THEME IS YOUR STORY'S LESSON, THE TAKEAWAY
for the readers who can then apply what they've learned
to their lives. In *The Wonderful Wizard of Oz,* the theme
"there's no place like home" doesn't come out until the very
end. In fact, you can read most of the whole book, or watch
the entire movie save the last bit, without realizing that was
going to be the final message. But without it, the fantastical
story would lack meaning and would probably not have
remained popular to this day.

Every piece of writing must have a theme in order for it
to be successful. This is true whether you are writing fiction
or nonfiction, poetry or prose. Many writers start out with
one theme, only to find it switching midway. Or, your theme
might not be apparent on your first draft, as Diane Johnson
suggests. However, as you edit and refine your work, a theme
should come through.

Your story should be a connection of scenes that communicate your theme. If not, see what you need to add in order
to reach a deeper meaning than what you've already created.

FRIDAY | BIOGRAPHY

> We need wilderness preserved—as much of it
> as is still left, and as many kinds—because it
> was the challenge against which our character
> as a people was formed. The reminder and
> the reassurance that it is still there is good for
> our spiritual health even if we never once in
> ten years set foot in it.
>
> —*Wallace Stegner*

WALLACE STEGNER (1909–1993) WAS BORN IN Lake Mills, Iowa. Over a sixty-year career, he wrote thirty books, including *The Big Rock Candy Mountain, Angle of Repose, The Spectator Bird,* and *Crossing to Safety.* He is best known as "the dean of Western writers," yet not all of his fiction is set in the West. His nonfiction, however, and one of his most eloquent statements about the environment, *Wilderness Letter*, have come to define his work.

Because he achieved financial independence as a writer and university professor, Stegner was able to pursue his interests in preservation and conservation. In 1960, he wrote his famous letter on the importance of federal protection of wild places. This letter was used to introduce the bill that established the National Wilderness Preservation System in 1964. In this way, Stegner used his craft to better serve his community.

SATURDAY | BOOKS TO READ

Native Son by Richard Wright

> In writing *Native Son*, Richard Wright had the
> courage to sit down next to his own fear and
> mould his literary child and alter ego, Bigger
> Thomas.
>
> —*Julia Wright*

J ULIA WRIGHT APPLAUDS HER FATHER'S COURAGE IN
writing a book that provoked, shocked, and, ultimately,
opened up new conversations in America about the country's
views on race and personal freedom.

Richard Wright's *Native Son* tells the story of Bigger
Thomas, a twenty-year-old living in grinding poverty on
Chicago's South Side. Bigger gets a job driving for a wealthy
Chicago family, the Daltons. Through a chain of events,
seemingly beyond his control, Bigger kills the Dalton's
daughter, Mary. In a frantic, out-of-control spiral, Bigger
then rapes and kills his girlfriend. Despite the heinous
nature of the crimes, Wright paints a portrait of a man who
is caught in his social, racial, and economic context. What's
more, the novel challenges the very concept of free will.

Upon its publication in 1940, the book was a runaway
bestseller. Like other great books, the novel met with controversy. Because of the violence and language, the book made
its way onto the list of banned books. Yet it remains in print
today because it serves as a powerful tool for generating
discussion about race and personal freedom. Scholar Henry
Louis Gates calls *Native Son* "the single most influential
shaping force in black literary history."

SUNDAY | WRITING PROMPT

*The most interesting person that I have
ever met . . .*

OFTEN, THE MOST INTERESTING PERSON YOU KNOW may not be someone you like or even respect. No one knows this better than Robert Caro, award-winning biographer of both Robert Moses and Lyndon Johnson. Caro was drawn to the stories of powerful men. In his words, he felt compelled to expose their less-than-ideal sides: "To show power truly you not only have to show how it is used but also its effect on those on whom it is used. You have to show the effect of power on the powerless."

For this prompt, see if you can discern the difference between someone you admire and someone truly interesting. You might find that these two features overlap. Or, you might discover that the most interesting fact about the person you have a high regard for is his or her less-than-admirable qualities.

MONDAY | WRITERS ON WRITING

> They say writing is lonely work. But that's an
> exaggeration. Even alone at their desks, writers
> entertain visitors: characters of a novel, famous
> and not so famous figures from the past.
> On good days, all these come to the table. On
> bad days, however, only unwelcome visitors
> appear: The specter of the third-grade teacher
> who despaired of your penmanship . . .
> —*Allegra Goodman*

AMERICAN NOVELIST ALLEGRA GOODMAN CAPTURES both sides of the writer's coin. On the head's side, writers have the luxury of working alone—luxury because they are alone with their thoughts and able to take the time to work through an idea and to "entertain visitors," perhaps the characters in a novel they are working on or a historic figure. There is, when everything is clicking, a certain bliss to this isolation.

On the flip side, writers can be dogged by doubts. Sitting alone, letting the mind race, writers can question all of their motives. Has someone already written this? Has that person done a better job? Is this writing business a fool's errand? These are the "unwelcome visitors," Goodman describes— visitors she works to keep at bay.

Writing can boil down to attitude rather than aptitude. On a day when the teacher who despaired of your penmanship looms large, put those negative thoughts aside. Remember, it takes fewer muscles to smile than to frown. Put on a smile and start writing.

TUESDAY | MOTIVATION

> You know, cut and paste used to mean
> something completely different at one time.
> —*Michael Ondaatje*

MICHAEL ONDAATJE, THE AUTHOR OF *THE ENGLISH Patient,* still writes in longhand. When he is finished with a draft, he literally cuts it apart and tapes it back together in a new arrangement. Ondaatje is in good company. Annie Proulx, author of *The Shipping News*; Joe Haldeman, author of *The Forever War*; Pat Conroy; and Stephen King all do some of their writing and editing in longhand. Of course, there was a time when writers didn't have a choice. It was not until 1870 that the typewriter was tweaked enough to actually work faster than writing by hand.

Take a day off from using your computer and try writing longhand. Arm yourself with paper and a pen or pencil and begin writing.

Writing longhand will help you experience your writing in a different way. Your mind will think in a different manner, both because writing longhand is a slower process and also because you won't have the opportunity to backspace and erase the words you've just written. Writing in longhand is a more deliberate act.

There is an elegant simplicity to writing longhand: it takes writing back to a primal and pleasing place. As an added incentive, there's also a sense of instant gratification. The moment you make a mark, it is real. Unlike the sometimes dicey business of storing your writing on a computer's hard drive, the handwritten page won't disappear into a mysterious Ethernet void.

WEDNESDAY | WRITING CLASS

Write a skit about losing a winning lottery ticket.

S KITS ARE HUMOROUS AND LIGHT-HEARTED SHORT plays often performed in informal settings. For this skit, create two characters: the lottery winner and the rather indifferent convenience store employee who isn't buying the story about the lost ticket. As you write, read the dialogue aloud to make sure it has the cadence of real-life speech. Keep this skit lively and funny.

THURSDAY | EDITING

> *Who* is one of the few words in English that differs in the accusative (objective) case, when it becomes *whom*, often throwing native English-speakers into a fizzle.
>
> —The Economist Style Guide

WHOM SOUNDS LIKE OLD-FASHIONED CONSTRUCTION, but it's actually necessary. So if you use it, you must use it correctly, and don't worry about sounding stuffy.

When you are writing a question, Grammar Girl Mignon Fogarty suggests seeing if you could answer the question *who/whom* poses with the word *him*. If you can, the correct choice would be *whom*.

Who always refers to the subject of a clause (someone taking an action), while *whom* always refers to the object (the one the action is thrust upon). The same is true for *whoever* and *whomever*: *whoever* refers to a subject; *whomever* refers to the object.

FRIDAY | BIOGRAPHY

> There is only one recipe for a best seller. . . .
> You have to get the reader to turn over the
> page.
>
> —*Ian Fleming*

I AN FLEMING (1908–1964) WAS EDUCATED AT Eton College, where he excelled at athletics over academics. His first job was at Reuters news agency, where he mastered the basics of journalism and covered a notorious espionage trial in Russia. However, feeling that he was never going to make his fortune in writing, he turned down a Shanghai posting and went to work for a small bank, and then as a stockbroker.

Much of what Fleming saw during World War II found its way later into his James Bond adventures. For example, Fleming worked for British Naval Intelligence, much like his best-loved character, James Bond. His post took him overseas to the United States, France, Spain, Ceylon, Jamaica, Australia, Cairo, and Tehran, all of which ended up on the pages of his novels. Interestingly, he played a pivotal role in coordinating special intelligence: his own secret work contributed to the establishment of the Central Intelligence Agency.

In 1953, he published his first book, *Casino Royale,* which introduced Agent 007. He published a total of thirteen James Bond titles before his death, and two more were published posthumously. He is also the creator of the beloved *Chitty Chitty Bang Bang,* which he wrote for his only son, Caspar.

SATURDAY | BOOKS TO READ

Madame Bovary by Gustave Flaubert

> What is remarkable in *Madame Bovary* is that its mediocre beings, with their earthbound ambitions and pedestrian problems, impress us, by virtue of the structure and the writing that create them, as beings who are out of the ordinary within their ordinary manner of being.
>
> —*Mario Vargas Llosa*

WHILE WRITING HIS 1857 NOVEL, *MADAME Bovary,* Gustave Flaubert was so sickened by his main character that he had to take time off from writing it to recover his health.

The character of Madame Bovary is difficult to like. She is superficial and prone to awkward social gaffes. Her stolid husband becomes a country doctor. She dreams of being more than a country doctor's wife and fantasizes about escaping the dullard. She looks to these daydreams for her salvation, ignoring the adoring husband. She worries more about her window treatments than her family.

Authors writing before Flaubert usually relied on attractive characters to draw in readers. Flaubert challenged this convention. Instead of following in the steps of his predecessors, the Romantics, Flaubert created a Realist novel, one that exposed the self-destructive delusions of Emma Bovary. James Wood wrote, "Flaubert decisively established what most readers and writers think of as modern realist narration, and his influence is almost too familiar to be visible."

SUNDAY | WRITING PROMPT

An account of a visit to a fictional place . . .

THIS PROMPT IS PURE FANTASY WRITING. HAVE FUN as you create a world from its very beginning. This is one prompt where the backstory is just as important as the tale you are willing to share. You will have to think through how your very own Wonderland or Oz came to be, who lives there, what it looks like, and why the reader should be aware of it. Once that is accomplished, you can write about your visit.

An excellent example of this prompt is Narnia, the magical location where C. S. Lewis's *The Lion, the Witch, and the Wardrobe* and all the subsequent books take place. Lewis wrote the seven books in this series between 1949 and 1954 but started working on the creation of Narnia in 1939. While I'm not suggesting that you take ten years to work out this prompt, it does illustrate how important the setup is to its successful execution.

MONDAY | WRITERS ON WRITING

> To write is to write is to write is to write is to write is to write is to write is to write.
>
> — *Gertrude Stein*

AMERICAN EXPATRIATE GERTRUDE STEIN WAS famous for her brilliant but befuddling statements. As her partner Alice B. Toklas once said, "This has been a most wonderful evening. Gertrude has said things tonight it will take her 10 years to understand." Visitors to her famed Paris salon would be dazzled and puzzled by her words. Famous utterances include "A diary means yes indeed," and "Before the flowers of friendship faded friendship faded."

The quote that begins this devotional, then, almost seems straightforward. For Stein, writing was a form of being. She felt that to write today meant to write again the next day and to have a purpose to fulfill. To write meant having doors open to the future, to possibility, and to experience, and to have the opportunity to write about this.

Stein's phrase also speaks to creating a routine and a discipline. She suggests that if you write one day, then you will write the next, and the next, and the next. And then you are a writer.

TUESDAY | MOTIVATION

> I don't care who you are. When you sit down
> to write the first page of your screenplay, in
> your head, you're also writing your Oscar
> acceptance speech.
>
> — *Nora Ephron*

NORA EPHRON (1941–2012) WAS NOMINATED three times for the coveted gold statue. She got the nod from the Academy for writing the original screenplays for *Silkwood, When Harry Met Sally . . . ,* and *Sleepless in Seattle.* When that first blank page was waiting to be filled, Ephron could envision a successful outcome. Likewise, best-selling author Margaret Atwood recognizes the power of visualization. On overcoming writer's block, she recommends "visualization of the holy grail that is the finished, published version of your resplendent book."

In large part, success in life comes from the ability to envision a positive ending. Imagine holding a finished novel in your hand and create an image of the cover art or flap copy. Picture a poem you have written included in an anthology or a short story chosen for inclusion in a volume of stories. Envision an article you have written given front-page placement in your local newspaper.

With any project in life, from baking a cake to building a house, you need to imagine the finished product. Having the image makes the task of creating all the more enjoyable. Envisioning your finished writing will make it more rewarding to sit and write every day and make your success as a writer more likely.

WEDNESDAY | WRITING CLASS

Write an ABC poem about an animal.

I N AN ABC POEM, THE FIRST WORD OF LINE ONE begins with an A, the first word of line two begins with a B, the first word of line three begins with a C, and so on through the alphabet. Your poem, when complete, will have twenty-six lines. The lines needn't rhyme. Each line could be an entire sentence, a phrase, a fragment of a sentence, or even a single word. The idea is to create an image with words.

THURSDAY | EDITING

> Commonly known facts, available in numerous
> sources, should not be enclosed in quotation
> marks or given a source citation unless the
> wording is taken directly from another.
>
> —The Chicago Manual of Style

WHAT WRITER ON A DEADLINE, SELF-IMPOSED or otherwise, doesn't have a love/hate relationship with the Internet? The temptations are enormous: all that copy, already written, sitting and waiting for someone to cut and paste. I'm not talking about the opinions, of which there are many, but of the myriads of facts there for the taking. But before you hit "Ctrl-C" you might change your mind. Think "copyright infringement." And if that doesn't stop you, think "plagiarism."

Plagiarism is when you take someone's hard work and make it your own. It doesn't matter if it is a fact or opinion: if you didn't do the original research, it isn't your work. The best way to avoid plagiarism is to always name your source if you are taking language directly from another source. The second best way is to reword everything, and forgo the temptation of the "cut and paste."

As you write, keep a list of your original resources, especially if they are Internet sites. Then, when you are in the editing phase, make sure you can go back to the resource and double-check that you didn't plagiarize accidentally or otherwise.

FRIDAY | BIOGRAPHY

I don't necessarily start with the beginning of the book. I just start with the part of the story that's most vivid in my imagination and work forward and backward from there.

—Beverly Cleary

B EVERLY CLEARY (1916–   ) WAS BORN IN THE town of McMinnville, Oregon, and lived on a farm in Yamhill, a community without its own library. Her mother arranged to have books sent to Yamhill and acted as librarian in a lodge room over a bank. Cleary was often in the low reading groups, but by the third grade she could rarely be found without a book in hand.

Her school librarian suggested that she write children's books, an idea that appealed to her. After graduating from junior college and the University of California at Berkeley, Cleary finished an advanced degree from the School of Librarianship at the University of Washington, where she specialized in children's literature.

Her first book, *Henry Huggins*, was published in 1950. Sixty years and forty-one children's books and two autobiographies later, she has remained a favorite writer for both children and adults.

SATURDAY | BOOKS TO READ

Invisible Man by **Ralph Ellison**

Invisible Man . . . is a sensational and feverishly emotional book. It will shock and sicken some. . . . [But] it does mark the appearance of a richly talented writer.

— Orville Prescott

R ALPH ELLISON'S STARK ACCOUNT OF RACIAL alienation, *Invisible Man* was published to acclaim in 1952. Its unforgettable protagonist battles racial discrimination only to find himself disillusioned and humiliated.

Considered a Modernist masterpiece, *Invisible Man* opens with the haunting first lines: "I am an invisible man. No, I am not a spook like those who haunted Edgar Allan Poe; nor am I one of your Hollywood-movie ectoplasms. I am a man of substance, of flesh and bone, fiber and liquids—and I might even be said to possess a mind. I am invisible, understand, simply because people refuse to see me."

The unnamed narrator, at first idealistic, grows up in a segregated community in the South. After attending a Negro college, he moves to New York City, only to find disaffection and violence and a descent into invisibility. Ultimately, he finds himself being acted upon—rather than having the capacity to act for himself.

Some have called *Invisible Man* a protest novel, an epithet Ellison disliked. A musician, lecturer, artist, and writer, Ellison said that *Invisible Man* was both a social document as well as a highly stylized novel. The book received the National Book Award, rare for a first novel.

SUNDAY | WRITING PROMPT

When I take a look in the mirror this is what I see . . .

IT'S ONE THING TO WALLOW IN SELF-PITY, AND another to have the gumption to do something about it. Use this prompt to really look deep within yourself and discover not only who the "real" you is but what the possibilities of change are.

A perfect example of this type of exploration is the recent bestseller, *Eat, Pray, Love* by Elizabeth Gilbert. Unhappy with herself and her marriage, Gilbert chronicles her quest to find herself as she travels to three exotic locales: Italy, India, and Indonesia. Her ability to capture her downward spiral is as compelling as her journey.

While we all can't leave our lives behind for a year of indulgent travel in order to find the person in the mirror, we can begin the exploration right in our own homes. Remember, they call the place where you put on your makeup a "vanity" for a reason.

MONDAY | WRITERS ON WRITING

> At one time I thought the most important thing was talent. I think now that the young man or the young woman must possess or teach himself, training himself, in infinite patience, which is to try and to try until it comes right.
>
> —*William Faulkner*

EVERYONE SHOULD TAKE GREAT HOPE FROM novelist William Faulkner's belief. If you're not patient, then you need to train yourself to become more serene. When you start to feel frustration rising, take your fingers away from the keyboard and take some deep breaths. Tell yourself to relax. Or, do as America's third president, Thomas Jefferson, advised: "When annoyed, count ten . . . if very annoyed, count one hundred." Another path to patience is to exercise. Exercise helps you relax when you sit down to type.

You've probably heard that patience is a virtue. It is also healthy. People who are patient are much likelier to have low blood pressure. Low blood pressure results in overall better health.

So take heart with Faulkner's idea. While some writers are born with an innate talent that cannot be trained, anyone can master patience.

TUESDAY | MOTIVATION

> You have to stay in shape. My grandmother, she started walking five miles a day when she was sixty. She's ninety-seven today and we don't know where she is.
>
> —*Ellen DeGeneres*

NEVER BELIEVE IT IF YOU'RE TOLD IT'S TOO LATE to become a writer. Just as Ellen DeGeneres's grandma took up exercise at the age of sixty, many authors hit their creative stride later in life.

Beloved children's author Laura Ingalls Wilder's *Little House* books weren't published until the author was in her sixties. The series has gone on to sell more than sixty million copies. Mark Twain published *Adventures of Huckleberry Finn* at forty-nine. Twain's method of writing involved such extensive revision and tweaking that several times he gave up on writing *Huckleberry Finn.* In the end, it took him almost a decade to finish. Raymond Chandler's international bestseller *The Big Sleep* was published when Chandler was in his fifties. And almost half of Robert Frost's anthologized poems were written after the poet was fifty. *Heart of Darkness*, considered to be one of the world's literary masterpieces, wasn't published until the author Joseph Conrad was forty-five. In fact, the Polish-born Conrad did not learn to speak—let alone write—English until he was in his early twenties. Daniel Defoe published *Robinson Crusoe* at fifty-eight, and Charles Dickens's *A Tale of Two Cities* was published when the author was almost fifty. That historical novel of the French Revolution has gone on to sell more than 200 million copies.

WEDNESDAY | WRITING CLASS

Write a recipe using eggs as the main ingredient.

WHETHER THE DISH IS AN OMELET, A QUICHE, home-made mayonnaise, or *croque monsieur*, be sure to include every detail in your recipe. Start with the name of the dish. Second, note if any preheating is necessary. Then, with bullet points, list all the necessary ingredients and anything special that needs to be done to them before they are incorporated into the dish. Do the eggs need to be at room temperature? Separated? Whisked? At the end of the bulleted list, write a narrative telling your reader how to combine the ingredients and how to cook the dish. Note whether it should be served hot or at room temperature. How long will the dish keep? Leave nothing to chance. If the recipe is a family one, make a note of that, as well.

THURSDAY | EDITING

> Whenever I read good writing, I always
> find the same thing: a fairly high degree of
> subordination, a mastery of parallel structure,
> and a wide variety of structures used in all
> possible locations in the sentence.
>
> — *C. Edward Good*,
> A Grammar Book for You and I . . . Oops, Me!

TO MAKE YOUR WRITING MORE INTERESTING, YOU need to vary the pace and construction of your sentences. Every sentence needs a subject, a verb, and an object. ("Pam picks up the pencil.") But they don't necessarily have to go in that order. I'm not suggesting that you write like Yoda talks. ("The pencil, Pam must pick up.") You can, however, play around with punctuation, clauses, and phrases to make your words more engaging. ("Before she could catch her breath, Pam picked up the pencil.")

Grammatical subordination makes sentences more vivid because they accomplish two ideas at once. Subordination occurs when two clauses are joined with a subordinating conjunction, such as *after, because, since, when, although, before, unless, whereas, as, if* (and the now popular *as if*), *until*, and *while*. The clause following the subordinating conjunction is called a *subordinate clause* because it leans on the other clause to complete the meaning. Here's an example: "Pam will pick up the pencil when she leaves her desk for a break."

Parallel construction requires that expressions of similar content and function be outwardly similar. A good example is the opening sentence in Dickens's *A Tale of Two Cities*: "It was the best of times, it was the worst of times."

FRIDAY | BIOGRAPHY

> You can tell the deepest truths with the lies
> of fiction.
>
> —*Isabel Allende*

ISABEL ALLENDE (1942–) WAS BORN IN LIMA, Peru, the daughter of Tomas Allende, Chile's ambassador to Peru, who disappeared in 1945. Her mother, Francisca Llona Barros, moved her children often, from Beirut to Santiago, where Isabel attended private high schools and graduated at the age of sixteen. Ultimately, she settled with her siblings in the home of their grandmother—whose interest in astrology and mystic fortune-telling made a lasting impact on Isabel. She met and married engineering student Miguel Frias in 1962, and after stints in the United Nations' Food and Agriculture Organization, and Spanish translator for English-language romance novels, Allende turned her attention to her own writing.

When a prominent relative, Chilean president Salvador Allende, was assassinated in 1973, she fled with her family to Venezuela. During her exile, Allende was unable to get a job and instead started to write her first novel, *The House of the Spirits*, which became a bestseller in both Spain and West Germany. Many award-winning novels followed, and Allende became an international literary celebrity.

In 1995, she wrote her first nonfiction book, *Paula*, which focused on the long illness and death of her daughter in 1992. She continues to write and is regarded as one of the world's leading Spanish-language authors.

SATURDAY | BOOKS TO READ

Anna Karenina by Leo Tolstoy

> We might list the greatest artists in Russian
> prose thus: first, Tolstoy; second, Gogol; third,
> Chekhov; fourth, Turgenev. This is rather
> like grading students' papers and no doubt
> Dostoevski and Saltykov are waiting at the
> door of my office to discuss their low marks.
> —*Vladimir Nabokov*

FROM *ANNA KARENINA'S* UNFORGETTABLE OPENING line, "Happy families are all alike; every unhappy family is unhappy in its own way," to its dramatic close, readers have been passionate for Tolstoy's romantic yet realist novel since it was first published in serial form between 1874 and 1877. The complete novel was published in 1878. In fact, when it was on the Oprah Winfrey book club list in 2004, it sold an additional million copies and hit the number-one spot on the *New York Times* bestseller list.

In *Anna Karenina*, Tolstoy examines the themes of marriage, love, and family as he follows the lives of three families: the Oblonskys, the Karenins, and the Levins. Beyond their stories are the massive political changes that were sweeping through Russia in the late nineteenth century: the liberation of serfs, developing urban centers, industrialization, and Western political thought.

Tolstoy revolutionized novel writing with the stream-of-consciousness style used in the book, which influenced writers such as James Joyce and Virginia Woolf.

SUNDAY | WRITING PROMPT

The saddest day of my life . . .

THIS EXERCISE ALLOWS YOU TO MORE FULLY explore a disastrous day in your past. See if you can view the events from a perspective other than your memory. What were the facts that surrounded that day? Were other people involved, and can you speak to them now to get their recollections? See if you can write out this event as a stream of consciousness, not stopping until you've gotten the whole thing on paper.

Another tactic would be to imagine what a terrible day could bring. In the novel *Talk Before Sleep*, Elizabeth Berg creates a set of close friends, Ann and Ruth, one of whom will die of breast cancer. At the end of the book, the two women, as well as other friends, gather together to say good-bye. The story is heartbreaking and beautiful, sad yet sincere.

MONDAY | WRITERS ON WRITING

> The ideal view for daily writing, hour
> for hour, is the blank brick wall of a cold-
> storage warehouse. Failing this, a stretch
> of sky will do, cloudless if possible.
>
> —*Edna Ferber*

E DNA FERBER IS THE AUTHOR OF *GIANT*, THE BEST-selling novel set in Texas, which was later developed into the 1956 film featuring Elizabeth Taylor, Rock Hudson, and James Dean. For Ferber, writing required a virtual blank slate. In order to create, she needed to clear her work area of as many distractions as possible. There are few places starker than the blank walls of a cold storage warehouse. And, along with a shortage of visual distractions, Ferber assures that you won't be taking any catnaps as you write. You'll be too cold!

She also emphasizes the need for a distraction-free environment, one that many established writers recommend. While you don't need to set up writing in a room-sized refrigerator, keeping the temperature a bit cooler than normal is a good device for staying alert and focused.

Ferber focuses on enjoying life as a writer. She says, "Life can't ever defeat a writer who is in love with writing." Ferber encouraged writers to enjoy the process, to seize the moment and feel joy in their ability to write.

TUESDAY | MOTIVATION

> "The king died and then the queen died," is
> a story. "The king died and then the queen
> died of grief" is a plot.
>
> —*E. M. Forster*

READERS WON'T BE DRAWN IN BY A STORY LINE. They will be drawn in by a strong plot.

Think of it this way: the story is what happens, the plot tells how and why it happened. Plot can be broken down into five key elements:

» Introduction of characters and setting

» Rising action, keeping the reader involved by providing dramatic tension

» Climax, the moment of no return for the protagonist

» Falling action—the effects the climax has on the book's characters

» Resolution

As you read, look for these plot elements. Of course, authors use some variation. Donna Tartt's bestselling *The Secret History* turns plot structure on its head, with the opening lines of the novel describing who committed a murder. In essence, she has opened her novel with the climax. Yet, masterfully, Tartt keeps the reader riveted for six hundred pages.

As you develop your own plots, remember your reader and the need to keep your reader engaged by developing and resolving a conflict. To paraphrase John le Carré: "The cat sat on the mat" is not a plot. "The cat sat on the other cat's mat" is a plot.

WEDNESDAY | WRITING CLASS

Create a protagonist for a character-driven movie.

MOVIE SCREENPLAYS FALL INTO TWO DIFFERENT camps: character-driven and plot-driven. Consider two Steven Spielberg movies: *Schindler's List* and *Jaws*. The first is an example of a character-driven movie, one that explores the complexities of Oskar Schindler. If not for Schindler, there would be no movie. In contrast, *Jaws* is plot-driven, as the movie is propelled forward by the actions and interactions of the shark and humans.

For this exercise, begin to create a main character that would act as the catalyst for a character-driven movie. It could be based on a historical person, like Schindler, or someone you create. Ask the five W's (who, what, where, when, why) of your character. This person must be multi-faceted to keep viewers engaged.

THURSDAY | EDITING

> The effect on language of the electronic age
> is obvious to all, even though the process has
> only just begun, and its ultimate impact is as
> yet unimaginable.
>
> —*Lynne Truss*, Eats, Shoots & Leaves

THE SHORTCUTS WE TAKE IN OUR E-MAILS AND TEXT messages cannot transfer to your regular writing, unless your regular writing is simply e-mails and text messages. This is particularly true when it comes to spelling and punctuation. These forms take all the formality out of writing, but they also take the burden of clarity away from the writer and put it on the reader. This is not what good writing is all about. What's more, you'll find out sooner or later that what you thought was cute in your texts to your friends may make you look not-so-smart when you're submitting an article to a newspaper or magazine.

There is, however, good news when it comes to all the e-writing we do: even if we spell poorly or take liberties with punctuation, we are becoming a nation of better writers, because we are writing more. Every time you write, you have the opportunity to write better. And you may just find that while you used to think that writing "C U 2day" was fun, you can take more pride crafting the perfect sentence and then pressing "Send."

FRIDAY | BIOGRAPHY

Words can sometimes, in moments of grace,
attain the quality of deeds.

—*Elie Wiesel*

ELIE WIESEL (1928–) WAS BORN IN SIGHET,
Transylvania. In 1944, his family, along with all the other
Jews in his small town, were deported to the Polish concentration camps. Wiesel was separated from his mother and sisters
immediately. He managed to remain with his father for only
the next year until his father's death at Auschwitz.

After the war, Wiesel found asylum in France and reunited
with his two older sisters. He mastered French and studied philosophy at the Sorbonne. He became a professional journalist,
writing for newspapers in both France and Israel.

In 1955, he first began to record his memories of the war.
His book was published only in Argentina, and many years
passed before he was able to find a publisher in French or
English. This book, *Night*, sold very few copies.

A year later, Wiesel was in New York reporting on the
United Nations and was struck by a taxi. His injuries confined him to a wheelchair for almost a year. He applied for
American citizenship and remained in New York, writing a
feature column for the popular Yiddish-language newspaper,
the *Jewish Daily Forward.*

Wiesel continued to write books and earned an international reputation as a novelist, journalist, and human
rights activist, culminating in receiving the Nobel Prize for
Literature in 1986. Today, *Night* is required reading among
middle- and high-school students around the world.

SATURDAY | BOOKS TO READ

To Kill a Mockingbird by **Harper Lee**

> It's one of the finest books ever written. The quiet heroism of Atticus Finch and the honesty of his children Jem and Scout as they face prejudice in the American South of the 1930s still ring true. If it's been a while since you read it, read it again.
>
> —*Sessalee Hensley*

SINCE ITS ORIGINAL PUBLICATION IN 1960, *TO KILL a Mockingbird* has never been out of print in hardcover or paperback—a remarkable feat for a book that almost didn't make it to the publisher. Midway through the writing process, author Harper Lee threw the manuscript out the window and into a pile of snow. Her agent convinced her to fish it out. Good thing. The book has sold more than thirty million copies and been translated into at least forty languages. It won the Pulitzer Prize in 1961.

To Kill a Mockingbird is told through the eyes of a child, Scout Finch. She describes both everyday events as well as the life-changing incidents that come to haunt her small Alabama town. In the novel, Lee takes on issues of race and discrimination as Scout's father, lawyer Atticus Finch, is asked to defend an innocent black man against a rape charge.

To Kill a Mockingbird remains an important book because it is both social commentary as well as a poignant coming-of-age story.

SUNDAY | WRITING PROMPT

This is my home . . .

TRY LOOKING AT YOUR HOME FROM A NEW ANGLE. Imagine that you are a first-time visitor to your home. What makes it unique? What would a visitor notice first? Would a visitor notice the bright colors of your walls, the interesting rug inside the front door, or the smell of something good cooking?

Or, use this prompt to chronicle your family and local history through a thorough description of your home. George Howe Colt successfully accomplished this in his book, *The Big House: A Century in the Life of an American Summer Home.* Colt used his family home to chart the history of Cape Cod as well as to create a memoir of his family, focusing on the time they spent in their rambling summer home.

By making your home a character, you can write about your family history and the special events that have taken place in your home or the unique people who have lived there.

MONDAY | WRITERS ON WRITING

> That's what I always thought I would do, write about my own life in some way that, in the best-case scenario, would constitute art or literature. I've never had any interest at all in being a journalist or writing some sort of historically accurate autobiography.
>
> —*James Frey*

J AMES FREY ACCOMPLISHED WHAT HE SET OUT to do in his devotional. He wrote a bestselling autobiography, *A Million Little Pieces*, which proved to be less than "historically accurate." Although this was his purported goal, readers of his book cried foul. Frey famously induced a temper tantrum from Oprah Winfrey and the rest of his acquired audience when it was revealed that *A Million Little Pieces*, the story of an alcohol and crack addict entering rehab, wanted by the police in three states, was more fiction than fact. Winfrey had handpicked the 2003 book for her book club, ensuring it bestseller status. When Frey reappeared on her show after the book had been revealed as a sham, Winfrey gave him a rather indelicate dressing down in front of her vast TV audience. It has been reported that she later (years later) apologized for this.

Although *A Million Little Pieces* did not prove to be truthful, it kept millions of readers captivated because of Frey's compelling storytelling, even after the hoax was exposed.

TUESDAY | MOTIVATION

> If there's a book you really want to read, but it hasn't been written yet, then you must write it.
>
> —*Toni Morrison*

HOW MANY TIMES HAVE YOU SAID, "I WISH I COULD find a book about that." Or, you've searched library or bookstore shelves only to come up empty-handed.

Using a complex algorithm, a Google research team came up with an estimate of an astounding 130 million books published in the history of humankind. Astonishing as it may seem, there are still books to be written and topics yet to be covered. That's where you come in.

Perhaps you would like to read a biography of a certain person and there is no book yet written. Maybe you are interested in a detail of history that has gone under the literary radar. Or, perhaps, you have an idea for a novel that you have not found in a work by another author.

This is a good starting place for any writer. What book would you like to pluck off the stacks of your local library or download on your Kindle? Perhaps, that is the book you are meant to write. Don't doubt your idea. The seed of any idea can grow into writing. As poet Sylvia Plath said, "Everything in life is writable about if you have the outgoing guts to do it. . . . The worst enemy to creativity is self-doubt."

WEDNESDAY | WRITING CLASS

> Write a Shakespearean sonnet about your
> favorite hobby.

A SHAKESPEARIAN SONNET IS COMPOSED OF fourteen lines: three quatrains (units of four lines) and one couplet. The rhyme scheme is ABAB, CDCD, EFEF, GG. Consider the first quatrain of one of Shakespeare's best-known sonnets:

> *Shall I compare thee to a summer's day?*
> *Thou art more lovely and more temperate:*
> *Rough winds do shake the darling buds of May,*
> *And summer's lease hath all too short a date:*

In it, the first line (A) rhymes with the third line (also A). Lines two and four (both B) also rhyme. Sonnets are often written in iambic pentameter. Iambic simply means an unstressed syllable followed by a stressed syllable: duh-DUH, duh-DUH, duh-DUH. Pentameter means that there are five of these duh-DUHs in every line. Choose any hobby— gardening, bowling, knitting, quilting, fishing, baking— and create your own sonnet.

THURSDAY | EDITING

> I like to make things as simple as possible, so
> I say that you use *that* before a restrictive
> clause and *which* before everything else.
> —*Mignon Fogarty*, Grammar Girl's Quick
> and Dirty Tips for Better Writing

M ANY A WRITER GETS *WHICH* AND *THAT* MIXED up, so if you suffer from this problem, don't panic. It's just that you have to get to the underlying issue. Before you can understand the meaning of this lesson, you first have to master the idea behind restrictive and nonrestrictive clauses.

The former (restrictive) can't be eliminated in a sentence because it works directly with the noun. A good example of a restrictive clause is "the butterflies that travel from Mexico to Canada amaze me." The clause that identifies the type of butterfly I'm specifying separates it from all other butterflies that might not amaze me at all. A nonrestrictive clause in the same sentence would refer to all butterflies, such as "butterflies, which have wings, can fly."

A quick way to tell which type of clause you are dealing with is Fogarty's best lesson yet: if you can throw out the *which* clause in a sentence and no harm is done to the meaning, you've used it correctly. However, if omission of the clause would change the meaning of the sentence entirely, you should use *that*.

FRIDAY | BIOGRAPHY

> Writing is an extreme privilege but it's also
> a gift. It's a gift to yourself and it's a gift of
> giving a story to someone.
>
> *—Amy Tan*

AMY TAN (1952–) WAS BORN IN OAKLAND, California. In California, the Tan family belonged to a small social group that called themselves the Joy Luck Club.

Tan's mother had high aspirations for her daughter, and she suggested that Amy pursue pre-med studies. Instead, Tan's college career was spent studying English and linguistics. She received her bachelor's and master's degrees in these fields from San Jose State University. After graduation, Tan moved to San Francisco, where she studied for a doctorate in linguistics, first at the University of California at Santa Cruz, and later at Berkeley. She left the doctoral program in 1976 to take a job as a language development consultant working with developmentally disabled children.

Later, she started a business-writing firm, providing speeches for salespeople and executives for large corporations. In 1985, she attended the Squaw Valley Community of Writers workshop, which gave her the encouragement she sought to start writing fiction. Her first novel, *The Joy Luck Club,* was published in 1989. It became an instant bestseller, remaining on the *New York Times* bestseller list for seventy-five weeks.

SATURDAY | BOOKS TO READ

The Complete Poems of Emily Dickinson
by Emily Dickinson

I'm Nobody! Who are you?
Are you—Nobody—too?
Then there's a pair of us!
Don't tell! they'd advertise—you know!
                              —*Emily Dickinson*

EMILY DICKINSON WAS FAMOUSLY RECLUSIVE. FROM 1830 through 1886, she rarely left her hometown of Amherst, Massachusetts. After her fortieth birthday, she seldom left her home, and when visitors called, she would speak with them from the other side of the door.

Literary critic Harold Bloom credits this reclusiveness to Dickinson's success as a poet. "Emily Dickinson had the inner freedom to rethink everything for herself and so achieved a cognitive originality as absolute as William Blake's." By limiting her physical space, Dickinson created unfettered space for her imagination. In her poetry she countered some of the norms—she used unusual punctuation, nonstandard capitalization, dashes, an elliptical style, and contracting metaphors.

Dickinson's work is important because she created a bridge between romantic and modernist poetry, creating a new type of poetic genre. She focused on the beloved nature around her as well as the themes of grief and passion, writing about universalities that remain rich and relevant today.

SUNDAY | WRITING PROMPT

If I could change the world . . .

P RESIDENT BARACK OBAMA'S 2008 PRESIDENTIAL campaign has reinvigorated a collective call to service. Many schools and cities have started to emphasize leadership and community activism on a broad scale. This has lead many a writer to thoughtfully consider how each of us can effect change and possibly save the world.

This topic is best suited for a nonfiction essay, but I can also see a poem lurking that covers the same ground.

MONDAY | WRITERS ON WRITING

> I spend half my time trying to learn the
> secrets of other writers—to apply them to the
> expression of my own thoughts.
>
> —*Shirley Ann Grau*

PULITZER PRIZE–WINNING AMERICAN NOVELIST Shirley Ann Grau has been called a fictional anthropologist. She studies the behavior, the social structures, the interactions, and the mores that make up the culture about which she writes, primarily America's South. In her prize-winning novel *The Keepers of the House*, published in 1964, she addressed the themes of gender, family relationships, and social structures unique to the South. Having grown up in Louisiana and Alabama, Grau knew the South firsthand.

However, Grau also knew that the old saying is true: imitation is the highest form of flattery. Grau has been compared favorably to other Southern writers, such as Eudora Welty, William Faulkner, and Carson McCullers. Yet, she is praised for having a unique writer's voice. By mining the work of other writers and learning their secrets she was able to elevate her craft. For instance, she has been likened to the writer Paul Bowles in her portrayal of a natural world that is unmoved by the humans inhabiting it. And, like Faulkner, Grau writes about themes—such as race—that transcend time and place.

TUESDAY | MOTIVATION

> Times are bad. Children no longer obey their
> parents, and everyone is writing a book.
>
> *— Cicero*

THE MORE THINGS CHANGE, THE MORE THEY STAY the same. Cicero wrote this famous line circa 43 BCE, but it still rings true today. It seems that everybody is writing a book, a story, or a memoir. View this as opportunity rather than competition.

Create a writing group. The group can meet at your home or, better yet, a neutral spot like a coffee shop, a conference room at your local library, or a bookstore. Choose how often to meet. Some writers groups meet weekly, others monthly. Develop a plan for exchanging work. Perhaps, each session will be devoted to the work of one member.

Set up some ground rules. First and foremost should be respect for one another and for the writing. You don't want a group of bloodletters, ready to tear into one another's work. But you do want members who will be willing to offer criticism. Shrinking violets need not apply.

You can find members by placing a notice in your local paper or leaving a flyer at your library or community gathering spot.

Consider how big the group should be. Large groups— more than ten or so participants—tend to get unwieldy. What will be the system for distribution of work? Will the participants e-mail one another or distribute hard copies of their work? The skill level of participants should be relatively even as well.

WEDNESDAY | WRITING CLASS

Write a very short story.

YOU CAN CREATE A COMPELLING CHARACTER AND engaging story line with a limited number of words. It just takes careful crafting and skillful editing. In this exercise you will write a 200-word short story about a missed airline connection and its consequences. Be sure to include the basic plot elements—introduction of the characters, rising action, climax, falling action, and resolution.

THURSDAY | EDITING

> A hook works because it creates a strong
> emotional bond between the readers and the
> central character.
> —The Writer's Digest Writing Clinic

YOUR HOOK IS ALSO WHAT MAKES YOUR WRITING relevant right now. It is the "high concept" of your plot or narrative that turns up the reader's interest at the very beginning and keeps their attention right to the end. When a reader falls in love with a character or a story on the very first page, or even in the first chapter, you've created a really good hook.

If you want to publish your work, you'll need to figure out what the hook is in order to sell your piece to an editor or literary agent. That person will in turn use your hook on every piece of marketing material until your work is published. In a magazine or newspaper article, the hook is your title. In a poem or blog, your hook is your first line of text.

Can you sum up your big idea in just a few words? If so, there's your hook.

FRIDAY | BIOGRAPHY

Belief gets in the way of learning.
—Robert A. Heinlein

R OBERT HEINLEIN (1907–1988) WAS FASCINATED by astronomy from a very early age and was an early reader of science fiction. He entered the Naval Academy in 1925 but had to reconsider a Navy career choice because he was continually seasick. Heinlein was at a complete loss as to what to do with his life. That same year, he read an ad in a science fiction magazine, *Thrilling Wonder Stories,* encouraging submissions from new writers. Over a four-day period, Heinlein wrote his first story, "Life-Line," but instead of submitting it to the magazine, set his sights higher and sent it to a more prestigious publication, *Astounding Science Fiction.* It appeared in the August 1939 issue.

Heinlein later sent in half a dozen more stories, all of which were rejected. However, he kept at it, getting published on a regular basis. By February 1940, Heinlein had been able to fully pay off the mortgage on his first home with the money he made from his short stories.

After World War II, Heinlein relocated to Colorado with his second wife and started writing children's adventure books and screenplays. His 1949 movie, *Destination Moon*, is considered the first modern science fiction film.

Over the next few years, one idea wasn't coming together. Eventually, in 1960, Heinlein was able to complete the 220,000-word *The Man from Mars.* It was unlike anything he had ever written before, a complex satire of sex and religion. After extensive cuts, it was published in 1961 as the iconoclastic *Stranger in a Strange Land.*

SATURDAY | BOOKS TO READ

Lolita by Vladimir Nabokov

> It is overwhelmingly nauseating, even to an
> enlightened Freudian. To the public, it will
> be revolting. It will not sell, and will do
> immeasurable harm to a growing reputation. . . .
> I recommend that it be buried under a stone
> for a thousand years.
> *—Rejection letter to Vladimir Nabokov*

FIVE MAJOR PUBLISHERS REJECTED VLADIMIR Nabokov's slim manuscript before G. P. Putnam and Sons agreed to publish it. Good call—it was the first book since *Gone with the Wind* to sell 100,000 copies during its first three weeks in print.

Lolita chronicles the relationship between middle-aged Humbert Humbert and twelve-year-old Lolita. Was the story pornographic, critics asked? There were loud voices in both camps.

Regardless, the book is a masterwork of wordplay. Russian-born Nabokov gives us an astonishing show of writing dexterity using and combining words in novel ways. Nabokov's acuity with English was at the virtuoso level. Every page of *Lolita* reveals puns, plays on words, double meanings, and other clever tricks. Perhaps the most famous is the character Vivian Darkbloom, whose name is an anagram of *Vladimir Nabokov*. There are multiple references to Edgar Allan Poe, because of Poe's interest in wordplay and the fact that Poe married his thirteen-year-old cousin, putting him in good company with Humbert Humbert.

SUNDAY | WRITING PROMPT

If I could go back in time . . .

M AKING THE ANCIENT WORLD—OR EVEN THE not-so-distant past—come alive is a challenge for both writers of historical fiction and biography. For biography, it is particularly difficult because you must rely solely on the facts or your best educated guess.

In the bestseller, *Hero: The Life and Legend of Lawrence of Arabia*, the former editor-in-chief of Simon and Schuster, Michael Korda, accomplishes this task through detailed and extensive research rather than the myths that surround this legend. Through his research, Korda presents a flesh-and-bones portrayal of this famous romantic hero and shows, for the first time, the contradictory nature of Lawrence of Arabia's personality. Korda describes a man who is at once a fearless leader and a warrior while at the same time being modest, shy, and wary of the limelight.

To try this prompt, pick one historical character you feel you would like to get to know better. See if you can develop a new angle or different way of viewing the person that hasn't been done before.

MONDAY | WRITERS ON WRITING

> Asking a working writer what he thinks about critics is like asking a lamp-post what it feels about dogs.
>
> — *Christopher Hampton*

CHRISTOPHER HAMPTON IS A BRITISH PLAYWRIGHT and screenwriter, perhaps best known for the play *Les Liaisons Dangereuses,* based on the French epistolary novel. He also wrote the screenplay for the popular movie version of the story, starring John Malkovich, Glenn Close, Michelle Pfeiffer, and Uma Thurman. Happily for him, since he seems not to hold warm and fuzzy thoughts about critics, the play and the movie were well received.

He has taken his lashings from critics, however. He especially took a beating for his 2003 film *Imagining Argentina*, starring Antonio Banderas and Emma Thompson. "Highly flawed," "awkwardly executed," "poorly conceived," "fidgety and incomplete." Ouch!

Hampton can keep this state of mind because he recognizes that writing involves risk. Every time writers create and publish—whether in the local newspaper or on movie screens around the globe—they are open to the judgment of others. In this way, writing, that most solitary of occupations, becomes dramatically unsolitary.

You shouldn't take his critic critique as disheartening news. Hampton affirms that there is nothing he would rather do than write. He says, "I'm aware of how rare it is for people to be able to do exactly what they want to do, so I'm always grateful."

TUESDAY | MOTIVATION

Letter writing is the only device for
combining solitude with good company.

—*Lord Byron*

I F YOU ARE EVER STUCK WITH AN IDEA THAT WON'T germinate on the page, consider taking a break and writing a letter to one of your favorite writers. If the author is no longer alive, that's okay. Write the letter as an exercise to limber up your mind before launching into other writing projects for the day.

Many authors love to receive fan mail and, with the advent of the Internet, it is easier than ever to track down either their home or e-mail address. Many authors have their own websites, which list contact information for snail mail or an e-mail address for sending your letter. Most publishers will also forward letters to their authors.

President Barack Obama, also a bestselling author, penned a fan letter to *Life of Pi* novelist Yann Martel. Martel celebrated the letter on his personal blog. By connecting with authors, you will continue to develop a foundation for your writing. Corresponding with other writers can help bridge the gap between the work you do on your own and your need as a writer to connect with others.

Writing letters is also, of course, another act of writing. Because all of your writing counts, so too do these letters. As Ernest Hemingway said, "[Writing letters is] such a swell way to keep from working and yet feel you've done something."

WEDNESDAY | WRITING CLASS

Write a travelogue about a day trip to a nearby town.

T O BE A GOOD TRAVEL WRITER DOESN'T NECESSARILY mean traveling to exotic locations. Rather, it is the ability to make the most routine destination more interesting. Travel to a town near your own. Your job is to introduce a destination that is "off the beaten path." Act like a reporter and take notes. Ask locals to describe their likes and dislikes about their hometown. Note details about buildings, landscapes, and the character of the residents. Are there interesting restaurants, shops, galleries? Is the town known for something special, like Mitchell, South Dakota, home to the one and only Corn Palace? Your goal in writing this piece—or any travelogue—is to propel your readers to want to visit this location.

THURSDAY | EDITING

> A dash is a mark of separation stronger than
> a comma, less formal than a colon, and more
> relaxed than parentheses.
> —*Strunk and White*, The Elements of Style

I AM CRAZY ABOUT DASHES AND USE THEM IN MY writing all the time when I want to make a particular point very clear. I love them because they are visually appealing—they really stand out on the page—and are more engaging than parenthetical remarks (which can often take you off topic). See what I mean?

Dashes are an immediate way to say to the reader, "Wake up! I've got some important information you need to know!" without using an exclamation point, which looks juvenile. The *Chicago Manual of Style* implies that the dash suggests decisiveness, and I agree.

However, like all great techniques of writing, it should not be overused. Dashes can be used no more than once a chapter, or once in an essay. When you do use them, they can be inserted into the middle of a sentence as a qualifying clause, or at the end of a sentence when you have an abrupt change in thought or an interruption in speech during dialogue. ("I think you're an angel—I mean an idiot.")

FRIDAY | BIOGRAPHY

> The most difficult task facing a writer is to find a voice in which to tell the story.
>
> —*John Grisham*

J OHN GRISHAM (1955–) MAJORED IN ACCOUNTING at Mississippi State University and later graduated with a law degree. He went on to practice law for nearly a decade, specializing in criminal defense and personal injury litigation. In 1983, he was elected to the Mississippi House of Representatives and served until 1990.

As a lawyer, Grisham was exposed to the darkest parts of the criminal justice system. He once overheard the testimony of a twelve-year-old rape victim, which inspired him to write his own novel exploring what would have happened if the girl's father had murdered her assailants. He took the time to write every morning for several hours before heading off to work, and three years later he was finished with his first novel, *A Time to Kill*. It was eventually bought by a small press following many other rejections, and in 1988, just five thousand copies were printed.

When he sold the film rights to his next novel, *The Firm*, to Paramount Pictures for $600,000, Grisham suddenly became "an overnight success." *The Firm* became the bestselling novel of 1991. Since then, Grisham has published a bestselling novel every year.

SATURDAY | BOOKS TO READ

Complete Letters of Vincent van Gogh
by Vincent van Gogh

[His letters] enable us to know more about van Gogh's life and mentality than we do of any other artist. The letters form a running commentary on his work, and a human document without parallel.

—Dr. Jan Hulsker

I N ALL, DUTCH ARTIST VINCENT VAN GOGH WROTE almost nine hundred letters weighing in at 850,000 words. These letters were first published in 1914 by Johanna van Gogh-Bonger, his sister-in-law.

The letters were written primarily to his brother Theo. In them, van Gogh covers wide-ranging topics, including the mundane (should he cut his hair?) to the profound (how he survives his battles with severe depression). The letters offer a complex and intricate autobiography of van Gogh's everyday life as well as opening a window into his psyche. His paper trail reveals his working process, his passion for color, the torment of loneliness, his worries about money, frustrations about his love life, his development as an artist, and his feelings of isolation and rejection.

These letters shine a spotlight on an artist's innermost thoughts and ideas, to which we are rarely privy. For those intrigued by autobiography and memoir, these letters show a unique way of disseminating personal information without the awkwardness or pomposity of self-reflection. As he beautifully wrote, "I wish they would only take me as I am."

SUNDAY | WRITING PROMPT

If I were on a deserted island . . .

INSTEAD OF PLAYING THE GAME WHERE YOU HAVE to whittle down your possessions to the few things you would bring to a desert island, see if you can imagine living on one right now. How would you survive? Would you thrive in solitude, or would you spend your time figuring out how to return to civilization? Hopefully you would do better than Tom Hanks in the movie *Cast Away*, and more realistically than Gilligan and his friends.

A wonderful example of this prompt is the memorable children's classic, *Island of the Blue Dolphins* by Scott O'Dell. First published in 1960, this award-winning story is the fictional tale (based on the true story) of a twelve-year-old girl, Karana, who lives alone on a Pacific island. Isolated for eighteen years, Karana forages for food, builds weapons to fight predators, clothes herself as she grows, and finds strength in her seclusion.

MONDAY | WRITERS ON WRITING

> If a writer of prose knows enough about what he is writing about he may omit things that he knows and the reader, if the writer is writing truly enough, will have a feeling of those things as strongly as though the writer had stated them. A writer who omits things because he does not know them only makes hollow places in his writing.
>
> —*Ernest Hemingway*

AS THE AMERICAN AUTHOR ERNEST HEMINGWAY explains: travelers on a cruise ship in the northern Pacific Ocean can imagine the immensity of the icebergs they pass even though only a small fraction of each iceberg peeks out from the water. Although not visible, people are aware of the icebergs lurking just below the ocean's surface.

Good writing follows the same idea. If the author genuinely knows of what he writes, then, almost by telepathy, it will be telegraphed to the readers. An English master gardener who writes a mystery about a murder taking place at the gardens of Buckingham Palace, needn't—and shouldn't—describe every scientific part of the flower or how the irrigation system works (unless, of course, it affects the outcome of the case). All of this detail would make for plodding reading. Instead, as Hemingway suggests, the reader will intuit this information.

The catch? You can't fake the knowledge. Don't write about deep-sea fishing if you've never set foot on a boat. Know well what you write. Avoid hollow writing.

TUESDAY | MOTIVATION

Do back exercises. Pain is distracting.
— *Margaret Atwood*

SITTING IN A CHAIR BENT OVER YOUR WRITING CAN mean trouble for your back and, for that matter, aches and pains for other parts of your body. Some of every writer's routine should include exercise, both to alleviate pain and to encourage the creative process. Research shows that virtually every type of thinking improves with thirty minutes of exercise. This includes creative thinking. Further, the effects of your half-hour exercise stint last for hours.

The type of exercise doesn't matter. Take your dog for a brisk walk—you'll be happier, and so will your pooch. If you have access to a pool, then swimming laps is a wonderful way to keep mind and body fit. Riding a stationary bike is another good choice. Some writers choose to break their solitary routines by working out at a gym or taking a group Pilates class.

Writers often turn to yoga as their exercise of choice. Yoga helps its practitioners find inner peace, tap into their creative energy, and to persevere—this last attribute being of particular importance when you are faced with writer's block. Yoga also trains its practitioners to visualize positive outcomes, an essential tool for successful writers.

WEDNESDAY | WRITING CLASS

Write a true crime story about a recent murder in your state.

D O YOUR RESEARCH BY COMBING THROUGH YOUR local and state newspapers, listening to newscasts (take notes on these), and by interviewing your own friends about their thoughts on the case. Draw your reader in by culling the newspapers to find lesser-known facts about the case. Or, begin with a quote from one of your friends, offering a new perspective. The thrill of true crime is in the details, so make sure you include everything that you've been able to uncover: the more gruesome and strange, the better.

THURSDAY | EDITING

> Avoid jargon.
> —*Frederick Crews,* The Random House Handbook

THIS PIECE OF ADVICE MAY AT FIRST SEEM TO FLY in the face of an earlier lesson (see Week 9), where I wrote about the benefits of using jargon, or specific types of language, when you are addressing specific groups of readers. Jargon is defined as "the specialized or technical language of a trade, profession, or similar group." However, while it's okay to use jargon when you know that your reader will understand what you are talking about, it's not okay to use it in a context where you come across as the "insider" and everyone else is not.

If you are writing nonfiction for a lay audience, you can introduce jargon as long as you include a full definition of what the word or acronym means. In this way, you are bringing the readers inside the circle and teaching them something new. Otherwise, use the definition without the jargon, and you won't have to worry whether or not you are sending your reader off to their dictionary, or worse, away from your article.

FRIDAY | BIOGRAPHY

> I do not just write, I write what I am.
> If there is a secret, perhaps that is it.
> *José Saramago*

J OSÉ SARAMAGO (1922–2010) WAS BORN IN THE small village of Azinhaga, Portugal, sixty miles northeast of Lisbon. He spent a lot of time with his maternal grandparents, who were poor rural peasants, while his parents went to work in the city. Though he was more than competent as a student, the Saramago family's financial situation prompted him to leave school at the age of twelve to pursue technical training as a car mechanic, where he could faster contribute to the family income. He then had a succession of jobs, including working as a welfare agency bureaucrat, a printing production manager, a proofreader, a translator, and a newspaper columnist.

Saramago published his first novel at the age of twenty-three, but nearly three decades would pass before he returned to novel writing. It wasn't until his employment options vanished following the 1975 countercoup that swept communists from power in Portugal that Saramago returned to writing.

"Being fired was the best luck of my life," he said in an interview in the *New York Times Magazine* in 2007. "It made me stop and reflect. It was the birth of my life as a writer."

His first major success after his return to writing full-time was the international bestseller *Baltasar and Blimunda*. He was awarded the Nobel Prize for Literature in 1998.

SATURDAY | BOOKS TO READ

The Corrections by Jonathan Franzen

> Funny and deeply sad. *The Corrections* is a
> testament to the range and depth of pleasures
> great fiction affords.
>
> —*David Foster Wallace*

WHEN JONATHAN FRANZEN'S *THE CORRECTIONS* was published in 2001, it was an immediate hit. Critic James Wood likened it to a Dickens novel, calling it a *Bleak House* of the digital age. Author Michael Cunningham favorably compared it to Thomas Mann's *Buddenbrooks*. Others invoked Tolstoy. Bret Easton Ellis called it one of the three most important books of his generation. In 2005, *The Corrections* was included in *Time* magazine's list of the 100 best English-language novels. The magazine lauded Franzen for taking up the mantle of Hemingway, Faulkner, and Updike by re-creating the great American literary novel with a postmodern twist. He masterfully straddled the gap between mainstream and highbrow.

The Corrections brings to vivid life the story of a Midwestern family. At its heart are the family patriarch and matriarch, Alfred and Enid Lambert. Alfred is suffering from Parkinson's and dementia, and Enid calls upon their three adult children, living in the Northeast, to attend "one last Christmas" to make decisions about their roles in Alfred's care.

With *The Corrections*, Franzen established himself as one of the preeminent American writers of his generation. The novel won the 2001 National Book Award for Fiction and the 2002 James Tait Black Memorial Prize.

SUNDAY | WRITING PROMPT

Weather can affect my life . . .

WRITING ABOUT WEATHER AND ITS CONSEQUENCES can make for a riveting story. The book, *The Perfect Storm: A True Story of Men Against the Sea* by Sebastian Junger, comes to mind as an effective example. In this book, Junger reconstructs "the perfect storm," which has entered our collective lexicon, referring to how a confluence of events can greatly (and mostly negatively) affect a situation. The *Andrea Gail* was a seventy-foot, steel-hulled vessel that had to face unrelenting weather caused by a hurricane off Bermuda, a cold front coming down from the Canadian Shield, and a storm brewing over the Great Lakes. His images were so vivid that it was no wonder that it was made into a major motion picture.

For this exercise, see if you can imagine, or retell, a day in your life when you were greatly affected by severe weather. The trick is to see if you can make the weather a fully realized character in the story, not just something that was going on in the background.

MONDAY | WRITERS ON WRITING

> To be a writer is to throw away a great deal,
> not to be satisfied, to type again, and then
> again, and once more, and over and over. . . .
> —*John Hersey*

PULITZER PRIZE–WINNING AMERICAN AUTHOR John Hersey was known primarily for his innovative account of the World War II bombing of Hiroshima, titled *Hiroshima*. It was published in 1946, when the emotional and physical scars from World War II were still raw. Readers clamored for books like it to help explain this unprecedented period in global history.

When you read a book like *Hiroshima*, one that practically refuses to let you put it down because it is that engaging and compelling, it can be challenging to believe that the writer struggled while creating it. As Hersey describes here, though, the task of writing, even for a professional writer, can be onerous. Being a writer is about destruction as much as construction. Writers throw work away. They delete whole passages, sometimes whole paragraphs and chapters.

The key word in the quotation above is *satisfied*. Hersey cautions writers not to be satisfied. Can the piece you are working on be done better? Differently? Would you be satisfied to be the reader of the piece you are creating? As you grow and mature in your work, you will learn to know when your written work is finished and satisfying to you and your readers.

TUESDAY | MOTIVATION

> Begin with an individual, and before you
> know it you find that you have created a
> type; begin with a type, and you find you
> have created—nothing.
>
> —*F. Scott Fitzgerald*

THE CHARACTERS IN *THE GREAT GATSBY* TELL A story that has become one of the cultural touchstones of twentieth-century American life. Fitzgerald began with an individual, the poor North Dakota farm boy Jimmy Gatz, and turned him into a type: the American symbol of the self-made man. The author was so successful that people began to refer to real-life, self-made millionaires as "Gatsbys."

Similarly, in writing his 1987 bestseller, *The Bonfire of the Vanities,* author Tom Wolfe took individuals Sherman McCoy and his wife, Judy, and developed them into types. Sherman became a "Master of the Universe," and Judy became a "Social X-ray," a WASP-y, too-thin blonde socialite. Both types have remained a part of the American cultural lexicon.

The greatest literary works have fully developed characters. You can practice character development by asking—and then answering—background questions about your characters' family, employment, childhood, adolescence, religion, likes and dislikes, friends, and values. Let them speak for themselves, rather than projecting your voice through them. Find out if a character has any secrets. What does he fear? Does he have allergies? No question is too small. Whether or not you use any of this information directly is not that important. But take time to see your characters from every angle, so when you write about them, they are more fully realized.

WEDNESDAY | WRITING CLASS

Write a short biography of a historical figure.

IT'S NOT ENOUGH TO COPY DOWN BASIC FACTS FROM the Internet. You have to take those facts and create your own unique perspective on the individual. Give the reader your impression of that person beyond the headlines or history. Set the person in the context of the time in which she or he lived, and show how that time is similar or different than what we are living in today.

Another route would be to take a little-known story of a historical figure and blow it out: capture details that may have gone missing over the years or were never fully explored. These are the types of things that make biography one of the bestselling genres in the nonfiction market.

THURSDAY | EDITING

> On words now accepted as English, use
> accents only when they make a crucial
> difference to pronunciation.
> —The Economist Style Guide

MANY LANGUAGES RELY HEAVILY ON THE USE OF accents. If you are incorporating foreign terms into your work, as either a proper name or descriptive word, use the accents as appropriate. You can choose from the following:

Acute accent	*étudiant*
Grave accent	*città*
Circumflex	*maître*
Umlaut	*müesli*
Cedilla	*soupçon*
Tilde	*mañana*

However, if the foreign word is now commonly used in the English language, you only need to include the accent if it makes a significant difference in the word's pronunciation. For example, you should include accents on words like *café* and *cliché*, but not with words like *chateau* or *elite*.

American English is filled with many foreign words, some of which we simply assume have been English all along. Two of my favorites are Icelandic in origin: *geyser* and *berserk*. *Raccoon, squash,* and *moose* all have Native American origins. *Cookie* and *stoop* are Dutch; *barbecue* and *stevedore* are Spanish.

FRIDAY | BIOGRAPHY

I've been as bad an influence on American literature as anyone I can think of.

—Dashiell Hammett

S AMUEL DASHIELL HAMMETT (1894–1961) DIDN'T see much future for himself in school, and, after dropping out at the age of thirteen, he thrust himself into the adult workforce, securing one menial job after another, from railroad laborer to stevedore. But it was a low-paying stint as an operative at the Pinkerton National Detective Agency in San Francisco where Hammett struck gold, mining his experiences there into the hardboiled detective stories that would later gain him fame.

Hammett enlisted in the U.S. Army in 1918, but after contracting tuberculosis, he was unfit for duty and confined to an Army hospital in Tacoma, Washington. He returned to San Francisco, but his health prevented him from going back to Pinkerton, and he decided to give writing a try. By 1922, he had published his first story in *The Smart Set*, a prominent literary magazine, but he soon realized that his hard-scrabble style of writing was better suited to pulp magazines. In 1923, the popular magazine *Black Mask* published his first hardboiled crime story. He continued to publish in that magazine for five years and, at the same time, began writing novels and screenplays for Hollywood. By 1930, Hammett had built a strong following for both his novels and his magazine stories. He decided to create a new character: the now-famous Sam Spade.

SATURDAY │ BOOKS TO READ

The Haunting of Hill House
by Shirley Jackson

I think there are few if any descriptive passages
in the English language that are any finer than
[the opening lines of *The Haunting of Hill House*]
—*Stephen King*

S HIRLEY JACKSON'S 1959 THRILLER *THE HAUNTING
of Hill House* opens with these chilling lines:

No live organism can continue for long to exist sanely
under conditions of absolute reality; even larks and
katydids are supposed, by some, to dream. Hill House,
not sane, stood by itself against its hills, holding darkness within; it had stood for eighty years and might
stand for eighty more.

Jackson's terrifying ghost story focuses on the Hill
House and its four occupants, as it is explored by Dr. John
Montague, an investigator of the supernatural. One of
the occupants is Eleanor, and as the novel progresses, she
becomes increasingly affected by the supernatural events
occurring in the house. Or, does she?

Jackson's writing has an eerie quality that has influenced
the masterworks of Stephen King, Neil Gaiman, and a host
of other thriller writers. The reader is glued to the page.
With her subtle hand, it is impossible for us to know until
the very end whether the supernatural has taken hold of
Eleanor or if she is descending into madness.

SUNDAY | WRITING PROMPT

Everyone needs help sometime . . .

CAN YOU RECOUNT A TIME WHEN YOU EITHER needed help or unselfishly lent a hand to someone in need? The stories shared on the *NBC Nightly News with Brian Williams* feature "Making a Difference" are a daily reminder of just how many people in our world continue to need help and can offer you a little inspiration as you take on this prompt.

You can also look to literature. *A Tale of Two Cities* by Charles Dickens is one of the best-loved and classic stories about choosing to help others. In it, Sydney Carton, who spends most of the novel indulging in a life of sloth and apathy, chooses to make the ultimate altruistic act to save his friends and to help save France. You can use this prompt to write about a small act of kindness or a large act of kindness such as Carton's courageous act.

MONDAY | WRITERS ON WRITING

> To write fiction, one needs a whole series
> of inspirations about people in an actual
> environment, and then a whole lot of hard
> work on the basis of those inspirations.
>
> —*Aldous Huxley*

E NGLISH AUTHOR ALDOUS HUXLEY, WHOSE 1932 futuristic novel *Brave New World* changed science fiction forever, focuses on the need for a writer to find inspiration, particularly when writing fiction. Finding and acting upon this inspiration involves two very different modes.

In the first, you must actively observe your environment. Go out and look. Really look. Too often, you might find yourself in the middle of a daily routine and realize you aren't observing, just going through the motions. Change this mindset and observe. Take notes to force yourself to observe. As Jack London, author of *White Fang* and *The Call of the Wild*, put it, "You can't wait for inspiration. You have to go after it with a club."

The second mode is in stark contrast: Huxley recommends here that one needs to get to work and use these inspirations as seed for writing. This is the solitary part of a writer's life and involves creating a workspace and time that allow for thought and germination of the inspiration you've found in your daily living.

TUESDAY | MOTIVATION

> Every day I get up and look out the window,
> and something occurs to me. Something
> always occurs to me. And if it doesn't, I just
> lower my standards.
>
> —*William Stafford*

JUST AS YOU DEPOSIT YOUR CHECKS IN THE BANK, start keeping an account of your ideas. Consider this exercise as prewriting. Just as there are preparations that must be made for preparing a meal—shopping and chopping, for instance—there are preparations for writing. This includes brainstorming ideas.

In your journal, keep track of any ideas that cross your mind. Don't worry if an idea feels too small or insignificant. If it struck you as interesting, then write it down. Don't fret about the quality of prose. Rather, focus on getting the idea in print.

On a day when the words are refusing to flow as you sit at your computer, refer to your idea journal and choose one. Write a page or two on this idea. It can be a small idea: Why is Maine the toothpick capital of the world? When was chewing gum invented? How many calories are on the back of a stamp? Take this small idea, and enjoy filling a page or two. Don't get tight with your writing. This is a chance to have fun and limber up your mind, like a pianist running through her scales before playing a sonata.

WEDNESDAY | WRITING CLASS

Write the book review you would like to receive.

WHAT ARE YOUR FAVORITE ASPECTS OF YOUR OWN writing? What do you think you do well that others cannot master? Use this information, and write a review of an imaginary book or one that you are actually working on. Describe for others what your motivations and interests are and what brought you to develop this project. See if you can link it to other published books in similar genres and show how it is better. (Of course it's better: it's your book!)

THURSDAY | EDITING

> There never was a golden age in which the rules for the possessive apostrophe were clear-cut and known, understood and followed by most educated people.
>
> —The Oxford Companion to English Literature

A POSTROPHES CAN BE USED FOR JUST TWO PURPOSES: to show possession and to form a contraction. Most writers can easily form a contraction (but try not to overuse them). It's the possessive that causes problems (in this sentence, *it's* isn't possessive, it's a contraction).

When you are signaling possession or ownership of something or someone by a singular noun, an apostrophe followed by an *s* is always used, whether or not the word ends in an *s*:

The principal's office was quiet.

My brother John's friends are coming over.

This is Henry Jones's wallet.

Create the possessive of names that have two or more syllables and end in an *eez* sound by adding only an apostrophe.

Take the time to study Sophocles' writings.

Plural nouns are another story. For these, just an apostrophe is added:

All of the girls' coats were in the closet.

Irregular plural nouns require the addition of an apostrophe and an *s*, as in the following:

Tommy told me to meet him in the men's locker room.

FRIDAY | BIOGRAPHY

Literature is analysis after the event.

—*Doris Lessing*

DORIS LESSING (1919–2013) WAS BORN IN PERSIA (now Iran). Both her parents were British: her father was a clerk in the Imperial Bank of Persia and her mother a nurse. In 1925, the family moved to what is now Zimbabwe. Lessing has described her childhood as an uneven mix of pleasure and pain. She was sent to a convent school and then to an all-girls high school from which she dropped out at the age of thirteen.

Lessing continued her education on her own, primarily through reading. She ordered books from London, which fed her imagination. Independent from the start, she left home for good when she was just fifteen and took a job as a nursemaid. She also began writing stories and sold a few to magazines in South Africa.

By 1949, Lessing had been married, divorced, remarried, and again, divorced. She had abandoned her first two children and moved to London with her young son. Soon after arriving, she published her first novel, *The Grass Is Singing*, and began her career as a professional writer. She wrote more than fifty books, many of them highly politicized novels that dealt with racial relations in Africa and feminism. She was awarded the Nobel Prize for Literature in 2007.

SATURDAY | BOOKS TO READ

The Great Gatsby by F. Scott Fitzgerald

> . . . one day *The Great Gatsby* flashed upon
> us. The promise of the first novel of the so
> greatly gifted young writer was fulfilled.
> —*Alice B. Toklas*

WHEN *THE GREAT GATSBY* WAS PUBLISHED IN 1925, it met with a lukewarm response. The book went through only two printings, and years later many copies remained unsold. Most of the critical reviews were positive, but it did not sell as well as F. Scott Fitzgerald's previous novels, *This Side of Paradise* and *The Beautiful and the Damned*. Now, a first edition with a dust jacket can fetch as much as $250,000.

The Great Gatsby is a classic coming-of-age novel set in the 1920s. North Dakota farm boy Jay Gatz re-creates himself as the dashing and mysterious Jay Gatsby. Written at the then peak of American prosperity and set in a wealthy community on Long Island Sound, the book captures the heart of the Jazz Age. Using a deft hand with language, Fitzgerald creates an allegorical reflection of an America on the verge of descent.

The Great Gatsby, with its universal themes of unrequited love, the inescapable temptations of wealth, and the desire to escape one's past, has become one of the must-read novels of the American twentieth and twenty-first centuries.

SUNDAY | WRITING PROMPT

My first love . . .

PERHAPS THE MOST PERSONAL PROMPT AND THE one you might not feel like sharing, writing about your first love may take time . . . and patience. See if you can recall the thrill of meeting the person you thought was "right" for you and then the subsequent happiness and sadness that came with this experience.

One of the most powerful tales of first love is the young adult novel *Forever*, by Judy Blume. First published in 1975, this tale of teen sexuality is so evocative that it remains high on the list of the 100 Most Frequently Challenged Books by the American Library Association.

What's more interesting is that this story of first love continues to be read as "fresh" and original more than thirty years after it was published. Will yours? Do you think your story stands the test of time, or are the circumstances locked in the moment in history when it happened?

MONDAY | WRITERS ON WRITING

*The most valuable of all talents is that of
never using two words when one will do.*
—*Thomas Jefferson*

THOMAS JEFFERSON ADMIRED THE BEAUTY OF brevity, urging writers and speakers to do more with less. Jefferson urged authors to remember that the goal in writing is to communicate an idea. If you can do it with fewer words, then that is the route to take, says Jefferson.

How do you achieve brevity in your writing? Write first, then edit. Take out all the words you can live without and still tell your story. Does your piece still make sense? Is your idea clearly communicated? Then, your editing made sense, and you have tightened your writing. Think of all those in your life who tweet daily: if they can get it down to six words, so can you.

Sometimes, authors are not aiming for brevity (consider James Joyce's stream-of-consciousness novel *Ulysses*), but it is good to keep Jefferson's words present as you write. After all, he (with a little help from other Founding Fathers of America) wrote the Declaration of Independence, the document establishing the right to be an independent nation, using less than fourteen hundred wisely selected words.

TUESDAY | MOTIVATION

> A blog is in many ways a continuing
> conversation.
>
> —*Andrew Sullivan*

I N 2000, ANDREW SULLIVAN BECAME THE FIRST mainstream journalist to experiment with blogging. His blog, *The Daily Dish*, soon gained a large following, enabling him to interact with his readers and garner almost instantaneous responses to his work.

There are thousands of blogs available to writers that allow you to have conversations with editors, agents, authors, and readers. Blogging is an effective way to receive an immediate response to an idea or question. It is also a method for finding advice and information. Blogger beware, though. Not all advice you will receive through a blog will be of equal value. Check out a variety of blogs to find one that matches your interests and ideas.

There are blogs for all types of writers. Whether you write romance, adventure, history, memoir, journalism, fantasy, or any other genre, there is at least one blog to help you. These blogs are useful to aspiring as well as established writers.

Be careful about spending too much time reading other blogs. It shouldn't become a distraction that takes you too far from your own writing.

WEDNESDAY | WRITING CLASS

Write a blog about something funny that happened to you this week.

LOTS OF PEOPLE TURN TO BLOGS FOR PRODUCT information, reviews of books and movies, and even medical help. But the ones that really stand out are the bits of people's ordinary days and the fans that follow them. Blogging can be like a public diary, but you have to make it really interesting in order for people to come back for more. Choose something that really amused you this week: something funny you saw at the grocery store, or on the Internet, or even at work. Remember, you don't want to hurt feelings or disparage coworkers, so keep those real names to yourself.

THURSDAY | EDITING

> It offends those who wish to confine English usage in a logical straitjacket that writers often begin sentences with "and" or "but." True, one should be aware that many such sentences would be improved by becoming clauses in compound sentences; but there are many effective and traditional uses for beginning sentences thus.
>
> —*Paul Brians,*
> Common Errors in English Usage

WE HAVE BEEN TOLD NOT TO BEGIN SENTENCES with conjunctions: the fear is that you would be left with a sentence fragment and not a fully formed idea. But there is nothing grammatically wrong with starting a sentence with a conjunction such as *but*, *and*, or *or*. (See? I just did it myself.)

There are plenty of good examples from literature that show that it's perfectly acceptable to begin a sentence with the word *but*. One instance is Sherlock Holmes's reply, as created by Sir Arthur Conan Doyle: "But, my dear Watson, the criminal obviously wore expensive boots or he would not have taken such pains to scrape them clean."

When you are editing, review your sentences that begin this way. Consider whether the sentence beginning with the conjunction really ought to be combined with the previous sentence. Would it be just as effective, or would it lose the emphasis you've created? Like every other technique we've talked about, use this sentence starter sparingly, or it will lose its emphasis altogether.

FRIDAY | BIOGRAPHY

> Far away there in the sunshine are my highest
> aspirations. I may not reach them, but I can
> look up and see their beauty, believe in them,
> and try to follow where they lead.
>
> —*Louisa May Alcott*

LOUISA MAY ALCOTT (1832–1888) WAS HOME-schooled by her father, Amos Bronson Alcott, and his literary friends Henry David Thoreau, Ralph Waldo Emerson, and Theodore Parker, all of whom lived in the tight, progressive community of Concord, Massachusetts. Although well educated, Alcott did not come from a family of means, and as an adult, she was sent to work as a domestic servant. She later secured a position as a private teacher. During the Civil War, Alcott traveled to Washington, D.C., to serve as a Union nurse.

Unbeknownst to most of her friends and family, Alcott began publishing poems and short stories as early as 1851 under the name Flora Fairfield. In 1862, she adopted the pen name A. M. Barnard, writing melodramas that were produced in Boston. She began to publish Civil War stories based on her experiences as a nurse under her real name in magazines, including the *Atlantic Monthly* and *Ladies' Companion*. Her first big success was the novel *Little Women*, which secured her fortune and allowed her to continue writing for the rest of her life.

SATURDAY | BOOKS TO READ

The Diary of a Young Girl by Anne Frank

> I have often been downcast, but never in
> despair; I regard our hiding as a dangerous
> adventure. . . . My start has been so very full
> of interest, and that is the sole reason why
> I have to laugh at the humorous side of the
> most dangerous moments.
>
> —*Anne Frank*

THE DIARY OF ANNE FRANK, WHOSE FAMILY WAS forced into hiding in Nazi-occupied Amsterdam, would become one of the most important documents of the Holocaust.

In the diary, which she received on her thirteenth birthday, the young Dutch girl described her daily experiences. Initially, Anne wrote the diary as a personal document, and like many diaries, it reveals both the mundane thoughts as well as a young girl's hopes and aspirations. What makes the diary truly unique is that while Anne was in hiding, she heard a radio broadcast encouraging people to write memoirs to be published after the war. Anne took this to heart and began deliberately writing a historic and public document.

In 1944, the family was discovered by the Nazis and sent to the Bergen-Belsen concentration camp where Anne died of typhus. The only family member to survive was her father, Otto, who was given the diary by a family friend who found it. The diary was first published in America in 1952 and has been updated to include material Anne's father first refused to publish. This extended version is worth reading because it puts a very human face on a tragic period in history.

SUNDAY | WRITING PROMPT

He seemed like a nice neighbor; who would ever believe that he was really . . .

THIS PROMPT CAN BE FOLLOWED BY MANY DIFFERENT techniques and writing styles. It can be the feature of a nonfiction exposé. It can delve deep into fantasy (à la *Harry Potter*) or humorous fiction (as in the television classic *The Munsters*). Or, it can be one element in a more complex and disturbing story.

Bestselling author Alice Sebold chose the third technique for her novel *The Lovely Bones*. (Spoiler alert!) This is a twist on the exercise because we don't know that the prompt has been employed until the ending. Nevertheless, it is the critical piece in the novel, a murder mystery told from the perspective of the deceased victim.

MONDAY | WRITERS ON WRITING

Don't tell me the moon is shining; show me the glint of light on broken glass.

—*Anton Chekhov*

RUSSIAN AUTHOR ANTON CHEKHOV IS CONSIDERED one of the absolute greats of the world's literary canon. He is especially renowned for his short stories, of which he wrote hundreds. Early in his writing career, he began submitting work to a magazine, and the editor there limited each piece submitted to a page and a half. It is thought that this length limitation helped Chekhov create his concise style of writing.

One of his gifts was the ability to beautifully describe a scene by showing rather than telling. It is pedestrian to write "The moon is shining." It is brilliant to show the reader it is snowing by describing reflected light.

Chekhov encourages writers to show rather than tell in order to be more believable. If you tell your reader that your protagonist is a world-class musician or an Olympic-level swimmer, she may not believe you. Your character won't feel fully developed. Likewise, if you describe a garden as "lovely," you haven't given your reader much information. Instead, says Chekhov, describe your character's experience of the lovely garden. Show, don't tell.

TUESDAY | MOTIVATION

> I'm always pretending that I'm sitting across
> from somebody. I'm telling them a story, and
> I don't want them to get up until it's finished.
>
> — James Patterson

WHEN YOU GO TO THE MOVIES, THE CREATORS of the film—the directors, actors, and screenwriters—are charged with keeping you in your seat until the lights come back on. James Patterson uses this approach in his writing, and it has been a recipe for monumental success. He has sold more than 170 million copies of his work worldwide, and it is estimated that one out of every seventeen hardcover fiction books sold since 2006 is a James Patterson title.

Patterson's page-turning formula works because his readers are so engaged that they struggle to put down his books at night when it is time to turn off the lights and go to sleep.

Think about what keeps you involved in the books you read. Is it the vivid descriptions, engaging dialogue, suspense, conflict, character development, or the action? What are the elements of a book that engage you? Then, try Patterson's model the next time you sit down to write. Tell a story that will keep the imaginary listener across from you entertained and eager to stay tuned.

You may not want to use this model every time you write, but, by using it on occasion, it will remind you that while you are sitting alone with your writing, ultimately, it may face an audience, one you must keep engaged.

WEDNESDAY | WRITING CLASS

Write a caption for a gossip magazine
photograph.

THINK "CELEBRITY CAUGHT IN THE ACT," AND LET
your imagination go wild. You have two lines of text,
so use them well, and make sure to capture all five Ws: who,
what, where, when, and why. It might be fun to put yourself
in the photo as well.

THURSDAY | EDITING

The phrase "working mother" is redundant.

—Jane Sellman

A REDUNDANT EXPRESSION SAYS THE SAME THING twice. Some writers mistakenly use redundant expressions because they might not understand the precise definition of a word. For example, *close proximity* is redundant because *proximity* means *nearness*. Can there be any other kind of nearness than close nearness?

Other times people use redundant expressions because they think they are writing for emphasis or believe that they are clever. Instead, the writing looks clichéd, and we certainly do not want that (see Week 17).

The following are some of my favorite redundant expressions. In each case, only one of these words is sufficient.

advance forward	lower down
close intimates	more better
completely unanimous	new innovation
consensus of opinion	past history
continue on	raise up
empty void	rejected outcast
end result	same identical
exact same	share together
famous celebrity	sudden impulse
free gift	true fact
fundamental basis	unexpected surprise
future ahead	unimportant triviality
join together	wealthy millionaire
leave from	yearly annual

FRIDAY | BIOGRAPHY

> Nothing you write, if you hope to be good,
> will ever come out as you first hoped.
>
> —*Lillian Hellman*

LILLIAN HELLMAN (1905–1984) WAS BORN IN New Orleans but soon moved to New York City, where she attended public schools. Throughout her childhood, she spent half her time in New York, and the other half living in her aunts' boarding home in New Orleans. Later, she went to college at both New York University and Columbia but never graduated.

At the age of nineteen, Hellman married *New Yorker* writer and press agent Arthur Kober, who helped her find editorial work in newspapers and magazines, and together they traveled to Germany in 1929. The couple moved to Hollywood in the early 1930s, where she worked as a reader for MGM. Hellman organized her fellow readers into a union, and it was there that she first met the writer Dashiell Hammett. She worked as a press agent and scenarist before she had the confidence to allow others to read her own plays. Hammett, who became both her mentor and her lover, is often credited as the impetus that kept her writing. In all, Hellman published five successful plays before she was blacklisted by the House Un-American Activities Committee (HUAC) in the 1950s. She then turned her attention to writing about social injustices and finishing her memoirs, which were published in three volumes, all of which became bestsellers.

SATURDAY | BOOKS TO READ

On the Road by Jack Kerouac

> The stars bent over the little roof; smoke
> poked from the stovepipe chimney. I smelled
> mashed beans and chili. The old man growled
> . . . A California home; I hid in the grapevines,
> digging it all. I felt like a million dollars; I was
> adventuring in the crazy American night.
>
> —*Jack Kerouac*

KEROUAC, WHO COINED THE TERM "BEAT GENERATION" in 1948, wrote *On the Road* over a three-week period and on one scroll (several twelve-foot-long sheets of paper taped together). The entire book is written as one continuous paragraph, and readers can actually feel the energy that impelled Kerouac to write this classic work. Kerouac claims that he was fueled by caffeine alone while writing it.

Jack Kerouac's 1957 *On the Road* is the bible of the Beat Generation. The "Beats" were adventurers, taking on the freedom of the open road. Set in the 1940s, *On the Road* chronicles the adventures of Dean Moriarty and his pals as they restlessly crisscross the United States over a three-year period. While the Beats—Allen Ginsberg, William S. Burroughs, Lawrence Ferlinghetti, and Gregory Corso—sought out the gritty reality of life, they also were interested in making spiritual connections and in communing with nature.

Kerouac's words struck a chord with a generation of readers who were themselves examining post–World War II American life.

SUNDAY | WRITING PROMPT

I've discovered a letter . . .

A RECENTLY DISCLOSED LETTER IS A CLASSIC fiction element for solving a mystery, beginning a journey, uncovering a lost romance, or even filling out the details for a well-researched biography. Books written in the form of personal letters are known as *epistolary* and have been widely successful and popular.

Collections of personal letters give readers a unique perspective into the subject and can often show a person in an entirely different light than his or her public image. Novels told in this fashion can also share two perspectives: what the characters are willing to share in the privacy of their own letters as opposed to their public life. Or, in the case of the novel *Possession* by A. S. Byatt, readers are treated to the story that develops from personal correspondence; they also watch the modern-day love affair unfold between the researchers who have found these letters.

However you choose to follow the prompt, realize that the letters must follow a voice of their own, separate from the language you use for your other characters.

MONDAY | WRITERS ON WRITING

> It is advantageous to an author, that his book should be attacked as well as praised. Fame is a shuttlecock. If it be struck only at one end of the room, it will soon fall to the ground. To keep it up, it must be struck at both ends.
>
> —*Samuel Johnson*

SAMUEL JOHNSON WAS A BRITISH AUTHOR WHO lived during the 1700s. He was the subject of the 1791 biography, *The Life of Samuel Johnson* by James Boswell. The groundbreaking biography, often credited with helping to create the genre of contemporary biography, remains in print today.

Samuel Johnson was amazingly prolific, writing poetry, crafting essays, publishing magazines, editing Shakespeare, and compiling a dictionary. Of course, given the number of projects and the wide scope, some were better received than others. Johnson felt that having critics weigh in on both ends helped keep his perspective as a writer. If a work is only praised, he thought that the momentum for the writer might ease and he might feel less compelled to continue to write to the same high standards.

What are the benefits of negative reviews? Johnson suggested that they could compel the writer to work harder in response to the critics. When your work is reviewed, you do not have to take to heart every criticism. Some you simply won't agree with, but less-than-glowing reviews, as Johnson points out, can help you to develop drive and energy to continue writing and to continue improving.

TUESDAY | MOTIVATION

I'm writing a book. I've got the page numbers done.

—*Steven Wright*

COMEDIAN AND AUTHOR STEVEN WRIGHT'S comment is not as off-the-wall as it sounds. Getting down to writing often involves getting something—anything—on the page. If putting down a page number helps motivate you, then that is a good strategy.

Wright's spot-on point is that you need to start somewhere, and if you need to take baby steps to begin, that is okay. Take those small steps. Try writing one sentence on each blank piece of paper, or write one paragraph.

Seeing any words on the page can help to jump-start your work. As the days and weeks go by and you develop a writing routine, you will discover your mind becoming more limber, and you will be better able to find the words to write.

Good writing is a process that usually occurs in incremental steps. E. L. Doctorow said, "Writing a novel is like driving a car at night. You can only see as far as your headlights, but you can make the whole trip that way." Write as far as you can see on each given day, and eventually your trip will be complete.

WEDNESDAY | WRITING CLASS

Create a new action figure.

START AT THE BEGINNING, AND CREATE THE BACK-story of a new character, à la Spiderman, Batman, or Storm. What would that character look like? What would his or her superpower be? What would be the single flaw that makes the action figure compelling to the reader and relatable to a wide audience? The assignment here is to quickly establish a character based on art and limited text: to set something up that is sustainable and at the same time universal. You have to make sure that you've come up with something wholly unique, not a rehash of the myriad heroes who have come before.

THURSDAY | EDITING

> Without any doubt, the most prevalent grammatical
> mistake is subject-verb disagreements in number.
>
> —*C. Edward Good,*
> A Grammar Book for You and I . . . Oops, Me!

THIS NOTE OF WARNING IS GOOD ADVICE, ESPECIALLY if you write with expletives. I'm not referring to words that in good company look like *\$%! Expletive expressions refer to a particular sentence structure that takes on the responsibility of another word. Expletives include *there is, there are, this is, these are, here is*, and *here are.* When you use these expressions, especially in a contraction (like *there's* or *here's*), the number of the singular or plural form of the verb will be determined by the noun that follows the expression. If the noun is singular, the verb should be singular (*is* or *was*). If the noun is plural, the verb will be plural (*are* or *were*). The grammatical subject, not some other word, always determines the number of the verb.

This becomes particularly confusing where there is a collective noun, which refers to a word describing a bunch of people or things, such as a group, team, or office. In this case, the collective noun takes a singular verb when you are using it to refer to the group acting collectively as one. However, if individual members of the group are acting alone, the sentence takes the plural. In this instance, it's best to add a descriptive plural noun (e.g., *the orchestra members*) for clarity.

FRIDAY | BIOGRAPHY

> If you don't know where you are going, any
> road will take you there.
>
> —*Lewis Carroll*

L EWIS CARROLL (1832–1898) WAS THE PEN NAME OF Charles Lutwidge Dodgson. Dodgson was the eldest son in a family of seven girls and four boys. He was a shy child who stammered.

The Dodgson children were raised in a rectory, living an isolated country life. At the age of twelve, young Dodgson began writing for the rectory magazines. However, his first love was mathematics. He entered Christ Church, Oxford, where he received a scholarship. Upon graduation, he was appointed a lecturer in mathematics at Christ Church.

Because of his stammer, Dodgson always found it easier to talk with children rather than with adults. One of his duties at Christ Church was to entertain Alice Liddell and her sisters Lorina and Edith, the children of the dean of the college. In July 1862, Dodgson and his friend Robinson Duckworth rowed the three girls up the Thames from Oxford. Dodgson later wrote: "On which occasion, I told them the fairy-tale of *Alice's Adventures Underground.*"

Soon after, Dodgson was able to write down the story. He illustrated it with his own crude drawings and gave the finished product to Alice as a gift. The novelist Henry Kingsley noticed the book on the family drawing-room table, read it, and urged Mrs. Liddell to persuade the author to publish it. The book was published with new illustrations as *Alice's Adventures in Wonderland* in 1865. By Dodgson's death, *Alice* had become the most popular children's book in England.

SATURDAY | BOOKS TO READ

A Room with a View by E. M. Forster

> I have always found writing pleasant and don't understand what people mean by "throes of creation." I've enjoyed it, but believe that in some ways it is good. Whether it will last, I have no idea.
>
> —*E. M. Forster*

B RITISH AUTHOR EDWARD MORGAN FORSTER needn't have worried about his work lasting. His novels, including *A Room with a View, Howards End,* and *A Passage to India,* have become perennial bestsellers and have been made into blockbuster movies and *Masterpiece Theater* productions.

A Room with a View was published in 1908. The novel features Lucy Honeychurch, a young English lady taking a grand tour of Italy. She is accompanied by her overbearing older cousin, Charlotte Bartlett. Armed with her *Baedeker* travel guide, Lucy learns about the world outside of England as she learns about herself. During her travels she is pursued by two suitors, George Emerson, a free spirit very much in contrast to Lucy's much more uptight English persona, and Cecil Vyse, who mirrors Lucy with his proper Edwardian English manner.

This popular book is a domestic comedy in the vein of Jane Austen. Forster's skewering of Edwardian values, particularly in the character of the prissy Cecil Vyse, is unforgettable. It's also a memorable book about breaking out of one's social class and finding love in unexpected places.

SUNDAY | WRITING PROMPT

And you thought dragons didn't exist . . .

THIS PROMPT MAY SEEM JUVENILE AND, TO THE writer who does not take it seriously, I can assure that it will end badly. However, dragons are like unicorns and fairies: loads of children, and many adults, can't get enough of them.

The most recent dragon tale is *Eragon* (The Inheritance Cycle), written by Christopher Paolini. The author, then a home-schooled fifteen-year-old, used this prompt to create an entirely different universe that is both engaging and compelling. It is the story of Eragon, a young farm boy who finds a mysterious blue stone, which turns out to be a dragon egg. When the egg hatches, Eragon bonds with the dragon and discovers that he is the last of the Dragon Riders, a cult of heroes that must defend their way of life against an army of deadly mythical creatures.

Try your hand at this prompt, either by following Paolini's lead or incorporating your dragon into "the real world."

MONDAY | WRITERS ON WRITING

> Honest criticism is hard to take, particularly
> from a relative, a friend, an acquaintance, or
> a stranger.
>
> —*Franklin P. Jones*

AMERICAN AUTHOR AND HUMORIST FRANKLIN P. Jones tells it like it is. While critics have their role in helping writers develop their craft, criticism usually comes with a sting. That's because many who are asked to be honest respond to the opportunity by being brutal.

Keep that in mind when you are reading your own bad reviews, or receiving the feedback from a friend willing to tell you what she *really* thought of your work. It's hard not to feel frustrated, angry, or ready to throw in the towel.

When this happens, bring Jones's words to mind. Even the most successful author feels some sting when the reviews are pans. If you feel wounded, it just means that you are human. Take the bits of criticism that you feel are relevant and helpful, let the other bits go, and don't continue dwelling on them.

Remember, even great works of art have been subjected to the wrath of critics. John Keats's "Endymion" received such negative reviews that some attribute Keats's death, soon after the poem was published, to the critical onslaught.

As Jones quips, "Experience . . . enables you to recognize a mistake when you make it again."

The experience of reading your reviews and sharing your work with friends will help you recognize mistakes when you make them again, even if the mistake was showing it to your friend in the first place.

TUESDAY | MOTIVATION

> Somehow I can't believe there are many
> heights that can't be scaled by a person who
> knows the secret of making dreams come
> true. This special secret can be summarized
> in four C's. They are: curiosity, confidence,
> courage, and constancy, and the greatest of
> these is confidence.
>
> — *Walt Disney*

CREATOR OF THE BELOVED MICKEY MOUSE, Walt Disney needed a large dose of confidence to open Disneyland in 1955. He began dreaming of creating an amusement park almost twenty years before Disneyland actually opened. As he took his two young children to parks and zoos, he would watch them spin endlessly on the merry-go-rounds and think about making something more imaginative.

As Disney began planning his amusement park, he found doubters and naysayers at every turn. Even his brother Roy had doubts about the success of the venture. Disney was forced to stretch his personal finances to the limit in order to fund the park. After all, he said, "I could never convince the financiers that Disneyland was feasible, because dreams offer too little collateral."

Disney's confidence paid off with the July 18, 1955, opening of this "happy place." One year later, the park was earning a profit. Nearly sixty years later, the profitable park has had than 450 million visitors.

Be confident about your writing. Don't let naysayers erode your belief in yourself. Create a vision for your writing and remain true to it as Disney did to his vision.

WEDNESDAY | WRITING CLASS

Create a new craft with "found" objects from home.

S HARE YOUR ENTHUSIASM FOR REPURPOSING found objects to create something new and wonderful (and best of all, inexpensive). Whether your medium is beer bottle caps, Popsicle sticks, rubber bands, or nails, break down your artwork into the simplest steps so that any reader can replicate your genius invention. As before, create a materials list and a numbered list of step-by-step instructions. Use diagrams if necessary, but don't get carried away with the artwork. Tell, rather than show, what someone would need to do to create this craft.

THURSDAY | EDITING

> Superlative modification involves three or
> more things.
>
> —The Writer's Digest Writing Clinic

WHEN YOU ARE MAKING A COMPARISON IN YOUR writing, you have two choices. *Comparatives* are adjectives like *more, better, taller,* and *stronger,* and they are handy when you are comparing two items, as in: "This blouse is *softer* than my wool sweater."

When you have three or more items to compare, all three can be *soft*; one can still be *softer* than another; but only one can be the *softest*. In a group, only one item can ever be the *best*.

Beyond this, don't fall into the trap of overusing superlatives, as in, how can everything be "awesome"? Save these types of words for when you really mean it. What's more, absolute terms do not need comparative or superlative modifications. Nothing needs to be "more unique" or "more dead" than anything else.

FRIDAY | BIOGRAPHY

> Neil has the ability to write characters—even
> the leading characters that we're supposed
> to root for—that are absolutely flawed. They
> have foibles. They have faults. But, they are
> human beings. They are not all bad or all
> good; they are people we know.
>
> —*Jack Lemmon*

MARVIN NEIL SIMON (1927–   ) WAS BORN IN the Bronx, New York, and raised in Washington Heights in upper Manhattan. After a brief stint at New York University, Simon enlisted in the Army Air Force Reserve in 1945, and enrolled at the University of Denver. By the 1950s, however, Simon made his mark in television when he began writing for Sid Caesar's *Your Show of Shows*.

It was Simon's older brother, Danny, who was a major influence on Neil. Danny was one of the most respected comedy writers in the business, working on some of the most popular shows of the time, including *The Colgate Comedy Hour* and *The Phil Silvers Show*, and he took his younger brother under his wing. It is believed by some people that Neil Simon's hit play *The Odd Couple* was based on brother Danny's experience rooming with another man following a divorce. In much the same way, Simon was able to draw extensively on his own life and experiences to create a long list of plays that chronicle the American experience.

SATURDAY | BOOKS TO READ

The Wonderful Wizard of Oz
by L. Frank Baum

I've always taken *The Wizard of Oz* very
seriously, you know. I believe in the idea of
the rainbow. And I've spent my entire life
trying to get over it.

— Judy Garland

INSPIRED BY THE WORK OF THE BROTHERS GRIMM, Hans Christian Andersen, and Lewis Carroll, writer L. Frank Baum set out to pen a modern fairy tale without the horror often found in folk tales. As for the setting, Baum said that he came up with the name for Oz when he glanced at his file drawer, which was labeled "O-Z."

The book was an immediate success with a 10,000-copy first printing that sold out within days. Ninety thousand copies were sold within the first year. The original book spawned dozens of sequels, thirteen of which were written by Baum. Baum wrote the book for children, "to keep them out of mischief on rainy days, [which] seems of greater importance than to write grown-up novels."

Today, the book resonates in our collective subconscious, and we turn to it not only for its fantastical elements (Munchkins! Flying monkeys!) but also for its resounding message that there is absolutely no place better than home.

SUNDAY | WRITING PROMPT

The nation is controlled by . . .

I KNOW, IT'S TEMPTING TO RESPOND WITH "IDIOTS" and move on to read tomorrow's entry. But don't. Dig out your inner conspiracy theorist or, on a more positive note, be the class president you always thought you could be. See if you can convey your political beliefs in five hundred words or less.

Or, take the science fiction point of view. In *I, Robot*, Isaac Asimov blended science fact and fiction in a short story collection where he created a world that ultimately came under the control of robots. His idea was so compelling that a major motion picture of the same name was loosely based on his work.

MONDAY | WRITERS ON WRITING

> The artist's only responsibility is to his art.
> He will be completely ruthless if he is a good
> one. . . . If a writer has to rob his mother, he
> will not hesitate: The "Ode on a Grecian Urn"
> is worth any number of old ladies.
>
> —*William Faulkner*

FOR WILLIAM FAULKNER, NO PRICE IS TOO HIGH for pursuing his art. Faulkner often turned to alcohol to give him the inspiration and the courage to write. The famed Southern writer even gave his writing precedence over his relationship with his wife. "I will always believe that my first responsibility is to the artist, the work. It is terrible that my wife does not realize or at least accept that."

For many, art trumps all else. Italian Renaissance artist Michelangelo chose to create great works of art rather than marry or have children. Louisa May Alcott and Jane Austen both chose writing over having a personal life. Ironically, they both wrote love stories but never found love themselves.

TUESDAY | MOTIVATION

A man only learn in two ways, one by reading, and the other by association with smarter people.

—*Will Rogers*

ALTHOUGH MUCH OF WRITING INVOLVES SOLITUDE, good writing also involves the involvement of other people. And, while they may not always be "smarter people," they should be people who can help you to achieve your goals and offer support.

Some people find writers groups too critical or too confining. Your friends and relatives cannot always be counted on to give realistic feedback. But your local booksellers are a great source to reach out to. These people know firsthand what sells and what doesn't. What types of books are customers clamoring for? Librarians are another great source of information. Ask your librarian for a list of his or her favorite books and make a point to read at least one of them.

The more you know about books, the better a writer you will become. By reaching out and connecting with other book people, you are forming the foundation for a writing community that will support, encourage, and help you critique your work.

WEDNESDAY | WRITING CLASS

Devise a hidden words puzzle based on your favorite television show.

M AKE A LIST OF FIFTEEN ELEMENTS OF YOUR favorite television show. They can be names, places, recurring themes, reappearing objects, and so forth that define this show for others. For example, if your favorite show is one of the *CSI* dramas, you can include its location, the forensic investigators' names, and common phrases used in the dialogue. Then, graph out a box that can include all these elements written backwards, forwards, horizontally, diagonally, and vertically. The hard part is to come up with the list of hidden words: the easy part is placing them in the puzzle.

THURSDAY | EDITING

> Punctuation should be governed by its function, which is to make the author's meaning clear, to promote ease of reading, and in varying degrees to contribute to the author's style.
>
> —The Chicago Manual of Style

SOME WORKS BECOME FAMOUS FOR THEIR LACK of punctuation, like the poems of E. E. Cummings, or Cormac McCarthy's *The Road*. Others are memorable for their parenthetical remarks or dramatic usage of dashes. Some writers disregard quotation marks.

If you choose to make a statement with—or without—punctuation, make sure that you are consistent but not abusive. Play around with how it looks on the page and how it changes the context of your writing. Then, see if it's additive: Does it serve as more than just a gimmick? Does it make the reading seem more immediate? If so, you've successfully developed a unique style without changing a single word.

FRIDAY | BIOGRAPHY

> I have been doodling with ink and watercolor on paper all my life. It's my way of stirring up my imagination to see what I can find hidden in my head. I call the results dream pictures, fantasy sketches, and even brain-sharpening exercises.
>
> *—Maurice Sendak*

MAURICE SENDAK (1928–2012) WAS BORN IN Brooklyn, New York, to Jewish immigrants from Poland. Health problems confined the young boy to his bed, forcing him to remain inside during much of his formative years. Primary entertainments were books and the bedtime stories of his dressmaker father. Instead of playing with other children, the boy began to draw.

His hobby soon turned to something more serious, and after graduating from high school, Sendak was commissioned to provide illustrations for a textbook in 1947. A year later, he was hired to create window displays for F.A.O. Schwartz, the famous Manhattan toy store. After studying at the New York Art Students League, Sendak's talents were in high demand, and the artist kept himself busy for much of the 1950s as an illustrator for children's books.

But Maurice Sendak gained his fame in 1963, when his book *Where the Wild Things Are* was published to great acclaim, if not controversy, as some parents believed the monsters depicted in the book might be too frightening for children.

SATURDAY | BOOKS TO READ

The Kite Runner by **Khaled Hosseini**

> I was probably eight or nine years old when
> I began writing. I really loved it . . . I felt so in
> my element when I was writing. And pretty
> much since then, I haven't stopped writing.
> —*Khaled Hosseini*

AFGHANI AUTHOR KHALED HOSSEINI LIT UP THE world's literary stage in 2003 with his debut novel, *The Kite Runner*. The first novel published in English by an Afghani, the novel has been translated into more than forty languages and has sold over eight million copies. Likewise, it has been made into an award-winning film. And still, it has not yet been published in Hosseini's native Afghanistan.

In the novel, he describes Afghanistan on the brink of turmoil from the point of view of two children living in Kabul, a city filled with warmth and humor. This evaporates when the Taliban invade and Kabul becomes a very dangerous place. This sweeping novel, which travels from Afghanistan to California, deals with universal themes ranging from loyalty and forgiveness, the strength of friendship, the power of family bonds, and issues of race and class.

This book serves as an important cultural bridge between the West and Afghanistan. When the book was released in 2003, Americans were still reeling from the September 11 attacks and trying to understand the U.S. military's role in faraway places like Afghanistan and Iraq. *The Kite Runner* helped to fill in the information gaps.

SUNDAY | WRITING PROMPT

It wasn't going to be easy, but somehow I had to confront my mother...

MOTHER-CHILD RELATIONSHIPS MAKE FOR GREAT drama, both in print and on the big screen. One reason is that everyone can relate to them, no matter how dysfunctional these pairs seem. If you are a woman, can you reflect on your own relationship with your mother, or your daughter, and see what you can teach others based on your experiences?

Men can get into the act, too. In the novel, *Terms of Endearment*, bestselling writer Larry McMurtry, who is more commonly known for novels set in the Old West, created a compassionate and realistic appraisal of a vibrant, over-the-top mother and her much more ordinary daughter who struggle to live with and love each other. See if you can capture the female voice, as McMurtry does, with authenticity and candor.

MONDAY | WRITERS ON WRITING

> I just try to create sympathy for my
> characters, then turn the monsters loose.
> —*Stephen King*

STEPHEN KING IS ONE OF THE REIGNING KINGS OF the horror and suspense genre, penning terror classics like *Carrie, Misery,* and *The Shining.* In all, he's sold an estimated 350 million books.

Lots of writers attempt to master the horror genre, thinking it is one of the easier genres to break into. They couldn't be more wrong. As King writes, he has been able to gather an audience of millions because he spends the time and uses a deft hand in creating sympathetic characters.

For all writers, fiction and nonfiction, King's words are valid. It is impossible for a reader to engage with flat, one-dimensional, unsympathetic characters. Yet, writers try to take the shortcut to action, particularly in certain genres like horror. Writers who don't develop the characters before "turn[ing] the monsters loose" lose their readers. Readers made *Carrie* a bestseller because they felt they had come to know her, to feel the pain the protagonist felt as a shy high-school girl who is subjected to merciless teasing. These readers felt they understood Carrie and her motivations when she turned her telekinetic powers on her fellow classmates with gruesome results.

TUESDAY | MOTIVATION

> The thing always happens that you really
> believe in; and the belief in a thing makes
> it happen.
>
> — *Frank Lloyd Wright*

BELIEVE IN YOURSELF AND YOUR WRITING SKILLS. On the most basic level, if you anticipate success you will begin each day feeling more optimistic and energized. If you anticipate failure or disappointment, it will be more challenging (if not impossible) to write.

Wright had plenty of reasons to feel discouraged. As a youngster, he was uprooted several times as his dad tried to find employment to support his growing family. When he was just fourteen, his mom and dad divorced, leaving Wright to support the family. There is no record that he was able to complete high school.

Later in life, when he found work as an architect, critics often panned his work. A review in the *New York Times* of Wright's Millard House in California said, "What kind of rich person, many wondered, would want to live in such a house? His motley clients included a jewelry salesman, a rare-book dealing widow and a failed doctor." Wright was unmoved by this criticism and responded by saying, "I would rather have built this little house than St. Peter's in Rome."

Wright is now considered one of the most important American architects of the twentieth century. He never let go of the belief that he could design and create innovative architecture. Don't lose sight of your belief that you can be a writer.

WEDNESDAY | WRITING CLASS

Re-create someone else's dream.

L ISTEN CAREFULLY TO SOMEONE ELSE WHO CAN tell you about their dream. Use the opportunity as a practice interview, pulling out the details that you need to flesh out the story. You are not allowed to add any of your own ideas to this dream: the object of this exercise is to re-create someone else's experience so that that person recognizes it as the same thing that happened to him or her.

THURSDAY | EDITING

> When proper names become parts of general expressions, they get decapitated: Danish, Russian, and Turkish become danish pastry, russian dressing, and turkish towels.
> —*William Safire*, How Not to Write

THE RULES OF CAPITALIZATION BECOME CONFUSING because there are no hard and fast rules. We capitalize proper nouns: John, Paul, Ringo, George. We capitalize places and their spoken and written languages: Spain/Spanish, Iceland/Icelandic, Russian/Cyrillic. We even often capitalize adjectives and adverbs that were created from proper nouns, such as Luddite, Christian, or Francophone. But we don't usually capitalize things that aren't that important—salad dressing, for example.

Historical periods have been elevated to the point of capitalization because they are so noteworthy they have become proper nouns. The following are always capitalized:

Black Death	Holocaust
Civil War (only when it refers to the war between the American states)	Middle Ages
	New Deal
	Renaissance
Cultural Revolution	World War II
Great Depression	

The rules get messy again when you write about politics. For example, a person can be a republican or a democrat by belonging to the Republican Party or the Democratic Party.

FRIDAY | BIOGRAPHY

> Poetry is the rhythmical creation of beauty
> in words.
>
> —*Edgar Allan Poe*

EDGAR ALLAN POE (1809–1849) WAS THE SON OF professional actors. Born in Boston, he lost both his parents by the age of three. Separated from his brother and sister, he went to live with a well-to-do family in Virginia. The Allans (which he borrowed as his middle name) raised him until he was ready to attend the University of Virginia.

After gambling losses, Poe left college and enlisted in the army, where he self-published his first book, *Tamerlane and Other Poems*. Upon his discharge, Poe worked briefly at West Point and then moved to Baltimore where he was as a book reviewer and literary editor. In 1833, he married a thirteen-year-old cousin and moved back to Virginia.

By the end of the 1940s, Edgar Allan Poe had already written much of his greatest work. Though he had a handful of admirers, his dark interests left him unable to successfully sell his work. He moved again to New York and took jobs as a magazine editor. But despite his editorial talents, he was unable to master the art of working with others, and his drinking habits did him no favors as he drifted from job to job.

"The Raven," a poem written in 1844, garnered Poe some literary attention but brought him no real monetary gains.

Poe was one of the earliest American practitioners of the short story and is considered the inventor of the detective fiction. His efforts to try to earn a living through writing alone resulted in a financially difficult life and career where his work was not fully appreciated until many years after his death.

SATURDAY | BOOKS TO READ

Nineteen Eighty-Four **by George Orwell**

> The society I depict in *Nineteen Eighty-Four* will
> not necessarily come about. But . . . something
> quite like [the society it depicts] could come
> about. I set the story in Britain to show that
> English-speaking countries are not above
> happenings of this kind: that totalitarianism,
> if not fought against, can triumph anywhere.
> It's a warning, not a prophecy.
>
> — *George Orwell*

PUBLISHED IN 1949, *NINETEEN EIGHTY-FOUR* WAS
an instant success. Winston Churchill said he read it
twice in a row. As one of the definitive books of the twentieth
century, it has sold millions of copies and been translated
into sixty-five languages. In combination with Orwell's
satiric novella *Animal Farm*, the duo has sold more copies
than any two books by any other twentieth-century author.

In this dystopian novel, Orwell creates a terrifying society
in which human rights are crushed and privacy is obliterated
by an intrusive government. Many of the terms he coined in
the novel—"Big Brother," "Thought Police," "Doublespeak,"
and "Newspeak"—are now part of the American lexicon.
The description "Orwellian" refers to a state-controlled society
and the widespread dissemination of inaccurate information.
Some hotels still refuse to have a room numbered 101: in the
novel, this was the room that contained all of the things the
occupants found impossible to endure.

SUNDAY | WRITING PROMPT

My favorite hobby . . .

E VERYONE HAS A HOBBY, EVEN IF HE OR SHE ISN'T aware of it. Watching television counts and so does surfing the Internet. Better still, you may be engaged in something really unique, and others might like to know about it.

Most of the time, writing about your hobby is a magazine article or a nonfiction essay at best. But what if you could turn your passion into a novel? That's exactly what Sophie Kinsella imagined in her "chick-lit" bestseller, *Confessions of a Shopaholic*, which went on to spawn not only a major motion picture but also an entire book series. In order to create your own success writing about your hobby this way, you'll need to find the humor in the activity. Figure out what's endearing about it to you, and then why others might find it worthy of a good laugh.

MONDAY | WRITERS ON WRITING

> Having been unpopular in high school is not
> just cause for book publication. . . . Your life
> story would not make a good book. Don't
> even try.
>
> —*Fran Lebowitz*

D EADPAN HUMORIST FRAN LEBOWITZ IS KNOWN
for her sardonic take on modern life. No one is spared
her caustic pen, including herself. Lebowitz often focuses on
the mundane with her razor-sharp wit: the average intelligence of children (not as smart as their parents say they are),
the benefits of vegetables (not so much unless accompanied
by meat), and the value of algebra in daily adult life (none).

She casts the same eye on writers who decide their life
stories are worth capturing on paper. Lebowitz is of the
mind, and likely she is right, that most people don't have
lives that will transfer to a publishable manuscript. Ready
to write a memoir about those tough adolescent years? Keep
in mind, says Lebowitz, that a majority of high-school kids
would probably describe a similar anguish. In other words,
your story is not unique.

Lebowitz is a bit disingenuous in this advice, however, as
she herself has made a living writing about the very things
she advises against: the things of daily life. She has done it,
though, with a style, wit, and flare that give commonplace
topics new life.

TUESDAY | MOTIVATION

Open your mind to new experiences,
particularly to the study of other people.
Nothing that happens to a writer—however
happy, however tragic—is ever wasted.

—*P. D. James*

BE OPEN TO ALL THAT HAPPENS AROUND YOU.
The next time you make a trip to the big-box store to
pick up sundries, rather than treating your outing as a bit
of ho-hum daily drudgery, consider it a spy mission for your
writing. Instead of racing in and out as fast as humanly possible, pause to take it all in. Notice how the mother is com-
forting her daughter who is keen for a new toy. Or, consider
why the couple standing in line in front of you is arguing
about the contents of their shopping cart.

Train yourself to treat every experience as valuable, and
to try to be open to new things. The next time you are at the
grocery store, buy a food you've never tried, or order something exotic at a restaurant. Visit someplace you have never
been. This doesn't necessarily mean a journey to a far-flung
destination. Perhaps, you have never been to the coffee shop
in the town bordering your own or never checked out the
stacks in a library other than the one in your community.
New experiences equal renewed energy and imagination.

WEDNESDAY | WRITING CLASS

> Write a three-paragraph essay that
> compares/contrasts two favorite fictional
> characters.

PICK YOUR TWO ALL-TIME FAVORITE CHARACTERS, and see why you relate to them. What are their similarities and differences? What makes them and their stories so memorable? How did they influence the decisions you've made as a child or as an adult?

THURSDAY | EDITING

> English does not have a neuter pronoun. Choosing the male pronoun is standard but arguably a little sexist. Choosing the female pronoun incurs the wrath of the anti-PC police.
>
> —June Casagrande,
> Grammar Snobs Are Great Big Meanies

GOOD WRITERS THESE DAYS ARE SUPPOSED TO strive for gender neutrality, but it doesn't always work. You cannot refer to a single person as *they*, as some try to do with varying degrees of success. In formal writing you can choose *s/he* or *he or she*, but where's the fun in that? When possible, you can recast your sentence from singular to plural, and then feel free to use the terms *they* or *them*.

Some nouns have distinct genders: ships are referred to as *she*; countries are no longer *she* (now they take *it*). Storms are now gender neutral: just look at the way the National Weather Service alternates the gender names of hurricanes.

When a noun clearly omits women, feel free to change it, or recognize that someone else already has. *Police officer, firefighter,* and *sanitation engineer* all work just fine.

FRIDAY | BIOGRAPHY

> I've always tried to be aware of what I say in
> my films, because all of us who make motion
> pictures are teachers—teachers with very
> loud voices.
>
> —*George Lucas*

G EORGE LUCAS (1944–   ) WAS BORN IN MODESTO, California, where his parents owned a stationery store and a walnut ranch. He was not much of a student, preferring race car driving to academics. But when he survived a near-fatal car accident just days before high-school graduation, he changed his mind and enrolled in Modesto Junior College. He later transferred to the University of Southern California film school where he met Francis Ford Coppola. The following year, Lucas worked as Coppola's assistant.

The two filmmakers were writers at heart and shared a common vision of starting an independent film production company. In 1973, Lucas cowrote and directed *American Graffiti*, which was based on his old high-school days and his love for cars. The film won the Golden Globe, the New York Film Critics Circle, and National Society of Film Critics awards and garnered five Academy Award nominations. Four years later, Lucas wrote and directed *Star Wars,* forever changing the way movies were made.

SATURDAY | BOOKS TO READ

The Making of the Atomic Bomb
by Richard Rhodes

It is *the* comprehensive history of the bomb—
and also a work of literature.

—*Tracy Kidder*

RICHARD RHODES'S 1986 BOOK BROKE NEW
ground for an event that had happened more than fifty
years before. It is both a scientific treatise on the creation
of the atomic bomb as well as a social history of the years
leading up to and including World War II.

The book resonates because of Rhodes's unique approach
to it. Although literally hundreds of books had been written
about the making of the atomic bomb, Rhodes chose a new
tack. "The early papers in nuclear physics were written very
clearly. Niels Bohr once said he could explain all of physics
without using a mathematical formula. So the archives are
full of those early papers that explain the ideas in ways
anyone could understand," Rhodes said.

During the research phase, Rhodes pored over thousands of pages of papers and journals and directly quoted
the participants who took part in the race for atomic power.
Those still living, he interviewed; those who had died he
brought back to life using the vast archives left behind. For
his efforts, Rhodes received the Pulitzer Prize, the National
Book Award, and the National Book Critics Circle Award.

The Making of the Atomic Bomb captures all aspects of the
making and implementing of the atomic bomb. The book is
compelling with a story line equal to the best novel.

SUNDAY | WRITING PROMPT

When I took a stand on an important issue . . .

F OR THIS PROMPT, ALL IMPORTANT ISSUES ARE created equal. It doesn't matter if your biggest position has been switching your family from white bread to whole wheat, or if you brought down a corrupt police department in your town. Explain, step by step, how you came to the conclusion that something was wrong, and then what you did about it.

If you need inspiration, look no further than the 1970s' classic *All the President's Men* by Carl Bernstein and Bob Woodward. The two reporters for the *Washington Post* began their investigation with the story of a simple burglary at Democratic headquarters, which unfolded into a headline-grabbing exposé of conspiracy and dirty tricks coming from Richard Nixon's White House. Their position to continue to report the story and let the public know the truth ultimately toppled the president and changed journalism forever.

MONDAY | WRITERS ON WRITING

> Great is the art of beginning, but greater the
> art is of ending.
>
> —*Henry Wadsworth Longfellow*

HENRY WADSWORTH LONGFELLOW WROTE "PAUL Revere's Ride," *The Song of Hiawatha*, and *Evangeline*. He was also the first American to translate Italian poet Dante Alighieri's *The Divine Comedy*.

Longfellow is correct in that the art of beginning bears great importance. Now more than ever, readers with short attention spans need a captivating start. Of greater import, says Longfellow, is the ending.

A good writer should leave his reader wanting more. You've had the sensation of finishing a book and wanting to start at the beginning again, to recapture the experience. That is what Longfellow is referring to here. You want to leave your readers with a powerful finish, one they will remember.

Consider the classic end to Charles Dickens's *A Christmas Carol*. As the book closes, Tiny Tim says, "God bless us, every one!" You have to hand it to Dickens: he opened and closed this novel with memorable lines. The opening, "Marley was dead, to begin with," is distinctive, a great start. The closing line is certainly a tad sappy, especially for today's readers, but equally memorable.

TUESDAY | MOTIVATION

> If you get stuck, get away from your desk.
> Take a walk, take a bath, go to sleep, make a
> pie, draw, listen to music, meditate, exercise;
> whatever you do, don't just stick there
> scowling at the problem.
>
> —*Hilary Mantel*

IT'S CONSOLING TO REMEMBER THAT EVERY WRITER has gotten stuck at one point or another. It's the nature of the business. When you find yourself getting bogged down, then it is time to take a break. As English novelist Hilary Mantel says, walk away from your desk. There is nothing worse than staying put and stewing about your problem.

When you find yourself getting stuck, don't treat it as a negative. If you're in a writing rut, it just means that your brain is working overtime to figure out where to go next. By walking away from your work, your subconscious will have an opportunity to percolate and process the ideas that are streaming through your mind.

You might need only a short walk to unstick yourself. Or, you might need to leave your writing until the next day. If so, don't fret. Enjoy the rest of the day, making that pie or listening to your favorite music, awaiting a fresh start tomorrow.

WEDNESDAY | WRITING CLASS

Record your family history of an event you didn't attend.

GRANDPARENTS, PARENTS, AND EXTENDED FAMILY members have experienced life in ways you can't imagine, unless they've been recorded. What is your family's best story? Get right to the source, if possible, and interview your relatives and record their experience. See if you can find a story with lots of drama: living through the Depression, life during wartime, or immigrating to the United States. See if you can capture the facts and the feelings that occurred.

THURSDAY | EDITING

Do not overuse the verb "to be."
—*Frederick Crews,* The Random House Handbook

THERE ARE TIMES WHEN YOU ARE USING THE VERB *to be* and don't even know it. Here are its conjugations:

Infinitive tense:	be
Past tense:	was, were
Present Participle:	being
Past Participle:	been

Present tense:	
I	am
You	are
He, She, It	is
We	are
You	are
They	are

No matter what form you use, this verb is a colorless action word. You can do better and make your writing more engaging by switching it out for a more descriptive verb.

When you review your first draft, one way to make your writing more interesting is to spot any repetition of key words within the same paragraph, and replace the repeated words with synonyms. Try to make each word in your story or essay count by having it work for you. While you won't be able to replace all forms of the verb *to be* all the time, by mixing up your language, you'll find that your writing makes for more satisfying reading.

FRIDAY | BIOGRAPHY

The critic has to educate the public; the artist has to educate the critic.

—Oscar Wilde

OSCAR FINGAL O'FLAHERTIE WILLS WILDE (1854–1900) was born in Dublin. His father, Sir William Wilde, was a well-known surgeon, and his mother, Jane Francesca Elgee Wilde, wrote popular poetry.

Wilde studied the classics at Trinity College, Dublin. His writing attracted a devoted group of followers early in his career. These men and women were purposefully unproductive, as was he, and believed in the glorification of youth.

Wilde's writing was both intense and sporadic. While at Oxford, he became involved in the aesthetic movement, which promoted the ideal "Art for Art's Sake." After he graduated, he moved to London to establish a literary career. In 1881, he published his first collection of poetry, which received mixed reviews. He then worked as an art reviewer and lectured about the aesthetic movement throughout the United States and Canada. His first and only novel, *The Picture of Dorian Gray*, was published in 1891, also to poor reviews. In 1891, Wilde began an affair with Lord Alfred Douglas, which ended his own marriage in 1893.

The love affair occurred at the same time that he began achieving literary success with his plays. In April 1895, Wilde sued Douglas's father for libel, for accusing him of homosexuality. As a result, Wilde was arrested and was sentenced to two years hard labor. After his release in 1897, he spent the rest of his life penniless, wandering around Europe.

SATURDAY | BOOKS TO READ

Wise Blood by Flannery O'Connor

No other major American writer of our century has constructed a fictional world so energetically and forthrightly charged by religious investigation.

—*Brad Leithauser*

W HEN *WISE BLOOD* WAS PUBLISHED IN 1952, critics weren't sure what to make of it. *New Republic* writer Isaac Rosenfeld said that *Wise Blood's* protagonist "is nothing more than the poor, sick, ugly, raving lunatic that he happens to be."

The book, now cited as one of the masterworks of the twentieth century, was challenging for readers. In it, the eccentric and unlikable war veteran Hazel Mote returns to Tennessee. The son of a preacher, Mote is disillusioned with the church and begins his own religion, The Church Without Christ.

Although O'Connor has always been lauded as a master of the Southern gothic, her writing on issues of faith and religion help sustain her importance. Through her characters, O'Connor examines her own connections with religion. Author Ralph Wood once said, "Flannery O'Connor is the only great Christian writer this nation has produced."

Born a Catholic, O'Connor was diagnosed with lupus at the age of twenty-five. She lived the rest of her brief life in Georgia with her mother and hundreds of peacocks and other birds she raised while she continued to write.

SUNDAY | WRITING PROMPT

My favorite piece of clothing . . .

D O YOU HAVE A FAVORITE PARTY DRESS IN THE back of your closet with which you just can't bear to part, or a pair of boots two sizes too small that once belonged to someone special in your life? These are some of the things to think about when you take on this prompt. You might have a favorite sweater or scarf that was given to you, or something you picked up during your travels. Or you might have a favorite pair of jeans that cannot be replaced.

Our collective obsession with comfortable jeans was taken to a new level with the young-adult novel-turned-movie, *The Sisterhood of the Traveling Pants* by Ann Brashares. This coming-of-age tale revolves around one seemingly ordinary pair of thrift-shop denims that four best friends buy together and pledge to pass around the first summer they are apart. Their stories unfold when the girls experience a first love, jealousy, fear, and sadness, while wearing the pants.

MONDAY | WRITERS ON WRITING

> Madame, all the words I use in my stories can
> be found in that dictionary—it's just a matter
> of arranging them into the right sentences.
> —*W. Somerset Maugham*

UNLESS YOU ARE EDWARD LEAR WRITING "THE Owl and the Pussycat" and creating the charming new phrase "runcible spoon," or William Shakespeare minting a variety of new words for his plays and sonnets, you don't need to create your own language to craft memorable writing. You will find all of the words you need in the same place every other writer is trolling: the dictionary.

In this way, all writers start out on a level playing field, and you can take a certain comfort in that. You have access to every word the next guy has. The trick, as British author W. Somerset Maugham points out, is in how you arrange the words. Just as an exceptional museum curator knows how to hang art for a show, a writer knows how to arrange words.

Think about it: if all writers have access to the same word bank, the only way to put a new spin on a piece of writing is to either come up with a completely original idea (challenging) or to put together language in a new way (also challenging but perhaps not quite as challenging as creating an idea that no author throughout time has taken on).

TUESDAY | MOTIVATION

> People who didn't live pre-Internet can't grasp
> how devoid of ideas life in my hometown
> was. I stopped in the middle of the SAT to
> memorize a poem, because I thought, "This is
> a great work of art and I'll never see it again."
>
> —*Mary Karr*

THE INTERNET OFTEN GETS A BUM RAP, ESPECIALLY from writers who find it a distraction. But as memoirist Mary Karr points out, the Net has also brought enrichment and the ability to explore new ideas.

Make a habit of learning something new every day by using the Internet. No, not the price of a plane ticket to Europe or the latest Hollywood gossip. Learn something meaningful. Discover a new poet. Learn about a city you've always wanted to visit. Read about a piece of art you have always admired. Explore a small idea that has always interested you. And then stop and start writing. Remember, the Internet is a rabbit hole you cannot always easily escape.

On average, an American spends about four hours online every day. That's a lot of surfing and social networking. Instead, try to use the time effectively to learn. Knowledge is one of a writer's essential tools. The Internet can bring a world of knowledge to you.

WEDNESDAY | WRITING CLASS

Write a haiku describing an emotion.

U SE THE 5/7/5 FORMAT TO CREATE A HAIKU THAT vividly captures an emotion, such as excitement, fear, loathing, grief, happiness, jealousy, anger, or boredom. Or, choose the emotion you feel most connected to. The haiku must have two distinct phrases that work together, each describing the other. Another loose rule for haiku is to write what can be said in just one breath.

THURSDAY | EDITING

> If you want to get technical, you can use *each* to emphasize the individual items or people . . . and *every* to emphasize the larger group.
>
> —*Mignon Fogarty,* The Grammar Girl's Quick and Dirty Tips for Better Writing

W HILE THE ABOVE STATEMENT IS TRUE, FOR THE most part, *each* and *every* are interchangeable. Some people think they are creating emphasis when they write "each and every," but all they are doing is being redundant. The same is true for *everyone* and *everybody*: they mean the same thing, so choose the one you like best and stick with it.

Each one and *everyone* are two entirely different terms: the former is singular, while the latter is plural. *Each other* and *every other* also cannot be interchanged. *Each other* refers to a pair. ("They like each other."). *Every other* refers to an alternating pattern.

Use *everyday* just as it's written—as one word—when you want an adjective that helps you describe something ordinary or common. ("These are my everyday shoes.") Use *every day* in two words when you're talking about how often you do something. In this instance, *every day* is an adverbial phrase. ("Every day I put on the same darn shoes, and I'm sick of them.")

FRIDAY | BIOGRAPHY

> When you work with people whom you
> respect and whom you like and you admire
> because they're so good at what they do,
> it doesn't feel like work. . . . It's like you're
> playing.
>
> —*Stan Lee*

S TANLEY MARTIN LEIBER (1922–   ) WAS BORN IN
New York City to Romanian Jewish immigrants. As
a child he was a voracious reader who enjoyed writing. He
worked part-time jobs throughout his teen years writing
obituaries and press releases, among other things.

Leiber graduated high school at the age of sixteen and
landed a job as an assistant at Timely Comics. There he
refilled the inkwells for the artists and proofread. He made
his comic-book debut writing filler for *Captain America
Comics* in 1941, using the pseudonym Stan Lee because he
had intended to save his given name for more literary work.

His creative life was interrupted in 1942 when he joined
the United States Army and served in the Signal Corps. After
the war, Leiber returned to the company then known as Atlas
Comics. By then the golden age of superheroes was over, and
Leiber was hired to write comics for such genres as romance,
Westerns, science fiction, and horror.

By the 1950s, Lee had become dissatisfied with his career.
However, DC Comics had successfully revived the superhero
archetype. In response, Lee was assigned to create his own
superheroes for Atlas (later to morph into Marvel Comics).
The first new characters were the Fantastic Four, followed by
the Hulk, Iron Man, Thor, X-Men, and Spider-Man.

SATURDAY | BOOKS TO READ

The Sheltering Sky by **Paul Bowles**

> Moving around a lot is a good way of postponing the day of reckoning. I'm happiest when I'm moving. When you've cut yourself off from the life you've been living and you haven't yet established another life, you're free. That's a very pleasant sensation, I've always thought. If you don't know where you're going, you're even freer.
>
> —*Paul Bowles*

IN 1947, AMERICAN AUTHOR PAUL BOWLES CONtracted with Doubleday to write a novel. The result, *The Sheltering Sky,* was perfunctorily rejected by his editor. Undeterred, Bowles found a home for it at New Directions, and the book became a bestseller (much to the chagrin of the folks at Doubleday, as Bowles was quick to point out).

The book centers on three Americans as they travel through the Algerian desert: Port; his wife, Kit; and their friend Tunner. Bowles has said that the characters are not autobiographical, but critics have often questioned this, as Port and Kit share many similarities with Bowles and his wife, Jane, not least their peripatetic nature. Tragedy strikes: Port dies and Kit spirals into madness as the travelers are unable to escape the cruel impassivity of the North African desert.

With *The Sheltering Sky,* Bowles established himself as one of the preeminent novelists of postwar America. The book is a groundbreaking and masterful depiction of the immovability of nature and humans' inability to overcome it.

SUNDAY | WRITING PROMPT

An alien visited my home . . .

THIS PROMPT IS PURE FUN. A GREAT EXECUTION OF this exercise is the movie *ET: The Extra Terrestrial*, whose screenplay was written by Melissa Mathison. Mathison envisioned her then-current world as seen through the eyes of children. It's a story more about friendship than science fiction, which is why it's an enduring classic. However, the prompt is clearly the premise.

How would your world change if an alien being visited your home? However you choose to complete this exercise, see if you can keep as many elements of the story realistic. In that way, the alien's experience will really stand out.

MONDAY | WRITERS ON WRITING

> I have never thought of myself as a good writer.
> Anyone who wants reassurance of that should
> read one of my first drafts. But I'm one of the
> world's great rewriters. I find that three or four
> readings are required to comb out the clichés,
> line up pronouns with their antecedents, and
> insure agreement in number between subject
> and verbs.
>
> —*James A. Michener*

SOME WRITERS HEAR THE WORD *REWRITE* AND HEAD for the hills. It can't be emphasized often enough that revision does not equal punishment. Just as a chef continues to refine a recipe or a gardener continues to prune her shrubs, a writer should take pleasure in the challenges of reworking a piece.

American author James Michener, author of more than forty novels, many of them bestsellers, would spend as many as fifteen hours a day working on his writing. The majority of this time was spent revising rather than doing the original writing.

As he put it, "You write that first draft really to see how it's going to come out." He believed that the first draft is like the framework of a house. It shows the skeletal outline but not the final outcome. As a house is being built, carpenters take the framework and form a house, complete with doors, windows, and other features. Likewise, Michener takes a first draft and uses it as a framework to create a finished piece.

TUESDAY | MOTIVATION

> Always carry a notebook. And I mean
> *always*. The short-term memory only retains
> information for three minutes; unless it is
> committed to paper you can lose an idea
> for ever.
>
> — *Will Self*

NOVELIST WILL SELF ISN'T EXAGGERATING. SHORT-term memory retains information for a *maximum* of three minutes. More commonly, ideas slip in and out of the mind in a minute or less. Sometimes, ideas can vanish from your consciousness within seconds.

Ideas can—and do—surface at any time, and sometimes at the most inopportune moments. Chopping onions when the next great thought arrives? Put down your knife, pick up a pen, and jot it down. A stroke of brilliance arrives while you are en route to the store? When you stop at a red light or pull into the parking lot, take a moment to write it down.

Record your thoughts on the memo pad in your smartphone or buy a small notebook, one that could fit easily inside a pocket, and make it your best friend. Carry it with you whenever you leave the house. Keep it close by while you are writing so any ideas can be quickly written down before you continue with your writing. Don't wait to write down your ideas and observations. These thoughts are fleeting and should be written down as they occur.

You can also keep this notebook by the side of your bed. When you wake up in the morning, record any thoughts that may have come to you in your dreams. Many writers find inspiration from their dreams.

WEDNESDAY | WRITING CLASS

Record your thoughts and feelings about
September 11, 2001.

ISTORY IS NOT JUST THE VERY DISTANT PAST: WE are creating our own history every day. For most of us, September 11 is a day we will never forget. Write a short piece about where you were on that day, how you heard about the devastating events, and what your thoughts and feelings were in reaction. Also include what your life looked like before and immediately after the event, and how it has changed your life since then.

THURSDAY | EDITING

> Remember that euphemisms are the stock-in-trade of people trying to obscure the truth.
> —The Economist Style Guide

EUPHEMISMS ARE THOUGHT TO BE A MORE PLEASANT-sounding way to say something that may be offensive to others. Some subjects are considered too personal, sensitive, or taboo to say aloud or appear in writing. For this reason, some people avoid mentioning them by name and instead use what they find to be a more humorous expression or a vague definition to refer to them. However, good writing should always strive to be clear and to the point, so there is really no room for euphemistic language. What's more, many euphemisms are degrading and not funny at all.

Euphemisms have been used for body parts (especially those belonging to women), giving birth, experiencing death, going to the bathroom, pain, unemployment, lying, and being poor. Politically correct language is also considered to be euphemistic, especially when it is used in works that deal with politics or the military. Corporations also take on euphemisms when they are trying to cover up bad behavior: for example, Enron's "document-management policy" referred to its practice of paper shredding.

If you are quoting an existing euphemism and want to point out its sarcastic nature, put the word or phrase in quotation marks.

FRIDAY | BIOGRAPHY

> I knew I was black, of course, but I also knew
> I was smart. I didn't know how I would use
> my mind, or even if I could, but that was the
> only thing I had to use.
>
> —*James Baldwin*

JAMES BALDWIN (1924–1987) CAME TO HARLEM, New York, as an infant during the height of the Harlem Renaissance. The oldest of nine children, James found himself in a caretaker's role, and by the time he was ten years old, after he had been beaten by police officers, he realized that an education might be the only way escape from a life of violence and poverty. Baldwin turned to books and the library, and he managed to attend DeWitt Clinton High School, a prestigious and mostly white school in the Bronx.

Though he made an attempt to follow in his preacher stepfather's footsteps by joining the Pentecostal Church at fourteen years of age, Baldwin did not see a future for himself in religion. He began spending time in New York's Greenwich Village, working various jobs, writing short stories, and imagining himself living the Bohemian artist's life. There, he met one of his literary heroes, the writer Richard Wright, and the two became friends. After World War II, Baldwin left for Paris and then Switzerland, where he would finish his first novel. *Go Tell It on the Mountain*, published in 1953, was a semi-autobiographical work. Baldwin was immediately recognized as establishing a profound and permanent new voice. In numerous essays, novels, plays, and public speeches, his uniquely eloquent voice continues to be heard.

SATURDAY | BOOKS TO READ

Persepolis by Marjane Satrapi

> I am just a small girl, it's not me who makes
> any decisions. . . . So the world around me
> changed, I am a witness of this big change
> around me. The war starts, and after a while
> it becomes completely normal, the situation
> of the war. That is the capacity of the human
> being, that everything suddenly becomes
> absolutely normal.
>
> —*Marjane Satrapi*

PERSEPOLIS IS AN ARRESTING AUTOBIOGRAPHICAL graphic novel. Published in 2000, using text and line drawings, many with a childlike, dreamy quality, Satrapi describes her childhood in Iran during the turbulent years surrounding the 1979 Iranian revolution.

During the course of the book, the child narrator grows from nine to fourteen years of age. The child of activist parents, Satrapi describes the contrasts in Iranian life. She recalls the first day that girls were required to wear the face veil at school. In counterpoint, she draws upon memories of wearing bootlegged jeans and Nikes, feeling free to argue political issues with adults, listening to punk music, and hanging posters of rock stars on her bedroom walls.

By superimposing the atrocities that occurred in Iran during the revolution on the mundane minutiae of her daily life, Satrapi shows us that in many ways her life is just like ours—filled with friends, family, and passions.

SUNDAY | WRITING PROMPT

A different way to tell that fairy tale . . .

NOVELIST GREGORY MAGUIRE HAS MADE A WRITING career of working this prompt. He first published *Wicked*, the story of *The Wonderful Wizard of Oz* told from the perspective of the Wicked Witch, in 1995, and since then he has followed it up with *Confessions of an Ugly Stepsister* (Cinderella) and *Mirror Mirror* (Snow White), among others. The exercise is formally known as creating "a parallel novel."

You may be equally successful. Take your favorite fairy tale, and explore it from another angle to see where it leads. Maybe you'll gain new insights into a much-loved classic. Who knows where it will lead? The novel *Wicked* was made into a Tony Award–winning Broadway musical that has been running internationally since its first show in 2003.

MONDAY | WRITERS ON WRITING

No tears in the writer, no tears in the reader.
— George Moore

IRISH NOVELIST GEORGE MOORE UNDERSTANDS that writers have to be involved with their subjects for the reader to be affected.

Think again of John Hersey, writing about the bombing of Hiroshima in the immediate aftermath of World War II. Certainly, as a writer he had tears and felt genuine emotion for the Japanese citizens of Hiroshima. This emotional connection was clear to readers. When the story was first published in the *New Yorker* magazine, the issue sold out within hours. The Book-of-the-Month Club felt that the book was so pertinent and important that it sent a free copy to each of its members. Thousands of books have been written about the atomic bombings that brought World War II to a close, but few have evoked this emotion. Moore would say it is because other writers took too academic a stance and readers could not find an emotional connection.

Moore's is good advice to heed when you are choosing a subject about which to write. Don't pick a topic just because it is "hot" or currently in the news. Choose something with which you have a connection, through experience or through a personal interest. Your sense of engagement in the topic will be clear to your readers who will respond to your enthusiasm or your anguish.

TUESDAY | MOTIVATION

> Words have weight, sound and appearance;
> it is only by considering these that you can
> write a sentence that is good to look at and
> good to listen to.
>
> —*W. Somerset Maugham*

SOMETIMES WRITERS OVERLOOK THE *SOUND* OF THEIR words. Just as words should look good on the page, they should ring true when spoken.

Bestselling author and journalist Anna Quindlen reads all of her work aloud—often more than once—before submitting a finished manuscript to her publisher. "[I always read everything aloud] before I hand it in. It's the only way to know if a sentence really works, without clunks or cul-de-sac clauses."

Likewise, British author and editor Diana Athill recommends, "Read it aloud to yourself because that's the only way to be sure the rhythms of the sentences are OK."

Try reading your work aloud. How does it sound to your ears? Especially take note of dialogue, as reading it aloud is the best way to know if it sounds true to colloquial language and casual speech. Is it convincing? Is it believable? Writing is as much about revision and editing as it is about putting the original words on the page. Just as you might add a dash of salt to a recipe once you have sampled it, you might adapt a work to change the tone and color of your written language once your own ears have heard it.

WEDNESDAY | WRITING CLASS

Write a stand-up joke.

JERRY SEINFELD OR CHRIS ROCK YOU ARE NOT, BUT everyone starts with these rules:

1. Start with five thoughts that you experience every day. Think of the different areas of your life, such as the office, a vacation, weekend events, members of your family, and so forth. Now, pick just one.

2. Write down five sentences that convey things you hate about your topic, or think are strange or unique. Choose the one that seems the oddest, funniest, or most ironic.

3. Write down five different ways that that same sentence could be seen as funny from an outside perspective. Imagine telling a stranger this sentence: How could you embellish your experience to show more emotion? This is called "the setup."

4. The second part of the joke is "the twist": this part takes the setup and turns it around so that others can see why it's funny. Or, it is a comment on the setup to hammer the point home. A great example is from the late George Carlin: "One nice thing about egotists: they don't talk about other people."

5. Say the joke out loud to see if it sounds right. You might have to edit word by word to get the best joke. An extra syllable might be all it takes to get the timing just right.

THURSDAY | EDITING

> Certain indefinite pronouns are always
> singular—even though plurality is implied—
> and always take a singular verb.
> —The Writer's Digest Writing Clinic

I NDEFINITE PRONOUNS REFER TO ONE OR MORE unspecified beings, objects, or places. They include the words *another, anything, each, either, everyone, no one, nothing,* and *someone*. Even though they may refer to a group, they always take a singular verb. The following sentences are correct:

Everyone on the team gets ice cream.

Someone in the parking lot is following me.

This rule needs to be taken into consideration when you are trying to achieve true gender neutrality. For example, by following this rule, the often-used phrase "everyone is entitled to their own opinion" is wrong. Instead, it should be written as "everyone is entitled to his or her own opinion." Then, you can sort that one out by reviewing Week 35.

FRIDAY | BIOGRAPHY

The secret of getting ahead is getting started.
—Agatha Christie

A GATHA CHRISTIE (1890–1976) WAS BORN IN Devon, England, to a conservative, affluent family. She was taught at home by a governess and tutors and never attended school. Yet her education was not lacking by any means.

In 1914, she married Archibald Christie, then a British fighter pilot. During World War I, she worked as a nurse and, while her husband was on duty, she decided to write her first detective novel, *The Mysterious Affair at Styles.* It was published in 1920, five years later.

The novel introduced her famous character, Hercule Poirot, who has since appeared in more than thirty novels.

When her husband left Christie for another woman in 1926, the writer disappeared from her home, resulting in a nationwide manhunt that ended eleven days later when Christie was found in a Yorkshire hotel, claiming that she'd lost her memory.

Christie is considered to be the bestselling author of all time. She has sold over two billion books and has been translated into more than forty-five languages. In a writing career that spanned more than half a century, Agatha Christie wrote eighty crime novels and short story collections, two autobiographies, and eight novels under the pseudonym Mary Westmacott. She also wrote more than a dozen plays, including *The Mousetrap*, which is the longest-running play in theatrical history.

SATURDAY | BOOKS TO READ

Pride and Prejudice by Jane Austen

> First and foremost let Austen be named, the
> greatest artist that has ever written, using the
> term to signify the most perfect mastery over
> the means to her end.
>
> — *George Henry Lewes*

M ANY OF US STILL AGREE WITH THE ABOVE assessment. Austen certainly makes almost every list of important and beloved English novelists. *Pride and Prejudice* sells at the brisk clip of 100,000-plus copies per year in America alone; it has spawned countless sequels and parodies, including the popular *Bridget Jones's Diary* and *Pride and Prejudice and Zombies,* and has been reproduced on *Masterpiece Theater* and in an Academy Award–nominated movie.

Published in 1813, *Pride and Prejudice* is set in rural England and is a comedy of manners, focusing on the relationship between Elizabeth Bennett and Mr. Fitzwilliam Darcy.

So what accounts for the phenomenal success of the book? In part it may be the very thing that critics cite as the book's flaw: that Austen didn't take on the class system of her time. Instead of fighting for social justice, Austen wrote cozy novels depicting English society at the end of the eighteenth century. Austen herself called the writing "light and bright and sparkling." She wrote to amuse rather than to provoke.

Although Austen herself never married, she spent her life writing about the affairs of the heart and exploring the intricacies of many kinds of relationships.

SUNDAY | WRITING PROMPT

Finding love on the Internet . . .

THE POPULAR DATING WEBSITE (OR AS THEY SAY, Relationship Services Provider) eHarmony.com says that finding love online happens all the time and, with the proliferation of other similar websites and social networking, it must be true. If you—or someone you know—has found a soul mate on the Internet, here's your chance to tell the story.

And if you don't know firsthand, can you envision how it works? That's what Claire Cook did with her debut novel, *Ready to Fall*. This story explores the surprisingly dangerous world of cyber-romance, where a disenfranchised housewife reunites with an old neighbor and sparks a seemingly harmless e-mail flirtation. If you can imagine what happens next, then you are ready to take on this prompt.

MONDAY | WRITERS ON WRITING

> The reader has certain rights. He bought your
> story. Think of this as an implicit contract.
> He's entitled to be entertained, instructed,
> amused; maybe all three. If he quits in the
> middle, or puts the book down feeling his
> time has been wasted, you're in violation.
>
> —*Larry Niven*

LARRY NIVEN IS AN AMERICAN SCIENCE FICTION writer, best known for *Ringworld*, published in 1970, which won the Hugo, Locus, Ditmar, and Nebula awards. In writing this captivating adventure, Niven recognized the implicit contract he had with his readers.

It is an interesting vantage point for a writer to take. When we are sequestered in our offices and writing spaces, we focus on the writing rather than on the reader. Not only does Niven acknowledge his reader, he gives the reader rights, insisting that a reader should receive a book that entertains, instructs, and/or amuses.

A successful writer acknowledges this responsibility to the audience. You never want to waste a reader's time. As Niven suggests, you should consider what motivates your writing: Do you want to entertain? To educate? To thrill, or to instruct? You don't have to commit this implicit contract to print, but keep your reader in mind as you write.

TUESDAY | MOTIVATION

> Leave a decent space of time between writing
> something and editing it.
>
> *—Zadie Smith*

YOUR FIRST THOUGHT UPON FINISHING A SHORT story, essay, poem, or other piece of writing might be to read it: to step away from your role as a writer and to take on the role of reader and critic. After all, you're excited to have finished a piece and eager to experience it as a reader.

You need to let your writing rest before you read it. Just as kneaded bread needs to rest before it is baked, you need to treat your words to the same.

By giving your piece some time, you will be able to distance yourself a bit from your role as a writer. Remember, when you read and edit your work, you are seeking to create the best writing possible. The editing is as much, if not more, a part of the creation as is the writing.

If the piece doesn't feel right and the revisions are extensive, it might be most beneficial to start afresh. Don't consider this a setback. In fact, it is a step forward. You have written a first draft, recognized what didn't work, and moved on.

Keep copies of all of your drafts. When a piece is finished, compare your first draft to your last. Don't worry if it takes a half dozen or more tries before you are happy with the results. Learn to view revision as progress. Just as a rock must be put in a polisher to become a gem, so too must your writing be polished.

WEDNESDAY | WRITING CLASS

Write a five-line limerick about your
next-door neighbor.

REMEMBER, LINES 1, 2, AND 5 SHOULD RHYME WITH one another and typically contain seven to ten syllables. Lines 3 and 4 are shorter, five to seven syllables, and also rhyme.

THURSDAY | EDITING

I won't not use no double negatives.

—Bart Simpson

WHILE A DOUBLE NEGATIVE DOESN'T ALWAYS TURN a negative statement into a positive one, it does make for some confusing reading. For example, the sentence "I'm not wearing no underwear" might mean that your panties are intact. It can also convey that you don't quite know what underwear is.

The only exception to this rule is following the word *not* with an *un-* statement when you are shooting for irony, sarcasm, or a little bit of understatement. You can say, "I'm not unhappy" if you are trying to convey that you aren't quite happy.

However, a better way to go is always sticking with the positive. Positive statements in general are more clear and to the point: they make your writing feel crisp. Negative words beginning with *un-* or *non-*, or words paired with *not*, can come across as wordy and indirect. It's hard enough to say what you mean as compared to what you don't, so stay positive.

FRIDAY | BIOGRAPHY

> I like to read a few lines from a favorite novel
> before I start writing, to sort of put me in the
> flow of things.
>
> —*Khaled Hosseini*

K HALED HOSSEINI (1965–) AND HIS FAMILY MOVED
to Tehran, Iran, in 1970 from their home in Kabul,
Afghanistan, when Hosseini's father became a diplomat with
the Afghan Foreign Ministry. They stayed for three years,
returned briefly to Kabul, then relocated to Paris and were
unable to return to Afghanistan when the Communist Party,
in the Saur Revolution, seized power.

The bloody coup left the Hosseinis virtually homeless, and
after being granted political asylum, they made their residence
in San Jose, California. Though he was multilingual, Hosseini
did not learn English until he began high school. His family,
which enjoyed significant wealth in Afghanistan, spent its
initial months in the United States subsisting on welfare.

Hosseini graduated from high school in 1984 and enrolled
at Santa Clara University, where he earned a bachelor's degree
in biology. Medical school was next, and he earned his medical degree at the University of California, San Diego School
of Medicine. By 1996, Hosseini had become a practicing
internist in Los Angeles.

Hosseini began to write before going to work. He focused
on short stories, mainly thrillers or gothic horror tales, which
he could only publish online. He began developing one idea
into a novel, which became *The Kite Runner*. Published in 2003,
its sales were not astonishing. However, strong word of mouth
made the paperback version an international bestseller.

SATURDAY | BOOKS TO READ

This Boy's Life **by Tobias Wolff**

> Tobias Wolff's first stepfather was not exactly a model parent. An alcoholic sadist who humiliated his young charge and regularly beat him up, he also stole his money and shot his dog. . . . [W]ere he to show up in a novel we'd probably say that he lacked credibility, that the author had overegged the custard.
>
> —*Joel Conarroe*

ALTHOUGH THE MEMOIR HAS NOW BECOME ubiquitous—Frank McCourt's *Angela's Ashes*, Mary Karr's *The Liar's Club*, Elizabeth Wurtzel's *Prozac Nation*, and Lucy Grealy's *Autobiography of a Face*, to name just a few—Tobias Wolff was the first to establish and to set the blueprint for the genre as an examination of one's own life rather than the examination of the life of a more famous person. Amazingly, he was the first to use the now customary subtitle *A Memoir,* according to Ben Yagoda, author of *Memoir: A History*.

Wolff describes an unsettled childhood, trying to escape the horrific beatings inflicted by his stepfather, Dwight, a mechanic and house painter. The book sings with a clarity and sureness of past events. "I've told these stories so often—in a way I've been writing it for 20 years," says Wolff. *This Boy's Life* was named a *New York Times* Notable Book of the Year and made into a movie starring Leonardo DiCaprio.

SUNDAY | WRITING PROMPT

The road trip I would take . . .

D ID YOU EVER WANT TO JUST GET AWAY FROM IT all? Well, where would you go, and who would you go with? Those are the questions that need to be answered to successfully complete this prompt. Or, if you have taken the trip of a lifetime, can you recall the details that made it so memorable?

One recent example was the buddy movie *Sideways* based on the novel by the same name by Rex Pickett. Pickett's setup is based on two longtime friends who leave Los Angeles for vineyard country on a weeklong bachelor party road trip. Along the way, the book explores the meaning of friendship, but the real treat is the trip itself and the two men's adventures.

MONDAY | WRITERS ON WRITING

> You could compile the worst book in the
> world entirely out of selected passages from
> the best writers in the world.
>
> — *G. K. Chesterton*

ENGLISH AUTHOR G. K. CHESTERTON WAS NOTHING if not prolific. He wrote eighty books, hundreds of poems, more than a gross of short stories, thousands of essays, and a handful of plays.

In this quotation, Chesterton makes an apt point that is often lost on novice writers: even the best-received pieces of writing drafted by the acknowledged masters of the writing universe, all contain less-than-lovely or less-than-profound passages. An eighty-thousand-word novel is not going to be perfection from stem to stern. There will be sentences, paragraphs, even chapters, that are less than memorable, to say the least.

All writers should take comfort in these words. An examination of any masterpiece will reveal sentences that are not up to par. Even writers on their game will have days when their words simply don't gel. As Chesterton suggests, don't worry. Even on the tough days you are in good company.

TUESDAY | MOTIVATION

> Read it pretending you've never read
> it before.
>
> —*Neil Gaiman*

A S YOU DEVELOP YOUR WRITING, THERE WILL BE time to consider it not only as the writer but also as the editor. In other words, it will be time to begin looking at your writing with a kind-but-critical eye.

View editing as you do your writing: as an act of creation. Yes, you may be deleting text. You may even decide to start anew. The end result, though, is the improvement of your written work.

Ask these questions:

» Do I have a compelling beginning?

» Are words spelled correctly?

» Is my piece grammatically correct?

» Is the tone correct for the type of piece I am writing?

» Is the piece always moving forward?

» Is the piece too "wordy"?

» In a nonfiction piece, are the facts correct?

» Do I show rather than tell my reader?

» Have I overused any words or phrases?

» Does the dialogue flow? Is it realistic?

Be honest as you answer these questions. If the writing doesn't work, then fix it. As Isaac Bashevis Singer, the novelist and Nobel Laureate, put it, "A wastepaper basket is a writer's best friend."

WEDNESDAY | WRITING CLASS

Write your own love story.

RECORD THE DETAILS FROM YOUR MOST FAVORITE romantic date. Try to remember every little detail, and focus on what made that night more special than any other. Think about what you wore, what you ate, and where you went. Think about what you were like at that time in your life. And if you've changed since then.

Or, write your love story as a letter you would send to remind that special someone of how you felt that day and why you remember and cherish it. This could be particularly fun if it's someone with whom you are not currently in contact. Whatever you do, don't follow up with a glass of wine and an hour on Facebook tracking that person.

THURSDAY | EDITING

> Whenever you introduce a sentence with any
> adjectival phrase, that phrase must modify
> the subject of the sentence.
>
> —*C. Edward Good,*
> *A Grammar Book for You and I . . . Oops, Me!*

D ANGLING PARTICIPLES SOUND DANGEROUS, BUT that's because the phrase itself scares most away from fully understanding them. The quote above doesn't make things any easier. The truth about them is that the rule is quite simple, even if the language describing it is complex.

What the quote above really means is that when you start a sentence using an -*ing* verb or phrase, you have to immediately identify your subject: "Relaxing in London, *Sheila* read the best book of her entire life." When you start a sentence with a past-tense verb or phrase, you have to immediately identify the recipient of that activity: "Caught in the act, *the burglar* was taken away by the police."

The second case is where most people make a mistake and create a dangling participle: when the subject of the sentence is not the recipient of the action. A poorly constructed version that creates a dangling participle would be: "Caught in the act, many people fled the burglar."

As you can see, the dangling participle isn't the bit at the end of the sentence; it's at the beginning.

FRIDAY | BIOGRAPHY

I work out what happens in every chapter and who the characters are. I usually spend a year on the outline.

— Ken Follett

KEN FOLLETT (1949–) WAS BORN IN CARDIFF, Wales, on June 5, 1949, the first born child to Plymouth Brethren parents whose conservative Evangelical Christian beliefs forbade Follett from watching television or even movies. But it was his strict religious upbringing that led Follett to develop an early interest in literature and story-telling, and when his family moved to London in 1959, his parents enrolled him at Harrow Weald Grammar School. Follett would go on to attend University College London, studying philosophy and politics before beginning his career as a reporter for the *South Wales Echo.*

Follett later became a columnist for the *London Evening News.* He became increasingly frustrated with his job and began to write fiction in the evenings and on weekends. But even when he began to make money from his writing, he did not give up his day job.

Follett became a master of the pseudonym, writing nearly a dozen thrillers under names such as Symon Myles, Zachary Stone, Bernard L. Ross, and Martin Martinsen, until his break-through mystery, *Eye of the Needle,* was published under his own name. The book has sold more than ten million copies, won Follett a 1979 Edgar Award from the Mystery Writers of America, and launched a career that has produced one bestseller after another.

SATURDAY | BOOKS TO READ

Charlotte's Web by E. B. White

> What the book is about is friendship on earth,
> affection and protection, adventure and
> miracle, life and death, trust and treachery,
> pleasure and pain, and the passing of time.
> As a piece of work it is just about perfect,
> and just about magical in the way it is done.
> — *Eudora Welty*

THIS BELOVED CHILDREN'S CLASSIC WAS PUBLISHED in 1952 with winning illustrations by Garth Williams. It has been called the bestselling paperback book of all time. It has sold an estimated forty-five million copies around the world and has been translated into dozens of languages.

A classic animal fantasy, set on the Zuckerman farm, *Charlotte's Web* tells the story of the pig Wilbur and his relationship with a spider named Charlotte. It is a story of friendship and mortality. Charlotte helps to save Wilbur from slaughter by weaving words, like *some pig* into her web, which hangs above Wilbur's farm stall. The animals on the farm can speak with human language and use it to converse and to formulate plans to help Wilbur survive.

Along with its abundance of charm and enchantment, *Charlotte's Web* found success for a very simple reason. E. B. White understood that even very young children are insightful, interested, and at times frightened by death. In this book, White takes on the issues of heartache, loss, and misplaced trust and entrusts them to his young readers.

SUNDAY | WRITING PROMPT

The whole story about my parents . . .

ONE THING I'VE LEARNED AS I HAVE GOTTEN older is that you never know what goes on in someone else's home. This prompt allows you to tell the story of what other people may not know about your parents. Here is an opportunity to share something very special about your relationship with them and some of the wonderful things they have done that have helped shape you and your relationships with others.

Or, you can recount their darker side, as was the case with the bestselling novel turned motion picture, *The Great Santini* by Pat Conroy. It's the story of Bull Meecham, a Marine fighter pilot, and his relationship with his family, particularly his oldest son, Ben. Bull Meecham is an absolute ruler in his house, and everyone's lives revolve around his decisions. The novel is based on Conroy's own childhood growing up in a military family; on publication, Conroy revealed that his own father, Donald Conroy, was the inspiration for Bull Meecham. Conroy again wrote about his relationship with his father in his autobiography, *My Losing Season*, where he portrayed his father as both violent and emotionally abusive toward him and his siblings.

MONDAY | WRITERS ON WRITING

> Most beginning writers . . . are like chefs
> trying to cook great dishes that they've never
> tasted themselves. How can you make a great
> . . . bouillabaisse if you've never had any? If
> you don't really understand why people read
> mysteries—or romances or literary novels or
> thrillers or whatever—then there's no way
> in the world you're going to write one that
> anyone wants to publish.
>
> —*Daniel Quinn*

MANY ESTABLISHED WRITERS ENCOURAGE BUDDING authors to write what they know. As Pulitzer Prize–winning novelist Geraldine Brooks once said, "Because I live in a long-settled rural place, I know certain things. I know the feel of a newborn lamb's damp, tight-curled fleece and the sharp sound a well-bucket chain makes as it scrapes on stone."

American author Daniel Quinn takes this advice one step further. As a writer, you need to read and truly know about the different genres, especially those that you would like to write. It is not enough for you to read a single mystery, says Quinn. Instead, you need to immerse yourself in the world of mysteries, not only by reading a variety of them but also by talking with readers of mysteries.

Quinn encourages writers to connect with readers before writing. Ask readers what makes one mystery better than the next. What draws a reader to choose one character series over another? Understand the people who are likely to read your work.

TUESDAY | MOTIVATION

> Find a subject you care about and which you
> in your heart feel others should care about.
> It is this genuine caring . . . which will be
> the most compelling and seductive element
> in your style. I am not urging you to write a
> novel, by the way. . . . A petition to the mayor
> about a pothole in front of your house or a
> love letter to the girl next door will do.
>
> —*Kurt Vonnegut*

AMERICAN NOVELIST KURT VONNEGUT WAS PAS-
sionate about issues of social justice. This moral vision
is reflected in his bestselling books, including his groundbreaking antiwar science fiction novel, *Slaughterhouse-Five*. The
novel, based on his firsthand experience of the firebombing in
Dresden by the Allied forces in 1945, was published against
the backdrop of Vietnam. In writing *Slaughterhouse-Five*,
Vonnegut picked a subject he cared about and one that was
very much in the hearts of Americans during the unrest of the
Vietnam War. The novel touched a nerve with readers.

Make a list of the things you care about. These do not
have to be profound. Do you want your grocery store to carry
more organic produce? Put this on your list. Are you concerned about the quality of schools in your town? Add this
to the list. Use this list to generate writing ideas.

Becoming a writer demands that you give clarity and
definition to your ideas and interests. Perhaps, you've never
stopped to consider the things you care about and about which
you would like to write. Your list might surprise even you.

WEDNESDAY | WRITING CLASS

Write a four-hundred-word product review.

P ICK ANY PRODUCT THAT YOU ALREADY HAVE IN your home, and describe it in detail. How does it work (or not)? Has it met or exceeded your expectations? What is unique about it compared to others on the market? Without going overboard, what adjectives can you think of that best describe it?

The trick to good magazine writing is to write lots of short paragraphs—four sentences at most—that convey a lot of information in very few words. A product review doesn't need a lot of personality, but it has to be engaging enough for the reader to read it. Most of all, use the title of the article as your hook to draw the reader in.

THURSDAY | EDITING

Italic print or underlining is used for emphasis, titles of major artistic works, books, and foreign expressions.
—The Writer's Digest Writing Clinic

WAY BACK IN THE DAY, MOST PEOPLE WHO WANTED to be writers had typewriters, and not even the self-correcting kind. And before typewriters, those writer-types actually wrote on paper, with pens that you couldn't erase. So there were rules for how to make small pieces within a work stand out. Everyone knew how to underline a word, which became the symbol for the typesetter—a person who actually set words into type letter by letter—to quickly switch to his italic font.

Today, many people think that half the fun of writing is picking your font, setting up your margins, and then finally, filling your computer screen with words. I recommend that format should follow writing: don't waste time making your page look pretty, because frankly, no one but you cares. If you are intending to show your work for possible publication, editors prefer the simplest fonts and the most words on the page in a legible type.

As for italics, don't overuse them. The quote above mentions that you can use them for emphasis, but keep in mind that you can't emphasize everything. You can italicize a word here and there but not a whole paragraph, because italic text is harder to read and, like ALL CAPS in e-mails, looks like you are adding unnecessary drama.

FRIDAY | BIOGRAPHY

> Writing the last page of the first draft is the
> most enjoyable moment in writing. It's one of
> the most enjoyable moments in life, period.
>
> —*Nicholas Sparks*

NICHOLAS SPARKS (1965–) WAS BORN IN Omaha, Nebraska. The family eventually settled in Fair Oaks, California, where Nicholas graduated from high school as the class valedictorian.

He attended the University of Notre Dame on a full track scholarship. Sparks graduated with honors and returned to California where he began to write while holding down a number of day jobs, including waiter, real estate appraiser, and telemarketer. Sparks eventually settled on a career that centered on the manufacturing of orthopedic goods, meanwhile completing two novels that never sold.

In 1994, he collaborated with his friend Billy Mills, an Olympic medalist, on a book called *Wokini: A Lakota Journey to Happiness and Self-Understanding*. The book sold moderately well and was later picked up by Random House, yet he was not making enough money to cover his bills. Sparks gave himself a timeline: he would write three more novels, and if none of them were published, he would move on.

For the next six months, beginning in June 1994, Sparks began a manuscript that would become *The Notebook*. When he finished in early 1995, Sparks found an agent, who found him a publisher. Within a shockingly short span of time, Sparks went from being a relative unknown to receiving a book deal and a $1 million movie-rights contract.

SATURDAY | BOOKS TO READ

Shakespeare's sonnets

My mistress' eyes are nothing like the sun;
Coral is far more red than her lips' red;
. . . .
I love to hear her speak, yet well I know
That music hath a far more pleasing sound;
I grant I never saw a goddess go;
My mistress, when she walks, treads on the ground:
And yet, by heaven, I think my love as rare
As any she belied with false compare.

—*William Shakespeare*

WILLIAM SHAKESPEARE'S SONNETS WERE FIRST published in 1609 and were composed between the years of 1591 and 1598. People were not attending the theater then because of the plague, so Shakespeare took this time to learn and master the form of the sonnet.

The sonnet gave Shakespeare a forum for displaying his genius for language and also provided a foreshadowing of the great works yet to come, including *Romeo and Juliet, A Midsummer Night's Dream, Hamlet, King Lear,* and *Macbeth.* Writing the sonnets enabled Shakespeare to develop the language he used in the plays he wrote afterward.

We really can't overestimate how Shakespeare's work influenced the trajectory of English-language development and writing. He created thousands of new words, and with his poetry, he introduced the concept of using streamlined language to convey and portray complex human emotion.

SUNDAY | WRITING PROMPT

I broke something that didn't belong to me . . .

T HIS SCENARIO BRINGS TO MIND A FAVORITE *I LOVE Lucy* episode, where Fred and Ricky each break a television set that belongs to the other. Your story can be just as effective and far less convoluted with the same hilarious results.

Take the movie *Risky Business* as another example. Written and directed by Paul Brickman, this coming-of-age classic features a twenty-something Tom Cruise playing a teenage boy who needs to raise money fast after he drives his father's Porsche into Lake Michigan. The movie covers the event, how the characters tried to "make it right," and the consequences.

MONDAY | WRITERS ON WRITING

On writing, my advice is the same to all.
If you want to be a writer, write. Write and
write and write. If you stop, start again. Save
everything that you write. If you feel blocked,
write through it until you feel your creative
juices flowing again. Write.

—*Anne Rice*

ON THE SURFACE, NOVELIST ANNE RICE, AUTHOR of bestselling *The Vampire Chronicles*, offers seemingly straightforward advice: to be a writer means to write. As straightforward as it may be though, many writers, both established and aspiring, lose sight of her advice. To be a writer does not mean having work published or even necessarily having your work read by others. To be a writer means to write.

It is easy to make excuses and to put writing on the back burner, but listen to Rice's sage advice and keep writing. To be a gardener means to work in the dirt and to grow plants. To be a painter means to lay paint on canvas. So it follows that to be a writer is to put words on paper.

If you feel blocked, write anyway. Write a silly poem or a one-page story of your life. Do whatever it takes.

TUESDAY | MOTIVATION

The writing life is lonely. Taking some of that
loneliness out of it helps you to hang in there.
Create a supportive environment that allows
you to give it the kind of time it takes.

—Po Bronson

AUTHOR OF THE *NEW YORK TIMES* BESTSELLER *What Should I Do With My Life?*, Po Bronson knows firsthand about the loneliness of the writing life. He spends hours alone writing nonfiction social documentaries, novels, profiles, opinion pieces, humor pieces, performance monologues, book reviews, screenplays, and television and radio scripts. He also writes for his own website.

Part of creating a supportive environment could include taking classes at a local college or university. You might choose a writing course or a literature seminar. Perhaps you have always been interested in the works of Victorian authors such as Charles Dickens and George Eliot. If so, try to find a class that looks at writers of this era. By learning about other books and writers, you will improve your own writing.

Some colleges and continuing education programs offer their classes online. If it is possible, you'll still get more out of the experience by attending the actual campus site for your class. The idea behind taking these classes is to get out from behind your computer, not to spend more time there.

By taking courses, you are learning and developing new ideas for your work. Just as important, you are escaping the solitude of writing and meeting other like-minded people who can help you to "hang in there."

WEDNESDAY | WRITING CLASS

Write the setup for your favorite detective's
next adventure.

MYSTERY SERIES ARE HOT SELLERS, BOTH IN THE
bookstore and on television, because the authors
have created characters that we love to follow. Imagine for a
moment that you are a staff writer for your favorite ongoing
television mystery series. What crime would you like to see
them solve? How would their particular personalities come
into play during the episode? Create a story that builds from
the last episode you saw, or one that could either start the
new season or even end the current one.

THURSDAY | EDITING

> If the number of numbers is infinite, how can there be a final number?
>
> —*Yevgeny Zamyatin*

JUST AS THERE IS NO FINAL NUMBER; THERE ARE NO real rules for how we are supposed to record numbers in the English language. It's merely a question of style. Your goal is then to make a decision and to stick with it throughout your piece. If you are writing "for your eyes only," then whatever you choose is correct. However, if you are writing with the intent of publication, your decisions may be modified by the publisher's own "house style."

Here are some tips many publishers of books and magazines use for their house style:

1. Use letters for numbers lower than 100, then numerals going forward.

2. Never start a sentence with a numeral: spell it out instead.

3. Always use numerals with units of measure (8 miles, 4 quarts).

4. Use numerals only in recipes and instructions (Add ¼ teaspoon salt, bake for 7 minutes).

5. Use words rather than numbers if you are trying to be rhetorical or sarcastic (a hundred years of solitude).

6. The following are real numbers: *million*, *billion*, *trillion*, and *quadrillion*. The largest number to actually have a name is called *googolplex*, and it means "a cardinal number represented as 1 followed by a googol of zeros (10 raised to the power of a googol)."

FRIDAY | BIOGRAPHY

> Collins is an efficient no-nonsense prose
> stylist with a pleasantly dry sense of humor.
> —*Stephen King*

S UZANNE COLLINS (1963–) WAS BORN IN Hartford, Connecticut. Her childhood involved frequent relocations because her father was in the Air Force.

Collins got her start writing for children's television, including *Clarissa Explains It All, Oswald, Little Bear,* and *The Mystery Files of Shelby Woo,* all for the American cable channel Nickelodeon. She also became head writer for Scholastic Entertainment's hit show *Clifford's Puppy Days,* and she earned a nomination for her role as cowriter for *Santa Baby!* from the Writers Guild of America.

It wasn't until she met children's author James Priomos while working on *Generation O!* for Kids WB that she gave serious consideration to writing her own books for children. Her first success was updating the classic *Alice's Adventures in Wonderland,* which she turned into *Gregor the Overlander,* the first book in her five-part fantasy/war series, *The Underland Chronicles,* which became a *New York Times* bestseller.

She then set her sights on tackling the science fiction genre, with her award-winning series, *The Hunger Games.* The first book in the series immediately hit the *New York Times* bestseller list as a crossover, appealing to teens as well as adults.

SATURDAY | BOOKS TO READ

The Color Purple by Alice Walker

> [In writing *The Color Purple*], I always felt [my ancestors'] help. . . . How many of [them] had to do whatever they had to do to make it possible for me to get educated, to actually end up sitting at a desk writing about them? I mean [when I was writing the book], I was just crying and laughing, and just really feeling love. You know, just love for them, their love for me.
>
> —*Alice Walker*

PUBLISHED IN 1982, ALICE WALKER'S GROUND-breaking novel received the Pulitzer Prize and the National Book Award. It became an Academy Award–nominated movie and was a Broadway play.

In *The Color Purple,* Walker poignantly describes the struggles of a young African-American girl growing up in the early 1900s in Georgia. Celie is the victim of abuse by both her stepfather and her husband. In this epistolary novel, letters and diary entries are used to show Celie's discovery of self-worth and empowerment.

The Color Purple is far more than a historical novel. While it is a compelling novel, it is also a treatise on gender, race, sexual orientation, and equality in this country. It lays bare the themes of friendship, relationships, and courage. Most importantly, *The Color Purple* has helped reframe the ways in which Americans think about race, and it has stimulated discussion about women's roles in society.

SUNDAY | WRITING PROMPT

The most valuable thing I own . . .

D O YOU LOVE YOUR STUFF? MAYBE NOT ALL OF it, but you must have one special thing that you enjoy contemplating. Can you share why it is special to you, and how it has changed your life? Can you give a vivid description of your possession, so that a reader can imagine touching or holding the item?

Another thing to consider is writing about what your prized possessions say about you. In her first book, *My Passion for Design*, Barbra Streisand gives a guided tour of her homes in California, including the furniture and art she has collected. Even though she puts herself in the background, readers get a vivid glimpse of her real life and come to a better understanding of this much beloved singer.

MONDAY | WRITERS ON WRITING

> A blank piece of paper is God's way of telling
> us how hard it is to be God.
>
> —*Sidney Sheldon*

A MERICAN AUTHOR SIDNEY SHELDON WROTE dozens of bestselling novels, including *The Other Side of Midnight*, award-winning television series, films, and Broadway plays. His books have sold more than 400 million copies, and most of his novels have reached the number-one spot on bestseller lists. With a resumé like this, it is evident that literally thousands of times, Sheldon has been confronted by the writer's nemesis: the blank piece of paper.

Sheldon conveys how difficult it is, even for a commercially successful author, to confront the empty page. Few acts in life are more challenging that the act of creating. And, unlike a textile artist who has her colorful fabrics, fibers, and ribbons from which to create, a writer has nothing except blank pieces of paper and a pen or a computer. Novice writers should be reassured by Sheldon's words. Sure, it is daunting as you start out to face an empty page. According to Sheldon, it remains taxing even after success. However, Sheldon's continued achievements over a forty-year career show that the empty page can be wrestled successfully into submission.

TUESDAY | MOTIVATION

> Try to think of others' good luck as encouragement to yourself.
>
> — *Richard Ford*

S OMETIMES AUTHORS GROUSE ABOUT THE GOOD fortune of other writers or engage in a healthy dose of *schadenfreude*, enjoying the rejection slips that a contemporary just received.

This is a funny quirk of human nature, and one you should work to tamp down. The fact is good news for one writer often means good news for *many* writers. Following the runaway success of the Swedish-born Stieg Larsson's fast-paced mysteries *The Girl with the Dragon Tattoo, The Girl Who Played with Fire,* and *The Girl Who Kicked the Hornet's Nest,* there has been a race by American publishers to "discover" more Nordic noir. Swedish author Camilla Läckberg had written seven noir novels that were all bestsellers in Sweden yet had no interest from American publishers until the success of the Larsson trilogy. Now, her American editor, Jessica Case, reports that Läckberg received "one of the highest advances we've ever paid." If not for the success of Larsson's books, it is likely that Läckberg would have remained unknown outside of Europe.

In another case of success begetting success, Stephenie Meyers's bestselling *Twilight* series has produced a host of successful copycat books about vampires. Just imagine how our world would look if Meyers had decided that Bram Stoker's success with *Dracula* meant that there was no room for another vampire saga.

WEDNESDAY | WRITING CLASS

Create an investigation of a local politician gone rogue.

THESE DAYS, YOU'VE GOT PLENTY OF EXAMPLES ON the real news that show how a little bit of power turns the nicest guy or gal into a felon (or at least, a philanderer). Imagine you are breaking a story about a local or national political figure who has just been linked to a heinous crime. Make sure you can answer the right questions:

» Who?

» What?

» When?

» Where?

» Why?

» How?

» Why does it matter?

THURSDAY | EDITING

Also, avoid all awkward or affected alliteration.
—*William Safire,*
How Not to Write

ALLITERATION IS THE REPEATING OF THE FIRST sound of either a consonant or a vowel to make a phrase memorable. A sixteenth-century alliteration that survives to this day is Chaucer's words, "Brown as a berry," which is interesting that it survived this long because berries are rarely brown. Stringing words together with the same first consonant but without the same first sound is not alliteration; "Sally sells seashells by the seashore" is instead a clever tongue-twister. However, neither alliteration nor the tongue-twister makes for good writing. While these devices work in spoken language, both are literally too cute for words. As Safire notes, "Straining for effect produces the effect of affectation."

The same goes for adopting trendiness into your written work. *Trendy* by definition, means "here today, gone tomorrow." Think of your writing as a long-term commitment: would you want to read over your work twenty years from now and have it sound dated? Leave your penchant for hipness behind, or risk sounding less than totally cool.

FRIDAY | BIOGRAPHY

> Vision is the art of seeing what is invisible
> to others.
>
> *—Jonathan Swift*

JONATHAN SWIFT (1667–1745) WAS BORN IN Dublin, Ireland. His Irish father died before he was born, and Swift was sent to live with an uncle when his mother returned to England. Swift attended Trinity College in Dublin and eventually became a priest within the Church of England. He was assigned to minister a small parish in Laracor, Ireland, with a congregation of fifteen people. This gave him abundant time for leisure, for cultivating his garden, and for writing. His topics spanned a broad range, from political commentary to social satire, and he also wrote under several assumed names.

It was during this time that he began writing *Travels into Several Remote Nations of the World, in Four Parts, by Lemuel Gulliver, First a Surgeon and Then a Captain of Several Ships,* which we know of today as *Gulliver's Travels.* Much of the material reflects his political point of view. First published as a political satire in November 1726, it was an immediate hit.

SATURDAY | BOOKS TO READ

Gone with the Wind by Margaret Mitchell

In the end what will happen will be what has happened whenever a civilization breaks up. The people who have brains and courage come through and the ones who haven't are winnowed out.

—Margaret Mitchell

WHEN *GONE WITH THE WIND* WAS PUBLISHED, the country had come out of World War I only to fall into the Great Depression. Hints of another global conflict were already emerging, but like the characters in Mitchell's novel, most Americans were optimistic that with courage all would be well.

Margaret Mitchell's sweeping, romantic novel was set in the antebellum and post-antebellum South. Mitchell created characters that remain etched in the minds of countless Americans: tough-as-nails Scarlett O'Hara (whom Mitchell originally wanted to call Pansy); the feminine yet immensely strong Melanie Wilkes; and, of course, the swashbuckling Rhett Butler, forever famous for uttering, "My dear, I don't give a damn" (in the movie the line was modified to "Frankly, my dear, I don't give a damn," and was uttered by the perfectly cast Clark Cable).

Famed Southern writer Pat Conroy, upon rereading *Gone with the Wind*, said, "It is an extraordinarily good book." That is why the book remains as popular today as at its publication. With a passion for her subject and skilled language, Mitchell vividly re-creates an important era in American history.

SUNDAY | WRITING PROMPT

A place that changed my life . . .

H AVE YOU EVER VISITED A PLACE THAT REMAINS stuck in your consciousness, long after you've left? Why was this the case? Was it the people you met, the architecture, or a singular experience while you were there? These questions form the premise of this prompt.

For *Esquire* magazine journalist John Berendt, that place turned out to be Savannah, Georgia. A lifelong New Yorker, he discovered in the early 1980s that a super-saver fare to Savannah cost the same as an entrée in a high-end Manhattan restaurant. Berendt then spent the next eight years traveling between Savannah and New York City, writing about this sleepy Southern town and its lively community. The result was his bestselling book, *Midnight in the Garden of Good and Evil*. While it read like a novel, it was a true piece of nonfiction: part investigative journalism, part travelogue. He was able to captivate the imagination of his readers to the point where tourism in Savannah has flourished: people from all over the world wanted to experience the sights and sounds to which they were first introduced in the book.

MONDAY | WRITERS ON WRITING

> The first chapter sells the book; the last
> chapter sells the next book.
>
> —*Mickey Spillane*

FOR SOME WRITERS, COMMERCIAL INTERESTS ARE the name of the game, and writing is all about getting published. Mickey Spillane, while receiving plenty of critical accolades, was a master at marketing. To date, more than 225 million copies of his books have sold, and in 1980, Spillane was responsible for a jaw-dropping seven of the top fifteen all-time bestselling fiction titles in the United States.

Spillane offers here his secret formula. Make sure that the first chapter is compelling. Throw in the big guns, and create a story that immediately captivates readers. Spillane was expert at this. Just as important, though, is to leave the reader wanting more. He wanted every reader to experience the feeling of finishing a book and feeling disappointed that it had ended. So he wrote his last chapters so they were as strong as the first.

Even if you don't have your eye on bestseller status, Spillane's advice makes good sense. Your reader will most vividly remember the beginning and end of your work. Make both parts as vibrant, strong, and compelling as possible.

TUESDAY | MOTIVATION

What's another word for thesaurus?
—Steven Wright

GOOD WRITERS USE WORDS THAT THEY KNOW. If you've never used a word in spoken conversation, it probably won't go over well in your writing, either. Using words you are not familiar with threatens to make your writing affected, artificial, and without depth.

To keep your interest in language vibrant and to expand your opportunities as a writer, create your own word bank through your reading and through your day-to-day activities. Maintain a journal of interesting words that you come across as you read or that you hear in conversation. Write down the definitions of the words and the books in which you found the words. Make it a point to learn at least one new word every day.

There will always be new words to learn. The *Oxford English Dictionary* estimates that there are three-quarters of a million words in the English language, with new words being thought up every year. In 2009, for instance, the *Oxford English Dictionary* added *muggle*, a creation of J. K. Rowling, who used it to describe humans without magical powers, and *cyberslacking*, describing someone who surfs the Net and reads e-mail during office hours.

Language is the most important tool of your trade. And as you incorporate new words into your language, they'll eventually find their way onto your pages.

WEDNESDAY | WRITING CLASS

Rewrite the ending of Charles Dickens's
A Christmas Carol.

IMAGINE THAT SCROOGE DID NOT LEARN FROM HIS mistakes. Rewrite the last scene, in play format, of what would happen instead. Make sure to include Tiny Tim and his family so that it's not just a monologue. Also, make sure to give instructions on how this is to be presented. All notes to the actors should be in parentheses.

THURSDAY | EDITING

> Happy the man who has never been told
> that it is wrong to split an infinitive: the ban
> is pointless. Unfortunately, to see [the rule]
> broken is so annoying to so many people t
> hat you should observe it.
>
> —The Economist Style Guide

THE INFINITIVE FORM OF A VERB IS THE WORD YOU would look up in the dictionary: it is the bare form of the verb all by itself in the present tense, such as *run, walk,* or *vote*. When an infinitive appears with the preposition *to* it forms the very fancily named "periphrastic phrase." The name alone should send people over the edge, but instead many have worked themselves into a lather over the related rule. It is this phrase that you have been taught to accept as sacred, and not to separate its parts by squeezing in another word such as an adverb. The truth is, people do it all the time, and it isn't grammatically incorrect. But if you want to make everyone happy, follow the dictum anyway.

"Correct" construction:

The squirrel does not want to upset the rabbit.

"Incorrect" construction:

The squirrel does not want to unnecessarily upset the rabbit.

Best construction:

The squirrel does not want to upset the rabbit unnecessarily.

FRIDAY | BIOGRAPHY

> A good book always keeps you asking
> questions, and makes you keep turning pages
> so you can find out the answers.
>
> —*Rick Riordan*

RICK RIORDAN (1964–) WAS BORN IN SAN Antonio, Texas. His parents were both teachers and artists: his mother a musician and his father was a ceramicist. Riordan attended public school and graduated from the University of Texas at Austin with a double major in English and history.

During college, Riordan worked for three years as the music director at a summer camp, much like the one he created in his bestselling *Percy Jackson* series. He then went on to become a middle-school teacher in Texas and then California, teaching for more than fifteen years. He taught mythology almost every year, which provided an excellent background for the characters in his bestselling series.

On an impulse, Riordan wrote a mystery novel, set in his hometown of San Antonio. Featuring a private-eye/English PhD named Tres Navarre, *Big Red Tequila* was published to rave reviews in 1997. Since then, this series has won the top three awards for the mystery genre: the Edgar, the Anthony, and the Shamus.

However, Riordan's real fame was cemented in his love for children's literature. His beloved *Percy Jackson* series has sold millions of copies and has been produced as a major motion picture series.

SATURDAY | BOOKS TO READ

The Wind in the Willows by **Kenneth Grahame**

Now I have read it and reread it, and have
come to accept the characters as old friends.
—*Theodore Roosevelt*

AMERICAN PRESIDENT THEODORE ROOSEVELT wasn't the only person to accept the animal inhabitants of *The Wind in the Willows,* published in 1908, as friends. Author A. A. Milne, famous for his *Winnie the Pooh* books, was so taken by Mr. Toad, one of the book's main characters, that in 1929 he created a stage play, *Toad of Toad Hall,* centered on the foppish fellow. The play still runs today.

Kenneth Grahame first created the animal characters in the book in stories he told his young son, Alastair. When he began writing *The Wind in the Willows,* he focused on four animals, Mole, Ratty, Mr. Toad, and Badger, frolicking in the English countryside. As they play, they learn about the virtues and challenges of friendship.

Grahame published *The Wind in the Willows* the same year Beatrix Potter published *The Tale of Jemina Puddleduck.* Both of these popular authors focused on the pleasures and coziness of home and hinted at nostalgia for a time they sensed was coming to a close: the Edwardian age in England. In fact, their views were prescient. World War I began in 1914, and England and the world were forever changed. Today's readers can catch a glimpse of a beloved bygone era in this work, which accounts for its ongoing popularity.

SUNDAY | WRITING PROMPT

A story centered on a song or a memory
associated with music . . .

HAVE YOU EVER OPENED A NOVEL OR NONFICTION work, and the first page features a singular song lyric? That's exactly how this prompt works. Start with your favorite lyric, and see if you can craft a story or poem around it. Ask yourself: Why is this song important to me? What have I always thought it meant? How else can it be interpreted?

Country music star Sara Evans and novelist Rachel Hauck collaborated on a sentimental novel, *The Sweet By and By,* based on a familiar Christian hymn of the same name. It reflects on the underlying themes of hopefulness and redemption that are present in this song.

MONDAY | WRITERS ON WRITING

> Fiction writing is great. You can make up almost anything.
>
> —*Ivana Trump*

IVANA TRUMP FIRST ACHIEVED FAME AS THE FABULOUS ex-wife of billionaire Donald Trump, and later took her wrath to the page. In this quote, she is having a bit of fun, playing with her image as a dumb blonde. Blonde she is, dumb she is not, as she has proven, creating her own profitable businesses and writing bestselling books.

Although Trump included a healthy helping of gossipy tidbits from her real life in her novel *For Love Alone*, she has also taken care to create fictional scenes for it as well. If you choose fiction, take care not to make the evil mother-in-law too much like your mother-in-law. Your mother-in-law (and, perhaps, your spouse) won't appreciate the resemblance, but also, as a writer, it doesn't allow you to exercise your imagination to its fullest. Don't remain fettered by drawing too many parallels between your fictional characters and the real characters who populate your life.

Writers beware: a friend may not appreciate being featured in your writing. Truman Capote found this out the hard way when he famously featured Bill and Babe Paley, leading society figures in New York City in the 1970s, in excerpts of his unfinished novel *Answered Prayers*, which were published in *Esquire*. The Paleys disliked how they were portrayed and ostracized Capote, leading others to do the same. Capote never recovered from this rejection and, worse, never fully understood it.

TUESDAY | MOTIVATION

> The best way is always to stop when you are
> going good and when you know what will
> happen next. If you do that every day . . . you
> will never be stuck. Always stop while you are
> going good and don't think about it or worry
> about it until you start to write the next day.
>
> —*Ernest Hemingway*

C AN THIS BE RIGHT? TO STOP WRITING JUST WHEN things are going well and the ideas are flowing. Doesn't this seem counterintuitive? Actually, by stopping when "you are going good" you will keep the ideas flowing and your writing momentum going.

Don't write until you reach the conclusion. If you do, then where do you begin when you next sit down to write? If you choose to stop working while the words are flowing, then you will be leaving your work on a fulfilling high note. It also means that when you begin working the next day, it's likely that your creative juices will be flowing and you will be less likely to procrastinate.

After you stop writing each day, put your brain to rest. Let your subconscious work on your writing rather than actively thinking about it. As Hemingway said, "If you think about [your writing] consciously or worry about it you will kill it and your brain will be tired before you start."

WEDNESDAY | WRITING CLASS

Create two stanzas of a rhyming poem
about fast food.

A N "ODE TO PIZZA"? OR AN "ODE TO FRIES"?
Your choice, but here are the rules: Each stanza should
be four lines. You can choose if all lines rhyme, or if you
want, you can create couplets. The goal is for the reader to
experience your favorite fast food just the way you do.

THURSDAY | EDITING

Join two independent clauses with a colon if the second interprets or amplifies the first.
—*Strunk and White*, The Elements of Style

COLONS AND SEMICOLONS CAN BE POWERFUL writing tools when used correctly. Unfortunately, many writers are scared of them. Don't be: as you can see, I used one right here.

Colons are used to join together two independent clauses, or even two complete thoughts that could be sentences in their own right, where the second modifies the first. In most cases the word following the colon is lowercased. You can also use a colon to introduce dialogue or a citation from another book.

Semicolons are much less formal. Some suggest using them when you want to evoke a longer pause than a comma. Others suggest using one when you have two related sentences that could use a conjunction like *and* or *but,* or where a comma would seem to be ungrammatical. Semicolons are also used as dividers in a list after a colon has already been employed and where commas might add greater confusion. For example,

> Here's what you need: a sleeping bag, warm enough for outdoors; a lantern that doesn't attract bugs; and a bathing suit.

Lastly, use a semicolon if you are joining two opposite phrases or clauses with a word such as *however*, *also*, and *consequently*. For example: "She mistakenly fed the dog rancid beef; however, he didn't eat much of it."

FRIDAY | BIOGRAPHY

The first four months of writing the book, my mental image is scratching with my hands through granite. My other image is pushing a train up the mountain, and it's icy, and I'm in bare feet.

—*Mary Higgins Clark*

MARY THERESA ELEANOR HIGGINS CLARK (1927–) was born in the Bronx, New York. She was just eleven years old, already writing stories and plays, when her father passed away. Higgins finished high school, then went immediately into the workforce as a secretary to help out. Her teenage years were challenging. She moved out of her bedroom so that her widowed mother could rent the room to a boarder. Then she gravitated to a series of jobs until she landed a highly coveted flight attendant position with Pan American Airlines.

In 1949, Higgins met and married Warren Clark. They settled in New York and she began taking writing courses at New York University, published her first story in 1956, and formed a writing workshop that lasted for almost forty years. When her young husband died in 1964, leaving Mary to raise five children alone, she knew that she needed to increase her income. To help pay bills, she wrote radio scripts for the *Portraits of a Patriot* series, when, encouraged by her agent, she made an attempt at novel writing. Although her first novel, *Aspire to the Heavens*, was a complete failure, she changed direction from historical fiction to suspense novels. *Where Are the Children?*, her second novel, became an immediate best-seller when it was published in 1975.

SATURDAY | BOOKS TO READ

As I Lay Dying by William Faulkner

> People need trouble—a little frustration to
> sharpen the spirit on, toughen it. Artists
> do . . . Only vegetables are happy.
> —*William Faulkner*

WILLIAM FAULKNER IS NOW CONSIDERED ONE OF America's most important writers, but he almost fell into obscurity. Although three of his books, *The Sound and the Fury, Light in August,* and *As I Lay Dying,* are now listed on the Modern Library list of 100 Best Novels, by the 1940s, only one of his works remained in print. Malcolm Cowley, an American poet, journalist, novelist, and literary critic, saved Faulkner from obscurity by publishing *The Portable Faulkner* in 1946. Cowley said, "Public estimation of his books sank so low that by the middle of the war, only one book, *Sanctuary,* was not out of print." Faulkner won the Pulitzer Prize (twice) for novels published after *The Portable Faulkner,* as well as the National Book Award and the Nobel Prize in 1949. Today he is recognized as a master of the Southern gothic novel and as a language virtuoso.

As I Lay Dying is a premier example of Faulkner's famed stream-of-consciousness narrative style. He uses this for Addie, a character who is dead and tells her story from her own coffin. A total of fifteen narrators populate the novel, and each chapter is titled only by the narrator's name. The shortest chapter reads, "My mother is a fish." Faulkner was known to admire cubist painting and fragments like this have led critics to call *As I Lay Dying* the first cubist novel.

SUNDAY | WRITING PROMPT

Something that I lost or was stolen . . .

WHILE OBJECTS ARE OFTEN MEANINGFUL WHEN you have them, they can also take on a life of their own once they are gone. This prompt can make for the perfect beginning to a mystery, where you can explore what happened after something was stolen and how it was returned to its owner.

Or, try something with even more of a twist. For example, "The Necklace" is a timeless piece of ironic writing by Guy de Maupassant, a master of the short story. First published in 1884 in a French newspaper, it is the tale of Mathilde, a would-be socialite who borrows what she believes is an expensive necklace to wear to a fancy party and subsequently loses it. She spends the rest of her life toiling away in order to pay for the borrowed piece of jewelry, not knowing that the necklace was a cheap reproduction.

MONDAY | WRITERS ON WRITING

> The essential element for good writing is a
> good ear: One must listen to the sound of
> one's own prose.
>
> *—Barbara Tuchman*

BARBARA TUCHMAN WROTE *THE GUNS OF AUGUST,* a Pulitzer Prize winner, in 1962. It was a book about the prelude and first month of World War I. Tuchman was a stickler for detail, and she tried to capture each historical aspect. As she writes in the author's note: "All condition of weather, thoughts or feelings, and states of mind public or private, in the following pages have documentary support." So accurate was her reporting that President John F. Kennedy made *The Guns of August* required reading for his staff: "I want you to read this," he told them, "and I want every officer in the Army to read it."

Like many other successful writers, Tuchman describes the importance of listening to one's own writing. As a writer, she says, it is vital to hear the words you have written, read aloud to ensure they ring true.

Just as important for her is to have every element backed up by real life, so that the story rings true for the readers as they hear it in their own heads.

TUESDAY | MOTIVATION

> Reading usually precedes writing and the
> impulse to write is almost always fired by
> reading. Reading, the love of reading, is what
> makes you dream of becoming a writer.
>
> —*Susan Sontag*

ASK ANY WRITERS TO NAME THEIR FAVORITE BOOK and, nine times out of ten, they will not be able to limit the choice to one. Instead, they'll rattle off a laundry list of top picks. Likewise, ask a writing instructor for a list of top-ten tips for writing, and reading will certainly hold the prime slot. In fact, for many writers, reading occupies more of their day than the act of writing. Portuguese Nobel Prize–winning novelist José Saramago, when asked to describe his daily writing routine, answered, "I write two pages. And then I read and read and read."

Keep a reading journal, noting both the books you have read and also the books you would like to read. When noting the books read, also jot down what struck you about the books. It is important to think about and understand why you liked one book more than another as you develop as a writer. This will inform your writing and help you understand the mind of your reader.

Gather titles for your reading wish list from friends, family, newspaper reviews, and the stacks at your local library or bookstore. Remember to branch out when selecting books. If you tend to prefer reading about history, try a new genre, perhaps historical fiction.

WEDNESDAY | WRITING CLASS

Enhance your favorite prepared meal with
five additional ingredients.

EVEN THOUGH A CERTAIN MIX FOR MACARONI AND cheese (in the blue box) is perfectly fine right out of the box, every once in a while you need to mix up your food options. Choose your favorite store-bought meal—frozen pizza, pasta, soup, salad, frozen burritos, or whatever—and add five more ingredients to make your dinner spectacular. These items can be either fresh or store-bought. Make sure to list exact measurements of what you are using and complete detailed instructions on how to prepare your dish.

THURSDAY | EDITING

> Whenever you have a noun or a pronoun,
> followed by a form of the verb "to be,"
> followed by another noun or pronoun
> that's basically the same as the first noun
> or pronoun, that's called the predicative
> nominative.
>
> —June Casagrande,
> Grammar Snobs Are Great Big Meanies

THIS QUOTE SUMS UP FOR ME THE REASON WHY people are stymied about grammar. Who really needs to know this? Unfortunately, writers do if they don't want to sound amateurish. Worse, didn't I already tell you to lay off the verb *to be*? (See Week 36.)

This rule is not so important if you are using two nouns with the *to be* verb in the middle, as in: "That short yet distinguished man over there is Robert Redford." If the first reference of the pair is a pronoun, you're also covered: "He is Robert Redford." However, if the second reference is a pronoun, choose the subject pronoun (*he, she, I*) instead of the object (*him, her, me*). So, the example above becomes "That short yet distinguished man over there is he," which doesn't sound so good. In this instance, feel free to break the rule and go with *him*.

FRIDAY | BIOGRAPHY

> I have learned to regard fame as a will-o-the-wisp which, when caught, is not worth the possession; but to please a child is a sweet and lovely thing that warms one's heart and brings its own reward.
>
> —*L. Frank Baum*

LYMAN FRANK BAUM (1856–1919) WAS BORN IN Chittenango, New York. His parents were affluent businesspeople involved in the oil fields of Pennsylvania. Frank, as he preferred to be called, was born with a weak heart and was a shy and timid child. He was homeschooled and spent hours reading in his father's library.

With his younger brother Harry, he started a newspaper, the *Rose Lawn Home Journal*. Baum wrote all of the articles, editorials, fiction, and poetry. When he was twenty-five, Baum tried his hand at theater in New York City. From 1881 to 1882 he managed an opera house and wrote a play, *The Maid of Arran.*

After he got married he became what was known as a "newspaperman." He and the family moved frequently across the country. Eventually Baum started to write down the nursery rhymes he had improvised and told to his sons. *Mother Goose in Prose* was published in 1897. It was met with rave reviews. His second book, *Father Goose: His Book,* was the bestselling book for that year.

In 1900, he published *The Wonderful Wizard of Oz.* It was an instant success. Encouraged by positive reviews, Baum turned his full attention to writing.

SATURDAY | BOOKS TO READ

Rabbit Run by John Updike

> When I was a boy, the bestselling books were often the books that were on your piano teacher's shelf. I mean, Steinbeck, Hemingway, some Faulkner. . . . You don't feel that now. I don't feel that we have the merger of serious and pop—it's gone, dissolving. Tastes have coarsened. People read less, they're less comfortable with the written word. They're less comfortable with novels.
>
> —*John Updike*

THE GREAT AMERICAN NOVELIST JOHN UPDIKE might be best remembered as the chronicler of America's middle class. In Rabbit Angstrom, the protagonist of the 1960 novel *Rabbit Run* and its sequels, Updike encapsulated the sturm und drang of middle-class Americans during the decades between 1960 and 1990.

Updike was a realist and used elegant, straightforward prose to convey the reality of Rabbit's everyday life: his marriage, his job as a demonstrator of kitchen gadgets, his role as dad to a toddler. Updike used the same accessible language to convey the inner debates waged by Rabbit about mortality and morality. In all, Updike wrote four *Rabbit* novels and one novella among dozens of books and frequent *New Yorker* articles. Two of the *Rabbit* novels received the Pulitzer Prize, elevating Updike to the small list of writers he would be happy to find on his piano teacher's shelf.

SUNDAY | WRITING PROMPT

My early memories of my faith . . .

Depending on (a) your nature and (b) your current relationship with your faith, you can take this prompt in many different directions. For those with a cynical streak, you might want to see the humor that resides in your faith. Take the book, *Growing Up Catholic* by Mary Jane Frances Cavolina, Jeffrey Allen Joseph Stone, and others, for example. First written in 1985, this classic collection of childhood memories of a Catholic upbringing endures because it is humorous without being blasphemous.

If you are more serious about your faith, there are hundreds of books that represent many different spiritual quests, each exploring early religious experiences. See if you can add to this rich tradition by exploring your early memories and how they have shaped your faith today.

MONDAY | WRITERS ON WRITING

A story isn't about a moment in time, a story is about the moment in time.

—*W. D. Wetherell*

AMERICAN AUTHOR W. D. WETHERELL CAPTURES the essence of good writing in this one profound quote. A skilled writer distills for her reader the heart and core of a given moment in time.

Any writer can research and write about the Vietnam War and the sweeping effects felt across America during those turbulent years. A good writer, says Wetherell, will define the story, making it the moment in time that everyone remembers. David Halberstam captured this moment in Vietnam with his award-winning 1972 account of the devastating effects of that war. Based on more than five hundred interviews, *The Best and the Brightest* captured the moment of the Vietnam War.

A writer does this by asking and answering questions for the reader: Why does this story matter? What impact did it have at the time, and how does it continue to resonate? What about this moment in time makes the story universal to all readers?

These are not easy questions to answer, which explains one of the divides between ho-hum writing and terrific historical writing. As Wetherell explains, a good writer is able to answer the questions and to make the answers valuable to every reader.

TUESDAY | MOTIVATION

> You can't put a limit on anything. The more
> you dream, the farther you get. I want to
> be able to look back and say, "I've done
> everything I can, and I was successful." I don't
> want to look back and say I should have done
> this or that.
>
> —*Michael Phelps*

THE 2008 BEIJING OLYMPICS ATTRACTED 4.7 BILLION viewers. That's 70 percent of the Earth's population, making it the most-watched television event in history. One reason so many tuned in was to watch U.S. swimmer Michael Phelps shatter Olympic and world records.

While Phelps made it look easy, the road to becoming one of the all-time Olympic greats has not always been smooth. He started swimming at the age of five. Soon after, he was diagnosed with Attention Deficit Hyperactivity Disorder. He used his time in the pool to release all of his excess energy. At the age of nine, his parents divorced, and Phelps told friends that he escaped to the pool to avoid the tensions at home. His training schedule is no cakewalk, either. It includes training for six hours a day, six days a week. His grueling hours at the pool often preclude time for hanging out with friends and family, although he makes time for his bulldog, Herman.

Phelps's thirty-eight world records and sixteen Olympic medals took tremendous effort. He has devoted his life to swimming and to training. For some, being a writer requires the type of discipline evidenced by Phelps. Whether you are writing for yourself or for an audience, to do something well takes effort. And as the adage goes, practice makes perfect.

WEDNESDAY | WRITING CLASS

Write a love scene for a romantic comedy.

I NTRODUCE TWO CHARACTERS, AND SHOW HOW THEY would interact on screen so viewers can better understand the entire context of their relationship. Be as graphic as you think necessary, yet make sure it is appropriate for a PG-13 audience. Keep the language witty and charming. Remember, this is a "feel-good" movie.

THURSDAY | EDITING

> A good story takes readers where they haven't
> been before in the company of interesting
> people they learn to care about who are
> forced to deal with adversity.
>
> —*Peter Rubie*, How to Tell a Story

CONFLICT IS THE BASIS OF DRAMA. IF YOU DON'T have a series of scenes with some sort of conflict in them, you don't have a narrative.

There are three major types of conflict, one of which must be found in your story: man vs. man, man vs. nature, or man vs. himself. Man vs. man is easy to identify: two guys are in a fight; two families disagree; a couple breaks up; a person takes on a corporation or a government. Man vs. nature brings to mind survival in the wilderness books and anything that has to do with "overcoming obstacles"—in this sense, nature is the "force to be reckoned with." Lastly, man vs. himself conflicts are often the quieter, more introspective books about personal change, coming of age, or dealing with death.

There are hundreds of references to works within this book for you to be able to pick out which conflicts were employed. That's a great exercise. A better one is to make sure that you've used conflict in your writing to move your story along.

FRIDAY | BIOGRAPHY

> Anything one man can imagine, other men can make real.
>
> —*Jules Verne*

JULES GABRIEL VERNE (1828–1905) WAS A FRENCH writer who was born and raised in the harbor city of Nantes, and from an early age he displayed an immense desire to escape from what he perceived to be his parents' traditional middle-class ambitions into a world of adventure.

One famous Jules Verne legend is that when he was just twelve, he ran away from home to work as a cabin boy on an ocean liner. The ship was prevented from sailing when his father came on board to "rescue" his son. Verne is said to have promised his parents that in the future he "would travel only in imagination"—a promise he kept.

Verne set out for Paris in 1847, with the desire to pursue a career in law. He befriended the author of *The Three Musketeers*, Alexandre Dumas, who helped Verne get his first play, *The Broken Straws*, produced. He continued to write comedies and operettas and began contributing short stories to popular magazines throughout France.

In 1857 he married the widowed mother of two daughters, Honorine de Viane Morel, and became a successful stockbroker—a career that he despised. He continued to write, however, with his wife's encouragement, maintaining a rigorous schedule in his hours away from the floor of the Paris Exchange. His first long work of fiction, *Five Weeks in a Balloon*, was published in 1863 and was an immediate success. He then decided to retire from his work as a stockbroker and to devote himself full time to writing.

SATURDAY | BOOKS TO READ

The Grapes of Wrath by John Steinbeck

> Little presses write to me for manuscripts
> and when I write back that I haven't any, they
> write to ask if they can print the letter saying
> I haven't any.
>
> — *John Steinbeck*

T*HE GRAPES OF WRATH* WAS PUBLISHED IN 1939 AND earned Steinbeck both the Pulitzer and Nobel prizes. Some critics complained that Steinbeck was a writer with a chip on his shoulder, who liked to complain about capitalism and the state of contemporary society without having any particular literary panache. Even Steinbeck, when asked if he deserved the Nobel Prize, said, "Frankly, no."

Written in just five months, *The Grapes of Wrath* takes on the plight of human suffering. It chronicles the misfortunes of the Joad family, Oklahoma sharecroppers who are forced to flee, along with thousands of other "Okies," for the greener pastures of California. Steinbeck opened his readers' eyes to the despair of agrarian America caused by the devastation of the dustbowl during the Great Depression.

Steinbeck said the novel has "five layers of meaning": literal, allegorical, moral, spiritual, and anagogical. This depth was lost on many early critics who saw it as either inflammatory (portraying both California farmers and Oklahoma migrants in unflattering light) or filled with generalizations. In fact, future generations have found *The Grapes of Wrath* to resonate, to remind us of the fate of humans forced by nature and destiny to be a part of the underclass.

SUNDAY | WRITING PROMPT

If I were suddenly rich . . .

THIS PROMPT SEEMS TO SURFACE EVERY TIME I TURN on the television to a new reality series or game show. It's the first question the emcee asks the contestant: What would you do with your newfound money?

In literature, one of the most evocative short stories is *The Lottery Ticket* by Anton Chekhov. In just 1,278 words, Chekhov was able to aptly describe the joys, perils, and sadness that can accompany wealth. He takes the reader on a quick ride through human nature, as a husband and wife contemplate winning the lottery.

MONDAY | WRITERS ON WRITING

I just write what I wanted to write. I write what amuses me. It's totally for myself.
—*J. K. Rowling*

WHO WOULD HAVE THOUGHT THAT STORIES ABOUT kids attending wizard school would strike such a chord, spawning hundreds of millions of copies of book sales, major motion pictures, and Harry Potter mania spreading around the globe?

English author J. K. Rowling, for one, apparently did not think her stories necessarily had tremendous commercial potential. In creating these captivating stories set at Hogwarts School of Witchcraft and Wizardry, she wrote about what amused her and captivated her imagination. In Rowling's case, commercial success followed. The seven *Harry Potter* novels have sold more than 400 million copies and been translated into seventy languages.

Instead of writing about something that you think might captivate a reader, Rowling recommends writing about what captivates you. Your enthusiasm could draw potential readers. It certainly was the case with the *Harry Potter* series.

TUESDAY | MOTIVATION

Learn poems by heart.
—*Helen Dunmore*

THE ART OF MEMORIZING AND RECITING POETRY began in Ancient Greece when Athenian schoolboys memorized the works of Homer. Shakespeare, at his school in Stratford-upon-Avon, learned language by memorizing large chunks of literature. This tradition carried on into twentieth-century America with schoolkids memorizing "Paul Revere's Ride" and college students taking on the opening stanzas of Chaucer's *Canterbury Tales*.

There is immense value in memorizing and reciting poetry. It helps writers gain a heightened feel for language by being able to show off the rhythms of language. Reciting poetry will help you choose flowing language as you write. It will enable you to better understand the intricacies of language and also introduce you to new words.

Memorizing poetry also teaches discipline. Start with a small poem, four lines or so, and work your way up to more challenging works. Try to memorize at least one poem every week. For those who question their capacity to memorize, consider the story of Connecticut resident John Basinger who, at the age of seventy-six, had memorized John Milton's seventeenth-century epic poem *Paradise Lost*. At 60,000 words, it took Basinger eight years to memorize.

WEDNESDAY | WRITING CLASS

Write an Italian sonnet about your favorite season.

WHILE ALL SONNETS ARE POEMS, NOT ALL POEMS are sonnets. And, not all sonnets are created equal. An Italian sonnet differs from its Elizabethan cousin because it comprises an eight-line "octave" of two quatrains, rhymed ABBAABBA, and followed by a six-line "sestet" usually rhymed CDECDE or CDCDCD. The transition from octave to sestet coincides with a "turn" in the mood of the poem or contrasts two opposing ideas. An example is this sonnet, "London, 1802," by Wordsworth:

Milton! thou shouldst be living at this hour:
England hath need of thee: she is a fen
Of stagnant waters: altar, sword, and pen,
Fireside, the heroic wealth of hall and bower,
Have forfeited their ancient English dower
Of inward happiness. We are selfish men;
Oh! raise us up, return to us again;
And give us manners, virtue, freedom, power.
Thy soul was like a Star, and dwelt apart;
Thou hadst a voice whose sound was like the sea:
Pure as the naked heavens, majestic, free,
So didst thou travel on life's common way,
In cheerful godliness; and yet thy heart
The lowliest duties on herself did lay.

Your task is to create an Italian sonnet about a season, showing two distinct ideas or themes that occur, or two disparate thoughts about that season.

THURSDAY | EDITING

> The difference between *bring* and *take* has to
> do with the location of the speaker and the
> location of any other actors who will be
> bringing or taking something from some place
> to some other place.
>
> —*C. Edward Good,*
> A Grammar Book for You and I . . . Oops, Me!

TAKE MEANS AN ACTION THAT WILL PROCEED AWAY from the location where the person is currently located. *Take* can always be thought of as the action "to take away" from where you are now to somewhere else. Yet many writers substitute the word *bring* in this instance. ("She should bring her umbrella because it is going to rain" is incorrect; "She should take her umbrella . . ." is correct.) *Bring* should instead be used when the actors in the sentence are returning, or "bringing back" something to where they are right now. In the sentence above, it wouldn't make sense to bring your umbrella when you are leaving the house, because it's raining outside, not inside.

The two verbs get more confusing when you are writing between two people who are not in the same place. For example, if Sally is visiting Ellen, Sally will be *taking* an apple pie, but Ellen will think that Sally is *bringing* the pie. Both are correct.

FRIDAY | BIOGRAPHY

The past is not simply the past, but a prism through which the subject filters his own changing self-image.

—Doris Kearns Goodwin

DORIS KEARNS GOODWIN (1943–) WAS BORN in Brooklyn, New York, and grew up in the Long Island suburb of Rockville Center, the Roman Catholic daughter of Michael Alouisius and Helen Witt Kearns. It was her mother's debilitating illness that prompted Kearns Goodwin's bedside appreciation for literature, while her father's love of baseball instilled in her a lifelong fascination with the game.

Kearns Goodwin received a liberal arts education at Colby College in Maine, where she graduated *magna cum laude* and landed prestigious internships at both the United States Congress and the U.S. State Department. She was awarded a Woodrow Wilson Fellowship in 1964, then went on to earn a PhD in government four years later from Harvard University.

Despite an article that she co-authored for the *New Republic*, "How to Remove LBJ in 1968," while serving as a White House Fellow, President Lyndon Johnson thought enough of the talented Kearns Goodwin to keep her around, and she was recruited to be Johnson's special assistant.

Her relationship with the president did not end when he left office in 1969. While teaching at Harvard, Kearns Goodwin assisted Johnson in the research and drafting of his memoir, *The Vantage Point*, which was later published in 1971. Six years later, Kearns Goodwin published a book of her own, *Lyndon Johnson and the American Dream*, based on her own vantage point and conversations with the late president.

SATURDAY | BOOKS TO READ

Remembrance of Things Past
by Marcel Proust

In *Remembrance of Things Past* . . . the narrator, who is a fictionalized Marcel Proust, dips this madeleine in some tea, and the spoonful of tea mixed with crumbs is kind of the point where the novel reaches escape velocity and he has this flood of memories that spark the whole rest of the novel.

—*Edmund Levin*

PUBLISHED BETWEEN 1913 AND 1927, FRENCH author Marcel Proust's *Remembrance of Things Past (À la recherche du temps perdu)* is a seven-volume autobiographical work. Amazingly, Proust paid to have the first volume published, as he could not find a publisher. The books have not been out of print since.

Proust's works break from the tradition of the realist novel. Rather than a straightforward plotline, the narrative often moves forward based on a memory or recollection of an occurrence. In fact, the role of involuntary memory is key to the novel's success. As noted in the quote above, the crumbs of a single cookie spurred all of Proust's senses.

Proust had a delicate nature. He wrote much of *Remembrance of Things Past* while tucked in bed inside a cork-lined room (to block out noise). He died at age fifty-one of pneumonia.

To savor Proust's long novel, read it slowly.

SUNDAY | WRITING PROMPT

When punishments do fit the crime . . .

D O YOU BELIEVE THAT OUR CRIMINAL JUSTICE system is effective, overbearing, or too lenient? Does it in some way have a direct impact on your life? This prompt lets you explore crime and its related punishments on any level that affects you: within your home, your community, your state, or even the country.

In the classic narrative poem, *The Rime of the Ancient Mariner* by Samuel Taylor Coleridge, the main character— the ancient mariner—is severely punished for killing an albatross that purportedly had mystical powers. The poem is vague as to whether the mariner believed the bird to be magical, and whether he agreed that his punishment he received, as well as what befell his shipmates, fit his crime.

MONDAY | WRITERS ON WRITING

> I just kept on doing what everyone starts out doing. The real question is, why did other people stop?
>
> —*William Stafford*

WILLIAM STAFFORD, AN ESTEEMED AMERICAN POET, never stopped working. At the age of seventy-nine, he was still writing. He wrote a poem the morning of the day he died:

> *"You don't have to*
> *prove anything,"*
> *my mother said.*
> *"Just be ready*
> *for what God sends."*

Many writers stop before achieving success for a myriad of reasons. Family intervenes, financial worries arise, careers interfere. For Stafford, it was never a question of stopping. He kept a personal journal for fifty years and wrote almost 22,000 poems, 3,000 of which were published. In 1970, he was named the Poet Laureate Consultant of the United States (this position is now called the Poet Laureate).

His advice for writers on writing is to continue on their path. When life events intervene, prune rather than delete your writing time. Take the time to compose a few lines even when only a few moments are available for you to write. Gertrude Stein didn't let life's events get in the way of her writing. When she had only a few moments free, she would scribble down her thoughts on scraps of paper while sitting in her parked Ford. Like Stafford, Stein wrote until the end of her life.

TUESDAY | MOTIVATION

I'm very proud of my flops, as much as of my successes.

—Francis Ford Coppola

DIRECTOR FRANCIS FORD COPPOLA WAS RIDING high on the success of his blockbuster movies, *The Godfather, The Godfather II*, and *Apocalypse Now*, when he decided to change courses and direct something more lighthearted.

In 1982, he chose *One from the Heart,* a musical romance set in a fantastical Las Vegas. Unfortunately, the story was overwhelmed by complicated sets, odd lighting, strange special effects, and questionable production values. Not only did Coppola take a hit from the audience and critics, but his wallet took a beating. He had invested $12 million of his own money to create the movie. He was not deterred. He learned from his mistakes and moved on to direct several more successful movies.

Everyone has failures. The key is to learn from mistakes and to incorporate this knowledge into life's further adventures. As Coppola's fellow movie director Woody Allen, no stranger to a few flops of his own, put it, "If you're not failing every now and again, it's a sign you're not doing anything very innovative."

WEDNESDAY | WRITING CLASS

Make a children's picture book.

A CHILDREN'S PICTURE BOOK IS LIKE A SHORT STORY in that you have a very limited number of words to convey an entire idea or sequence of events. The typical children's book is thirty-two pages (roughly twelve hundred words) for fiction and forty-eight pages for nonfiction (no more than two thousand words for younger readers). The fictional version must follow the same story arc as any good work: it must introduce characters, set the scene, and show both a conflict and its resolution.

You can make your picture book appropriate for any age group: the best children's books have a universal appeal, making them equally readable for adults as well as children. Don't worry about the artwork at this point: a good story is all you need to craft.

THURSDAY | EDITING

> A common mistake is to treat an unhappy
> coincidence as irony. It isn't ironic that your
> oven breaks on Thanksgiving morning or you
> run into your old boyfriend at the café where
> you used to hang out together.
> —*Mignon Fogarty*, The Grammar Devotional

HUMOR, SARCASM, AND IRONY ARE ALL TOOLS IN language that are really hard to deliver well when you are speaking, let alone writing. So when you are reviewing your work, make sure that you've used these tools correctly. Otherwise, your attempts will not be successful.

Sarcasm is defined as "expressing or expressive of ridicule that wounds." When you use sarcasm, you are intentionally hurting someone's feelings or poking fun at yourself. It is often employed in attacking a person or belief through harsh and bitter remarks that mean the opposite of what they say. For example: "Cinderella's stepmother would have been a nicer person if she just got out of the house more often."

Irony is different and much harder to write. Irony is the "incongruity between the actual result of a sequence of events and the normal or expected result." The difference is best noted by the Sarcasm Society (www.sarcasmsociety.com): "One main difference between irony and sarcasm is that irony is generally observed and sarcasm is generally created." An irony is: "At *Sports Illustrated* supermodel Elle Macpherson's wedding, she wore a gown that converted into a bathing suit." You just can't make this stuff up: you have to find irony where it lives.

And you are all on your own in defining humor. One person's joke is another's offense; proceed with caution.

FRIDAY | BIOGRAPHY

> Writers may be disreputable, incorrigible,
> early to decay or late to bloom but they dare
> to go it alone.
>
> —*John Updike*

JOHN UPDIKE (1932–2009) WAS BORN IN READING, Pennsylvania. His grandfather was a minister and his father was a high-school science teacher. An only child, Updike and his parents shared a house with his grandparents.

A voracious reader, Updike enjoyed popular fiction, especially humor and mysteries, and his mother, Linda Grace Hoyer, encouraged all of her son's artistic aspirations. An aspiring writer herself, Updike's mother inspired the young man, and he spent summers writing copy at the local newspaper, the *Reading Eagle*. As valedictorian of his high-school class (and class president) in 1950, Updike received a scholarship to attend Harvard University, where he studied English, contributed to the *Harvard Lampoon*, and ultimately graduated *summa cum laude* in 1954.

Soon after college, Updike was married to Mary Pennington, an art student from Radcliffe College, and he sold his first short story to the *New Yorker* magazine. A literary career looked promising. For a while, he studied art in England, and there he met E. B. and Katherine White, editors at the *New Yorker*, who encouraged Updike to return to New York and work at the magazine. He did, and was a staff writer there. After the birth of his son two years later, he decided to move to Massachusetts. He continued to contribute to the *New Yorker* and to write bestselling novels, articles, and short stories.

SATURDAY | BOOKS TO READ

Murder on the Orient Express
by Agatha Christie

> "As to who killed him—" He paused, looking
> at his audience. He could not complain of any
> lack of attention. Every eye was fixed upon
> him. In the stillness you could have heard a
> pin drop. He went on slowly.
>
> —*Agatha Christie*

BESTSELLING BRITISH AUTHOR AGATHA CHRISTIE wrote dozens of murder mysteries, none better than *Murder on the Orient Express*. First published in 1934, it featured the eccentric and beloved detective Hercule Poirot, known for his outsized moustache, his need for order, love of sweet liqueurs such as crème de menthe, and the ability to crack even the toughest case at hand.

In this book, the Belgian detective boards a crowded train as it is en route from Istanbul to England. When a snowstorm delays the train's journey, an American is found dead. Hercule must solve the murder.

Agatha Christie was a master of using the closed location—such as an island or a train—for her mysteries. By using a setting of this type, she ensured that every character could be considered a suspect in the murder. She was also a master of the red herring, so just as a reader says, "Aha," and presumes to have solved the case, Christie proves her reader wrong.

SUNDAY | WRITING PROMPT

Perseverance is the difference between good and great . . .

THE AMERICAN WORK ETHIC IS BASED ON THE IDEA that hard work is rewarded. Do you believe this to be true, or do you think that there are other mitigating factors to take into consideration when it comes to success? Is all that hard work really worth it?

For example, take the classic children's book, *The Little Engine That Could.* In print for more than 100 years and still selling 10 million copies annually in English alone, this story is a metaphor for America's can-do attitude. While larger locomotives insisted they couldn't get over the mountain, the smaller locomotive chugged along, all the while saying, "I think I can, I think I can." Even when faced with overwhelming odds, the little train persevered, finally getting to the other side of the mountain.

MONDAY | WRITERS ON WRITING

The virtue of books is to be readable.
—Ralph Waldo Emerson

RALPH WALDO EMERSON WAS AN AMERICAN essayist and poet as well as a founding figure in the Transcendentalist movement. Early in his career, in 1837, Emerson delivered a Phi Beta Kappa address in Cambridge, Massachusetts. The address was entitled "The American Scholar." He went on to publish five hundred copies of the address at his own expense; they sold immediately. The piece struck a universal chord with his audience because it helped create a roadmap for Americans to create their own identity separate from the European identity by which much of the nation was still bound. The speech was called "America's Intellectual Declaration of Independence."

Emerson was very concerned with creating and using language—both spoken and written—that would help America's emerging culture establish itself. Seven of his ancestors were ministers so Emerson knew about the power of the word spoken from the pulpit. He assisted in leading a group of Concord writers including Bronson Alcott, Henry David Thoreau, and Margaret Fuller, to write books that helped define the American tradition of writing.

TUESDAY | MOTIVATION

I think I did pretty well, considering I started
out with nothing but a bunch of blank paper.
—*Steve Martin*

CONSIDER IT A KIND OF ALCHEMY. JUST AS WIZARD-like figures in medieval times were famous for allegedly turning base metals, such as lead, into gold, modern-day writers are alchemists in their own right.

The act of writing is rather miraculous. From a blank sheaf of papers emerges a wholly invented character, a new town, or another world. Like the transmutation of one element to another, writers perform their own alchemy.

Pat yourself on the back for developing the focus and discipline to write. It takes a leap of faith to believe in your ability to transform blank paper into prose, and it is a leap that can be challenging to ford.

As the world changes and technology develops at a frantic pace, there is an almost greater need for writers and writing as a counterpoint to technology. Books and other written materials offer readers the opportunity to step away from the hectic pace of everyday life and to discover new worlds. The demand for books is strong. According to the Book Industry Study Group, more than three billion books are sold each year. Likewise, literary journals, both on- and off-line, continue publishing short stories, nonfiction, poems, and essays. Reading has always struck a common chord in humans, and writers provide for that need.

WEDNESDAY | WRITING CLASS

Write a travel piece about a recent vacation
you've taken.

S EE IF YOU CAN REMEMBER FIVE UNIQUE FEATURES
of your vacation. Review the place you stayed (even if
it was a friend's home), the weather you experienced, what
you ate, what you saw that was noteworthy, and anything
interesting about the culture. Load on as many adjectives as
possible to fully describe your experience. Then, pare down
the hyperbole until the writing rings true.

THURSDAY | EDITING

> In a series consisting of three or more elements, the elements are separated by commas. When a conjunction joins the last two elements in a series, a comma is used before the conjunction.
>
> —The Chicago Manual of Style

THIS RULE IS OFTEN REFERRED TO AS "THE SERIAL comma" rule and is open to interpretation based on a publication or publisher's "house style." However, I find that it's easier to locate a list within a paragraph by looking for the commas, so I adhere to this rule. If you think of a comma as a slight pause in your sentence, it makes sense to follow the serial comma rule.

Descriptive lists are an easy way to add variety to your sentences. They are particularly useful when you are describing inanimate objects, although they can be used to describe people as well. When you are using a descriptive list, save the most impressive detail for last. This makes the greatest impression on the reader, especially if the last point contrasts with the other items on the list. For example, you can say, "George is short, bald, yet handsome."

FRIDAY | BIOGRAPHY

*The use of language is all we have to pit
against death and silence.*

—*Joyce Carol Oates*

J OYCE CAROL OATES (1938–) WAS BORN IN
Lockport, New York, the daughter of Frederic and Carolina
Oates, and raised in a Catholic household. The Oates family
enjoyed a close and traditional bond in rural western New
York, and, in fact, Carol had attended the very same one-
room school as her mother. Early on, she had displayed a
sophisticated interest in literature and writing, and despite
the fact that her father (a tool-and-die designer) and mother
(a homemaker) had themselves had little exposure to the
intellectual benefits of higher education, they nevertheless
encouraged their daughter to pursue her interests.

She read Hemingway, Thoreau, Faulkner, and Dostoevsky,
and at fourteen, she was given a typewriter by her grandmother. The impact was immediate, and Oates set out to
make writing a part of her daily life—a habit she maintained
through college. She won a short story contest at the age
of nineteen, sponsored by *Mademoiselle* magazine, and after
graduating Syracuse University as valedictorian in 1960, and
receiving her MA from the University of Wisconsin–Madison
the following year, Oates was seeing her short stories published regularly by prestigious publishers such as Vanguard
Press. Her first novel, *With Shuddering Fall*, was published in
1964 when she was just twenty-six years old.

Since then, the prolific Oates has written more than fifty
novels, hundreds of short stories, volumes of poetry, and countless nonfiction works, including essays and book reviews.

SATURDAY | BOOKS TO READ

The Power of Myth
by Joseph Campbell with Bill Moyers

Follow your bliss and the universe will open
doors for you where there were only walls.
—*Joseph Campbell*

"FOLLOW YOUR BLISS" BECAME A CATCH PHRASE FOR a generation. With the publication of his 1991 post-humous book *The Power of Myth*, Campbell's message was accepted by millions: "If you follow your bliss, you put yourself on a kind of track that has been there all the while, waiting for you, and the life that you ought to be living is the one you are living."

The book, based on a 1988 Public Broadcasting Service television series featuring a series of conversations between Campbell and Bill Moyers, focused on the role of myth in everyday contemporary life. Whether examining the roles of *Star Wars'* characters or redefining John Wayne as a mythological hero, Campbell showed readers how to use the constructs of mythology to navigate and interpret contemporary life.

As much as Campbell brings an intellectual enthusiasm to mythology, he also brings his unbridled joy to the fore as he describes the myths' power as stories. From the tales of the Bible to the myths of ancient Greece and the tales of the Buddha, Campbell takes stories and strands from all periods of time and all points on the Earth to weave universal themes.

SUNDAY | WRITING PROMPT

What makes a great leader . . .

CAN YOU DEFINE LEADERSHIP AND THE QUALITIES a great leader possesses? You can write about any leader of your choosing: someone on the world stage, someone in your community, or the person who runs your household. How have they risen to this status, and why do others choose to be influenced by their decisions?

This prompt can easily be the basis of a biography. One interesting take on leadership comes from bestselling motivational writer Stephen R. Covey, the author of *The 8th Habit: From Effectiveness to Greatness.* He writes that true leadership is "communicating to people their worth and potential so clearly that they come to see it in themselves." His approach starts with developing one's own voice, one's "unique personal significance." Only then can you inspire others and create a community where people feel engaged.

Do you agree? Is this leadership style present in your world, or are you subjected to a more authoritarian point of view?

MONDAY | WRITERS ON WRITING

> In nearly all good fiction, the basic—all but
> inescapable—plot form is this: A central
> character wants something, goes after it
> despite opposition (perhaps including his
> own doubts), and so arrives at a win, lose,
> or draw.
>
> —*John Gardner*

AMERICAN AUTHOR JOHN GARDNER DISTILLS
fiction to its most basic elements: the desire for something, the chase after that something, and the outcome.
Gardner is best known for his 1971 work *Grendel*, a retelling
of the classic 1000 CE *Beowulf* myth. In Gardner's version,
the story is told from the viewpoint of the monster.

Examine any fictional book written and you will find
that Gardner's thesis holds true. A longtime teacher of fiction
writing, Gardner distills into one elegant sentence what he
feels is the heart and essence of good fiction writing. A plot is
driven by someone wanting something. There must be oppo-
sition to this desire to create conflict. And, there must be a
resolution that, as Gardner says, can be "win, lose, or draw."

This simple formula allows for an almost limitless land-
scape in which authors can work and publish. Estimates
suggest that there are about 100,000 new English, book-
length works of fiction published each year. Most authors
use Gardner's straightforward recipe to create a seemingly
endless panoply of fictional scenarios and outcomes. The
books that resonate are those that touch on universal themes,
include compelling and well-developed characters, and have
a plot that continues to draw in the reader.

TUESDAY | MOTIVATION

> Outside of a dog, a man's best friend is a
> book. Inside of a dog, it's too dark to read.
> — *Groucho Marx*

THE OLDEST KNOWN LITERARY WORK, *THE EPIC of Gilgamesh*, was composed three thousand years ago in Babylon on a series of clay tablets. The universal themes developed in these epic poems—love, the power of the gods, the inevitability of death—were once again tackled by the Greek poet Homer in *The Odyssey* and *The Iliad*. So began the chain that links all writing, connecting cultures and contexts. The same themes, first portrayed three millennia ago, still prevail today. Your desire to write and express continues this long global tradition. Your writing, whether a journal you keep for your own use or a novel you hope to publish, is a link in this three-thousand-year-old literary chain.

Beyond carrying on a written tradition, writers bring richness to the lives of their readers, beginning in the earliest stages of life. Albert Einstein said, "If you want your children to be intelligent, read them fairy tales. If you want them to be more intelligent, read them more fairy tales." Books and writing educate and inform, amuse and delight, pique curiosities and satisfy intellectual questions. Writing and reading are essential elements of the human experience.

WEDNESDAY | WRITING CLASS

Revisit an unsolved murder.

THE CHALLENGE FOR THIS PIECE WILL BE TO TAKE all of the available research and to condense it into a feature-length story. If you choose a homicide case that has been under investigation for years, especially if there was a trial, you will have to condense hundreds of pages of material into one compelling story. Once you have mastered all the facts, see if you can figure out exactly what happened and why the killer has been able to elude the police.

THURSDAY | EDITING

> Learn the rules; and then forget them.
> —*Bashō*

THROUGHOUT THIS BOOK I'VE GIVEN YOU LOTS OF rules to follow to improve both your grammar and style. However, the reality is that there is no single set of rules for correct usage of the English language. Other languages are not as flexible. French, for example, is a language closely monitored by a governmental body called the Académie Française (French Academy). The Académie consists of forty members, known as *immortels* (immortals), who hold office for life. The body has the task of acting as an official authority on the language. English takes a more inclusionary approach to language, which is why grammar is subjective.

Rather than view any of these rules as ironclad, consider them as suggestions. They should help to direct you rather than confine you. In many instances, great writing doesn't come from strict adherence to grammatical rules any more than great cooking comes from strictly following a recipe. Sometimes you have to improvise just a little to create a signature piece of work.

However, if you adhere to most rules and disregard just a few, your work will be clear and direct, which is the goal of any good writer.

FRIDAY | BIOGRAPHY

> I love writing. I love the swirl and swing of
> words as they tangle with human emotions.
>
> —*James A. Michener*

JAMES A. MICHENER (1907–1997) WAS ABANDONED at birth by his biological parents and taken in by a Quaker woman named Mabel Michener in Doylestown, Pennsylvania. Michener's adoptive mother did not have much in the way of material wealth for the young boy, but she did instill in him a love of music and literature, and encouraged his curiosities. He was still a teen when he decided to hitchhike his way around America, hopping rides aboard freight trains, taking odd jobs in small towns, and even working in traveling carnivals.

He graduated Phi Beta Kappa and *summa cum laude* from Swarthmore College in 1929, and further pursued his studies abroad at Saint Andrew's University in Scotland before returning to the United States to teach, first at Colorado State Teachers College and then at Harvard. He left teaching to edit textbooks for a New York publishing company, a position he enjoyed until he joined the Navy during World War II.

The Navy brought Michener to the Pacific. From his wartime experiences in the Solomon Islands, he created his first book, *Tales of the South Pacific*, which he mailed anonymously to his former employer. Published in 1947, the book won a Pulitzer Prize. Michener then returned to his job as a textbook editor. Richard Rodgers and Oscar Hammerstein, with Joshua Logan, adapted the story into the musical *South Pacific*. Over his lifetime, Michener published nearly fifty books.

SATURDAY | BOOKS TO READ

The Maltese Falcon by Dashiell Hammett

> I went mooning about in a daze of love [for Spade] such as I had not known for any character in literature since I encountered Sir Launcelot.
>
> —*Dorothy Parker*

THE MALTESE FALCON, BY DASHIELL HAMMETT, WAS published in book form in 1930. It originally appeared as stories in a pulp detective magazine.

In *The Maltese Falcon*, Hammett tells the story of private detective Sam Spade's dealings with three unscrupulous characters who compete to obtain a precious jewel-encrusted falcon figurine. Set in San Francisco, sardonic Spade lets the cops think he is in cahoots with the criminals while he single-mindedly works to solve the case. Spade's character is based on Hammett's time as a Pinkerton Detective Agency operative.

With this book, Hammett did several things that had not been done in mystery writing before. Sam Spade became the archetype of the hard-boiled, tough-guy detective, a stereotype that would soon become ubiquitous. *The Maltese Falcon* has been called America's first existential novel because there is no background given about the book's main characters—it is as if they had simply dropped onto the face of the earth that day. Another unusual aspect: Hammett used a device called a *MacGuffin*: an object, event, or character in a film or story that drives the plot. In the end, the object proves to be of no intrinsic value to the story. The Maltese Falcon is considered a classic example of this device.

SUNDAY | WRITING PROMPT

My favorite meal . . .

THIS LAST PROMPT LETS YOU EXPLORE ONE AREA of your life that you know best: eating. Many great food writers can create recipe after recipe, making the otherwise mundane sound interesting, or the highly complex appear to be easy. But another area of expertise is someone who can write about the foods they've eaten in either an immediate or historical perspective.

This prompt is a totally different perspective on one's life, but one worth trying. Can you single out a perfect meal, or a signature dish, that you relate to? What was your experience either making it or eating it? Were you alone, at a party, or with someone memorable?

One of the masters of this type of writing is Ruth Reichl. Her many books, including *Tender at the Bone* and *Comfort Me with Apples*, are memoirs told through food experiences.

RESOURCES AND REFERENCES

Bryson, Bill. *Bryson's Dictionary of Troublesome Words: A Writer's Guide to Getting It Right.* New York: Broadway Books, 2004.

The Chicago Manual of Style. Chicago: University of Chicago, 2010.

Casagrande, June. *Grammar Snobs Are Great Big Meanies: A Guide to Language for Fun and Spite.* New York: Penguin, 2006.

Crews, Frederick C. *The Random House Handbook.* New York: Random House, 1987.

The Economist Style Guide. London: Profile, 2010.

Fogarty, Mignon. *Grammar Girl's Quick and Dirty Tips for Better Writing.* New York: Henry Holt and Company, 2008.

King, Stephen. *On Writing.* New York: Pocket, 2002.

Leonard, Elmore. Elmore Leonard's *10 Rules of Writing.* New York: William Morrow, 2007.

Nickell, Kelly. *The Writer's Digest Writing Clinic: Expert Help for Improving Your Work.* Cincinnati, OH: Writer's Digest, 2003.

Rubie, Peter, and Gary Provost. *How to Tell a Story: The Secrets of Writing Captivating Tales.* Cincinnati, OH: Writer's Digest, 1998.

Safire, William. *How Not to Write: The Essential Misrules of Grammar.* New York: W. W. Norton, 2005.

Strunk, William, and E. B. White. *The Elements of Style.* New York: Penguin, 2005.

Truss, Lynn. *Eats, Shoots & Leaves: The Zero Tolerance Approach to Punctuation.* New York: Gotham, 2006.

INDEX OF LITERARY FIGURES & WORKS

INDEX OF DAILY ACTIVITIES

Note: For references on specific writing techniques and advice, see **Editing**; **Motivation**; and **Writers on writing**.

Writing prompts *(cont.)*